Gamification
for Business

Gamification for Business

Why innovators and changemakers
use games to break down silos, drive
engagement and build trust

Sune Gudiksen
and Jake Inlove

First published in Great Britain and the United States in 2018 by Kogan Page Limited

2nd Floor, 45 Gee Street
London
EC1V 3RS
United Kingdom

c/o Martin P Hill Consulting
122 W 27th St, 10th Floor
New York, NY 10001
USA

4737/23 Ansari Road
Daryaganj
New Delhi 110002
India

www.koganpage.com

© Sune Gudiksen and Jake Inlove, 2018

The right of Sune Gudiksen and Jake Inlove to be identified as the author of this work has been asserted by them in accordance with the Copyright, Designs and Patents Act 1988.

ISBN   978 0 7494 8432 3
E-ISBN   978 0 7494 8433 0

British Library Cataloguing-in-Publication Data

A CIP record for this book is available from the British Library.

Library of Congress Cataloging-in-Publication Data

Names: Gudiksen, Sune, author. | Inlove, Jake, author.
Title: Gamification for business : why innovators and changemakers use games
  to break down Silos, drive engagement and build trust / Sune Gudiksen and
  Jake Inlove.
Description: 1st Edition. | New York, NY : Kogan Page Ltd, [2018] | Includes
  index.
Identifiers: LCCN 2018012303 (print) | LCCN 2018013298 (ebook) | ISBN
  9780749484330 (ebook) | ISBN 9780749484323 (pbk.) | ISBN 9780749484330
  (eISBN)
Subjects: LCSH: Organizational change. | Gamification. | Organizational
  effectiveness.
Classification: LCC HD58.8 (ebook) | LCC HD58.8 .G824 2018 (print) | DDC
  658.4/0343–dc23
LC record available at https://lccn.loc.gov/2018012303

Typeset by Integra Software Services Pvt Ltd, Pondicherry
Print production managed by Jellyfish
Printed and bound by CPI Group (UK) Ltd, Croydon CR0 4YY

CONTENTS

11 Bizzbuilder: How to sustainably grow a professional services business 65

12 Business Branching: Balancing ongoing operations and innovation initiatives 72

13 Changesetter: Leading change 81

ABOUT THE BOOK

Gamification has been used as an umbrella term for the use of games beyond the entertainment industry. When first introduced, gamification was used inappropriately in marketing, only transferring extrinsic-based game elements such as point systems and scoreboards with simple *pointless* reward systems. Newer gamification approaches seek to address the core of what has always been part of games – story, rules, objects/tokens, challenges and meaningful interaction. Such approaches offer a more promising perspective and enduring experience. In this book, gamification simply means games applied in organizations with purposes beyond pure entertainment. These purposes are described in Part One and Part Two, but in general are connected to collaboration, communication and social interaction.

In the 21st century, business games have accelerated to become a vital ingredient in innovation pursuits and the process of change. Simply stated, this has happened because such games are highly interactive, participatory and immersive. They offer a method that takes a radically different route from the dominant managerial approach of the Industrial Age, an approach based on direct instruction. When applied well, these games invite meaningful experiences through practical, hands-on activities that enhance concrete organizational development and collaborative reflection on practice, and scaffold new learning incentives on mindset and approaches. This book collects and unfolds business game approaches from various geographical and cultural sources in Northern Europe – Denmark, Sweden, Finland, the UK, Germany and the Netherlands – to share an overview of how they can be applied to organizational challenges. This approach can be associated with New Nordic management movements, which invite organizational actors, including leaders, partners, employees, customers and other stakeholders, to engage in action-oriented, thought-provoking dialogue.

Part One illustrates seven obstinate organizational challenges that seem to influence all organizational structures, cultures and activities. It provides arguments for why game approaches can be an effective method to overcome these challenges. In the 21st century, with fast technological changes and rapid market changes, these challenges are vital to work with on an ongoing basis. Games have a proven record as an effective method for promoting innovation and change processes when they include a group of diversified organizational actors. Even though games cannot stand alone in such processes, they often function either as a particularly good opener for new projects or as a reflective closer for established ones that sets the stage for new initiatives.

Part Two provides a comprehensive list of games that are currently used to deal with organizational challenges in the industry. Here, specific organizational challenges are highlighted so readers can focus on the examples that are similar to the challenges they currently face. The examples also point to the overarching challenges and goals in applying these types of games. On the first page in this section keywords – formed in a visual cluster – direct readers to business game examples that could be most relevant for a specific challenge they are currently occupied with. Readers can choose to have a quick glance at a few examples that seem relevant to them or scroll through all the examples to get an overview.

Part Three first describes the concepts underlying the basic elements used in game situations through a comparison of perspectives on the game examples and organizational challenges discussed in the previous section. Models and frameworks convey further easy understanding of the core elements in business game application. After this, readers are invited to acquire a quick historical understanding of business games through perspectives from experienced contributors. The book closes with a glimpse at the future, as seen from a New Nordic management perspective.

ABOUT THE AUTHORS AND BIZGAMES

Sune Gudiksen

Sune Gudiksen is Associate Professor in Design and Innovation Management at Design School Kolding, Denmark. He is part of an unconventional and innovative research and development group called Design-for-Play, which aims to pioneer the understanding of playful designs and game-based approaches in life-long learning across age groups and applied domains. He holds a PhD in co-creation of business models with the use of open-ended games for radical framing, and has conducted research on the use and effects of games in innovation, strategy and change topics. He is a leading thinker within this field with the aim to bring together existing knowledge as well as challenging this to arrive at new understandings. His approach is direct game interventions in organizations to observe effects from concrete activities. He has written several book chapters and articles for prestigious international design, innovation and change publishers, journals and conferences. As co-founder of GameBridges he aims to bring design, application and research together to instantiate novel and impactful interventions in organizations.

Jake Inlove

Jake Inlove is co-founder of GameBridges, a company that makes games for organizations. Here, he has developed and used games to help a variety of organizations become more innovative. Described as 'a creative powerhouse with many talents', Jake uses his abilities within illustration, design, copywriting, research and game design to produce useful tools for organizations and people. As a devoted researcher of human behaviour and learning, Jake has a master's degree in Education Science from the University of Aarhus, Denmark. As a result of his exhaustive studying and researching, Jake has a thorough understanding of learning processes, game mechanics, innovation and human behaviour – and is dedicated to using it to build more engaging learning and development processes.

BizGames community

In order to assemble a diversity of practitioner knowledge, Sune Gudiksen and Jake Inlove initiated the founding of a community now called BizGames through a series of network meetings. In this community, practitioners and applicators of business, innovation and change games can share ideas and examples, and qualify the use of games in organizational development. Readers are welcome to dive into more content and join the BizGames LinkedIn group through www.bizgames.org.

FOREWORD

This book is an enthusiastic celebration of a playful learning through games. For too long 'fun' has been devalued and continues to be squeezed out of our formal educational institutions and organizations under the misguided view that play is immaterial to learning. Contrary to such a view, existing research on play and learning offers a critical link between play and human cognitive and social-emotional growth from childhood to adulthood. The authors, Sune Gudiksen and Jake Inlove, clearly establish an important and insightful link between intricately designed games and the powerful learning experiences they unleash in individuals, teams and organizations. Games enable the creation of a safe ludic space, the authors argue, where players feel free to take risks, learn novel approaches and enter into an open and trusting dialogue with others to develop a common vision and pathway that leads to innovation and change.

To create effective and engaging games, game designers adhere to seven key design principles drawn from challenges most organizations face in their day-to-day operation. These principles are: 1) games break the boundary among individuals and promote mutual understanding and shared communication; 2) they appeal to diverse learning styles by providing a multisensory experience through manipulation of three-dimensional objects; 3) they create a meaningful connection between theory and practice by structurally guiding the players to move around the experiential learning cycle; 4) games create a safe ludic space where players are free to imagine and experiment with new ideas and choices; 5) they help build capacity to navigate complexity; 6) they encourage players to overcome rigid power relationships by experimenting with different roles; and 7) games connect people through social interactions by bringing participants' own experiences into a clear focus.

For example, Align is an online game aimed at aligning organizational and individual core values by encouraging participants to express their values intrinsically in their daily work. The learning outcome it seeks is for the players to realize that an inside-out approach to life ultimately will benefit both the individuals and organizations. This game is appealing to me in that it encourages participants to take responsibility for their experiences. The message is simple but powerful: we experience our own reality by the choices we make. Changesetter is a game played in groups designed to manage change in organizations. It offers different game formats to be played in different settings in organizations. The game is designed around the Kolb experiential learning cycle and players move through the process of experiencing, reflecting, thinking and acting as they decide on a course of action, implement a specific change and receive feedback on the outcome of their choices. It is an attractive game for raising awareness about the process of change and resistance to change. Innovate or Dinosaur is a game that helps teams and organizations think creatively, generate new ideas and create new opportunities in business. The main attraction of the game is the playfulness it unleashes in participants, a key factor in innovation and creativity. I find this game to be particularly effective in posing teams with the dilemma between a 'winning at all costs' strategy versus being deliberate about focusing their attention in the process of the game. As the example in the book illustrates, the teams motivated by the competitive nature of the game were outperformed by the teams who succeeded in generating the best ideas by deliberately digging deep into a specific opportunity or challenge.

Although these represent a small sample of over 20 insightful and well-crafted games presented in the book, they amply illustrate the importance of playfulness and fun to help individuals and organizations develop innovative approaches to problem solving, acquire adaptive flexibility to deal with change in imaginative ways and learn to enter into an open and honest dialogue with others.

Gudiksen and Inlove can be confident that there will be many grateful readers of *Gamification for Business* in business organizations as well as in educational institutions who will benefit from a broad perspective of the transformative impact of games in the workplace and in classrooms as a result of their efforts.

Alice Kolb
Experience Based Learning Systems, Inc
Kaunakakai, Hawaii

PART ONE
Seven Obstinate Organizational Challenges

1

Breaking down silos

*And why games enable shared communication
and mutual learning*

One of the biggest challenges organizations face is the constant and instant formation of silos; that is, formation of specialized knowledge groups. Even in small companies, this phenomenon seems to result in a downgrading of allocated time to communicate across teams and among individuals. Departments and separate teams are not problems as such; we need those specialized workforces. However, a lack of cross-function communication can become a major problem. Managers know this issue will eventually arise and will result in potentially crucial declines in business if they do not attend to it regularly and systematically.

Communication across divisions, units, teams and individuals is not always regarded as an important factor in growth; however, we will argue that the ability to create time and space for communication impacts organizational culture as well as the ability to work together towards a common organizational goal. If this communication does not occur regularly, leaders risk unhealthy alienation between actors in organizations, long decision-making cycles, and a lack of alignment in terms of priorities and goals.

Horizontal–vertical communication challenges

Through education and organizational experiences, professionals develop highly specialized skills and vocabularies. This continues for most of our working lives. As we gain work experience and develop specialized knowledge and language, we risk losing the ability to engage in strategic conversations and understand each other's viewpoints, interests, perspectives and practices. We call this the *horizontal* communication challenge in organizations (Figure 1.1).

Big organizations must apply top-level decisions all the way down the line. With management too distant, a high risk for employee dissatisfaction is ever present. Decision making is slow and complex and can result in going in circles. Because the information flow has to go through a series of channels, running up against walls for no particularly good reason will happen on a regular basis. As a consequence, the organization becomes less able to act on changes that occur outside of their own territory due to the front personnel or the intrapreneurial employee having limited action and feedback possibilities.

It is well-known that this phenomenon occurs in hierarchical organizational structures, but flat organizational structures also tend to struggle with it.

Figure 1.1   Horizontal–vertical / internal–external silo challenge

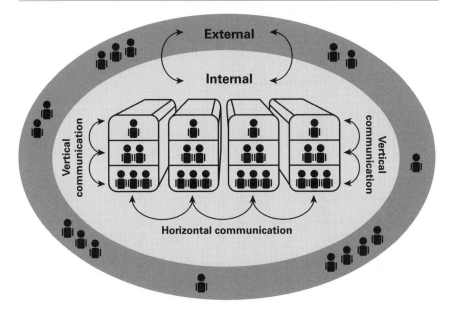

The road employees take to find the right decision-maker for a specific matter becomes a complex journey, as do leaders' and managers' ability to communicate from a distance and ensure that employees have shared goals. We call this the *vertical* communication challenge (Figure 1.1).

Internal and external communication challenges

We live in an age in which co-creation with customers, partners and stakeholders is increasingly common in complex organizational development situations (Table 1.1). In terms of consumer trends, employee motivation, partnerships and collaborations, people want to influence and co-create environments, tasks and solutions.

When organizational leaders and managers try to connect in different ways with employees, customers and partners, they must find common denominators and a communication format in which everyone can participate. This is a difficult task, since the process of putting organizational initiatives into practice is complex. Due to the increased number of organizations

Table 1.1 Co-creation directions and discourses

	Consumerism	Management	Policies and Politics	Strategic co-design
Why co-creation	Consumers want influence.	Customers and partners can be active contributors.	Citizens want influence. Public sector under economic pressure.	Design/innovation processes involve a circle of stakeholders.
Co-creation reasoning	Consumer influence on products/services.	Value and market differentiator.	Resources, ideas, ownership, collaboration.	Stakeholder ownership and organizational embedding.
Potential positive effect	Consumer receives unique products. Companies have unique products/services.	New value creation/capturing for both parties.	New policies and politics in line with citizen experiences. An active population.	Effective concepts that take into consideration stakeholder constraints.
Potential negative effect	Consumers become a free labour force.	Customers as idea bank with no real effect.	Pseudo-citizen involvement only to support political agenda.	Stakeholders are stuck with old system of thoughts. Stakeholder communication overload.

with departments and teams in various countries, and given the cultural differences among them, we expect horizontal and vertical communication challenges will continue and intensify.

A boundaryless organization

Some years ago, Jack Welch described the *boundaryless organization*, in which a series of structured and facilitated forums are systematically built into company activities (Ashkenas et al, 2015). Here, people with different functions and decision-making powers are brought together. Even though communication technologies have given us access to more information than we could ever have imagined, they have also led to increasingly complex matrix organizational structures. This means that the need for structured forums continues to exist and is perhaps more crucial today. According to Ashkenas and colleagues (2015):

> Each of these boundaries needs appropriate permeability and flexibility so that ideas, information and resources can flow freely up and down, in and out, and across the organization. The idea is not to have totally permeable boundaries or no boundaries – that would be 'disorganization'. Rather, you want sufficient permeability to allow organizations to quickly and creatively adjust to changes in the environment.

In the Industrial Age success factors included size, role definition, specialization and control, but according to experienced and successful change management practitioners Ashkenas and colleagues (who drove several initiatives for the former CEO of General Electric, Jack Welch) new factors come into play – not necessarily as a replacement but as supplement – in the 21st century such as speed, flexibility, integration and innovation.

To create this boundaryless organization in practice, new rules apply. There is less focus on command and control and more focus on enabling activities where common language, shared mindset, and engaged and empowered employee initiatives flourish – this is not to say that accountability for performance is out of the picture, but it does mean that this is viewed and 'measured' in different ways.

Third space communication

It is not enough simply to bring people together; they also require a structure for approaching the subjects at hand and, if possible, a somewhat neutral

Figure 1.2   *Third space* illustration

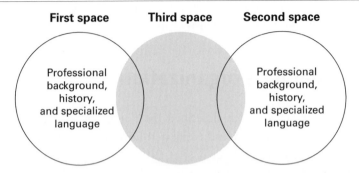

setting in which to discuss them. We tend to call this *third space* communication (Muller, 2003) or, in other words, collaborative settings, including tools and techniques, that can build bridges between parties.

Figure 1.2 shows that participants always bring their professional background and history into play through specialized language, but also need to attend to the backgrounds that other participants have. Subsequently, one needs to understand the terminology they use, which is often taken for granted, while at the same time leave space open for a third inspirational space. Thinking carefully about settings, game approach, and participant backgrounds and interests will lead to better results in terms of collaboration; this, in turn, will lead to increased commitment and ownership. Additionally, improved articulation of how value is created and captured across departments will, in the long run, lead to easier collaboration and frictionless action taking.

Reason 1: reach mutual understanding and shared communication

Games can advance the pursuit of boundaryless initiatives by targeting cross-communication internally between teams, units and so on, and between levels of hierarchy, as well as externally involving partners, suppliers and customers. Games are not a singular activity of such efforts, but they can open the ballet in an effective, highly engaged way. With the use of games, we seek to reach mutual understanding and shared communication. Above all, we want to establish a common language through which we can communicate and collaboratively engage in new organizational initiatives. This does not mean that conflicts – differences in opinions and interests – that arise when playing games are to be avoided.

On the contrary, they become positive and necessary incidents, as long as the games work with changes in perspective during the gameplay, since such changes increase understanding between parties. In addition, games either introduce novel approaches that take people beyond their routine practices, or they incorporate practices, experiences and working dilemmas, encouraging them to share these through the gameplay and in the context of a reflective knowledge-sharing agenda. All the games in this book build on this foundation and add thematic organizational challenges, to enhance quality, action-committed dialogues that will lead to new, concrete action in innovation initiatives or changes in practice.

Games are a common denominator for many people; very few have not at some point experienced a board game, a game-based activity or an online simulation. Given the structural layer of games, all participants are intuitively invited to participate; to some extent, this balances power among individuals. We regard this as a vital step towards understanding stakeholders with diverse viewpoints and professional expertise, and enabling alignment and ownership in organizational initiatives to arrive at beneficial alternatives to distant, instructional leadership.

Table 1.2   Quick recap of Challenge 1 and Reason 1

Challenge 1: Break down silos
Horizontal and vertical lack of cross-communication
Internal and external lack of communication
Finding *third space* opportunities
Reason: Reach mutual understanding and shared communication
Targeting cross-communication
Knowledge-sharing agenda
Quality, action-committed dialogues

References

Ashkenas, R, Ulrich, D, Jick, T and Kerr, S (2015) *The Boundaryless Organization: Breaking the chains of organizational structure*, John Wiley & Sons, New York

Muller, M J (2003) Participatory design: the third space in HCI, in *The Human-Computer Interaction Handbook*, ed A Sears and J A Jacko, pp 1051–68, Lawrence Erlbaum, New Jersey

2

Bursting out of the blah, blah, blah

And why games engage people through structured techniques and multisensory experience

We are stuck attending numerous confusing strategic meetings concerning organizational goals, and somewhat endless discussions, which are forgotten the moment we leave the room. Unless you are an excellent presenter and visionary to whom employees want to listen, we experience these non-productive and pseudo-inviting meetings all the time. Only a few people participate directly. Many might indicate that they are listening by nodding, but they are nonetheless indifferent. Engagement is low. Thus, annual strategic planning processes, according to chief executive officers (CEOs) and executives, rarely pay off (see, for instance, Beinhocker and Kaplan, 2002; and Mankins and Steele, 2006).

The only truly effective goal of these presentations is to help individuals cope with fear of the unknown. Strategic and organizational design plans are abstract, less inviting than they could be, and apparently static documents and summaries that seem to collect much dust. In general, people are not engaged or encouraged to participate intuitively in activities. They do not feel that they have a real say. Renowned visual thinker Dan Roam (2011) called these *blah blah blah* meetings. He stated the following:

> Powerful as words are, we fool ourselves when we think our words alone can detect, describe and defuse the multifaceted problems of today. They can't – and that's bad, because words have become our default thinking tool. (2011: Introduction)

We need vocabulary, but we are not created with only the ability to speak, or to see and visualize. In general, we think differently when working with more senses. In his seminal paper, MIT professor Seymour Papert, together with entrepreneur Idit Harel, coined the term *constructionism*, popularly known as learning-by-making. As they explained, constructionism 'favours forms of knowledge based on working with concrete materials rather than abstract propositions' (Papert and Harel, 1991: 2).

However, the introduction of tools and techniques that involve multiple senses must be done in a way that is not discomforting; one must start with familiar settings before moving on to more creative, unfamiliar acts. If you are not trained in drawing, for instance, a natural barrier arises to using pen and pencil. Similarly, some people have more training than others in using their full body in daily activities, so theatre-based activities, for instance, can be challenging, problematic openers. Games, on the other hand, are familiar 'material' for many, if not all. Board games have been around for a long time and digital games are part of the lives of the young people who are now joining the workforce.

Reason 2: engage in quality dialogue through structured techniques and a multisensory experience

Games are highly visual and tactile, and involve moveable objects. Add to this a suggested game structure with a proposed way forward, and participants can experience possible directions, and ways to proceed. One of the forefathers of what has become known as the *Lego serious play* approach, Johan Roos (2006), argued:

> When we fear losing track of all the entities that we juggle in our mind, we often recruit external elements to reduce the cognitive load. (2006: 78)

Three-dimensional objects let us think differently and create a space for experimenting as well as framing and reframing the specific challenges at hand. Several senses are involved, and three-dimensional objects appeal to a greater variety of learning styles. Game rules (actions participants can or cannot perform) and procedures (progression in the game) provide structure and can lead participants towards quality dialogue. Thus, games are not only related to constructionism but also *ludic (rules/procedures) constructionism*, as proposed by Gudiksen (2015) (Figure 2.1).

Figure 2.1   Participatory ludic constructionism

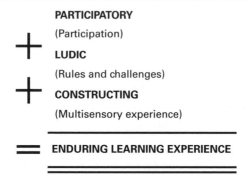

After a game session, there is clear documentation and visual mapping of the results and memory of the process. The use of supporting facilitative question techniques creates the opportunity to reflect on actions after the game has finished. When individuals move from being passive recipients to active participants using many senses, meetings are easier to remember and participants have an easier time processing the organizational initiatives and relationship of those initiatives to everyday tasks.

Table 2.1 Quick recap of Challenge 2 and Reason 2

Challenge 2: Bursting out of the blah, blah, blah
Non-productive and pseudo-inviting meetings
Direct instruction with no engagement
Only words
Reason 2: Engage in quality dialogue through structured techniques and a multisensory experience
Inviting for participation and engagement
Appeals to a greater variety of learning styles
Deep, immersive learning

References

Beinhocker, E D and Kaplan, S (2002) Tired of strategic planning, *The McKinsey Quarterly*, **2**, pp 1–7

Gudiksen, S K (2015) Co-designing business models: engaging emergence through design games, PhD dissertation, Aalborg University

Mankins, M C and Steele, R (2006) Stop making plans; start making decisions, *Harvard Business Review*, **84** (1), p 76

Papert, S and Harel, I (1991) Situating constructionism, *Constructionism*, **36** (2), pp 1–11

Roam, D (2011) *Blah Blah Blah: What to do when words don't work*, Penguin, New York

Roos, J (2006) *Thinking from Within*, Palgrave Macmillan, London

3

Closing the gap between theory and practice

And why games create a meaningful connection

Sometimes we witness a fantastic, inspirational lecture or are inspired by others' work; more often, however, we learn through concrete, hands-on experiences and actions that we can reflect on before moving on to a new experience. This brings to the table a learning style that is less based on *instructivism*, which involves an *instructor* and a *receiver*. The main problem is twofold: 1) the use of an academic, abstract theory with no attention to organizational situations, which can seem useless; 2) constant action, with no time to adjust, adapt or evaluate practices to search for new, better methods and approaches.

Theories, models, frameworks and terminology originating from research struggle to reach beyond narrow communities. The opposite also takes place on a regular basis. As Shakespeare's character Iago (in *Othello*) says, 'Mere prattle without practice is all his soldiership.' In the play, Iago plots to advance his social position, but causes a tragedy in which everyone loses. He was practising without reflective theory, the opposite of theorizing without practice. We suggest a better conjunction. We need practice to develop useful theoretical language, and we need theory to move beyond our normal approach to various issues.

From theory to practice

To have real impact, these theories must be matched with situated practices, problems and working procedures in organizations, and be described in accessible language. We see few bridges between these ideals and situated practices in everyday organizational work. A transfer is needed to make the theories relevant. As suggested by Randi and Corno (2007):

> Rather than apply theory to practice, teachers might be encouraged to adapt practice to theory, identifying teaching situations in which research principles might be relevant, and to change their practice accordingly to resolve the immediate problems of practice.

From practice to theory

According to the work by influential organizational change researcher Chris Argyris and colleagues (2010), we know it is important to create mechanisms that prevent us from falling into unhealthy routines. This is not to say that routines and standardized processes are not fruitful; we simply need to be aware of which practices should be turned upside down and when. Such practices can be best identified by systematic explorations and interventions that deal with the activities we take for granted and challenge our underlying assumptions.

For this to happen we need conceptual models and frameworks that challenge the underlying beliefs we have incorporated into everyday practices.

Reason 3: make a meaningful connection between theory and practice

In his influential book *Experiential Learning*, David Kolb (1984) argues that it is crucial that active experimentation is followed by reflections on these experiences in relation to practice. Afterwards, we can work more with conceptualization; that is, we create a language that is not detached from situated practices, but can be applied to evaluate practices and eventually lead to new experiments. It is, in many ways, similar to the ideas of Chinese Confucian philosopher Xunzi:

> Not having heard something is not as good as having heard it; having heard it is not as good as having seen it; having seen it is not as good as knowing it; knowing it is not as good as putting it into practice. (Knoblock, 1988)

In a later article, David Kolb and colleague Alice Kolb stated that setting up a ludic learning space can be considered one of the highest forms of learning (Kolb and Kolb, 2010). Kolb and Kolb argued that:

1 Learners take charge of their own learning based on their own standards of excellence.

2 Equal value is placed on the process and outcome.

3 Familiar experiences are experienced with a fresh perspective. (2010: 46–47)

According to Kolb and Kolb the ludic learning space (Figure 3.1) is characterized by elements such as the freedom to play, the chaos of uncertainty, the welcoming of foolishness and the stepping out of real life to enter deeper learning. We can discuss whether the players are entirely 'free' to play or they are still bound by group dynamics and power relations (see also Challenge 6), but encouraging and inviting for play is at least to be pursued.

Figure 3.1   Ludic learning model from Kolb

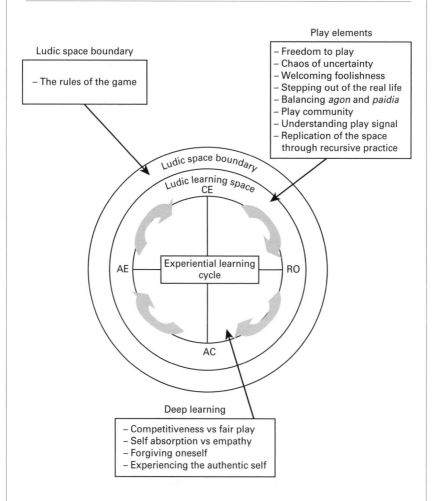

Participants in games continuously move between what Donald Schön (1987) called *reflections-in-action* (actions, reflections and surprises in the game activity) and *reflections-on-action* (transferring or debriefing on concrete happenings). In games, this occurs in a collaborative manner. Actions and reflections are interconnected rather than decoupled. Thomas Benedict, book contributor and book author to *The Winning Dialogue* (Benedict, 2010) from *InContextSimulations* argues that:

> When participants can quickly recognize their own processes, structures, ways of working and culture in a simulation it delivers a massive impact in a short space of time. (Personal communication)

Games can create a bridge to close the gaps between theory and practice. Good games do exactly that and challenge participants' perspectives on both. The games in this book were created from two different starting positions:

Outside-in

Theories are incorporated into games with openness towards situated, context-specific organizational practices. In this way, bridges are formed from the outside (theories from research) to the inside (the organizational context).

Inside-out

The experiences of skilled organizational developers and facilitators are incorporated into games. These experiences stem from observing problems and paradoxes in specific organizational contexts that are relevant to many organizations. In this way, a bridge is created from the inside (single cases) to the outside (working generic models for more organizations).

Table 3.1   Quick recap of Challenge 3 and Reason 3

Challenge 3: Closing the gap between theory and practice
Abstract theory far from practice
Constant action with no time to adjust
No conjunction between knowledge areas
Reason 3: Make a meaningful connection between theory and practice
Learners take charge of their own learning
Invites for freedom to play and a ludic space to enable new learnings
Outside-in and inside-out connection between knowledge areas

References

Argyris, C (2010) *Organizational Traps: Leadership, culture, organizational design*, Oxford University Press, Oxford

Benedict, T (2010) *The Winning Dialogue: Negotiation and communication for professionals*, CreateSpace Independent Publishing Platform

Knoblock, J (1988) *Xunzi: A translation and study of the complete works*, vol 1, Stanford University Press, Stanford

Kolb, D A (1984) *Experiential Learning: Experience as the source of learning and development*, Prentice Hall, Englewood Cliffs, NJ

Kolb, A Y and Kolb, D A (2010) Learning to play, playing to learn: a case study of a ludic learning space, *Journal of Organizational Change Management*, **23** (1), pp 26–50

Randi, J and Corno, L (2007) Theory into practice: a matter of transfer, *Theory Into Practice*, **46** (4), pp 334–42

Schön, D A (1987) *Educating the Reflective Practitioner: Toward a new design for teaching and learning in the professions*, Jossey-Bass, New York

4

CHALLENGE 4

Mitigating the clash between ongoing operations and innovation

And why games create a safe space for experiments and risk taking

Organizations struggle with maintaining the relationship between ongoing operations and the creation of a portfolio of new business opportunities on which to act. In terms of resources, these two purposes are sometimes at odds with each other; the need to realize short-term gains often means that the search for new, innovative value propositions loses that competition. However, the collapse of the movie/game-rental Blockbuster chain serves as a clichéd example of this competition turning out badly; disruptive competitor moves are just around the corner. Business thinker Rita McGrath (2013) argued that we can no longer rely on sustainable business advantages and need to work continually with temporary advantages. This means that we must use different managerial skill sets.

According to innovation researchers Govindarajan and Trimble (2010), when dealing with ongoing operations, we can predict the results of new moves based on previously developed value propositions. However, this is not possible when experimenting with new value propositions. Due to an apparent lack of time, organizations may launch new initiatives proposed by management that rely on numbers, metrics and parameters. Even entrepreneurs, who often test small samples of new products and services quickly and directly in the proposed market, need a place in which to experiment beforehand or gather experiences afterwards.

In Denmark, the Dogme 95 filmmaking movement has had a profound influence on filmmaking and, interestingly, some areas of organizational research. The manifest created by the directors that began the movement comprises a set of rules that should be followed when filming scenes for a movie. These rules were intended to ensure that filmmakers focused on deliberate creative strategy rather than on technology and budgets. Influential scriptwriter and teacher Mogens Rukov, who acted as a consultant on many movies produced according to the tenets of this movement, said: 'When fantasy is frameless, it becomes homeless' (Munch, 1999: 1).

As a result of this movement, *obstructions* and *constraints* in innovation and change processes are considered positive and necessary means in many areas in Scandinavia and are vital for identifying new ways to approach an issue. Of course, there are times when organizational issues can be too constrained. However, as a rule of thumb, constraints support novel thinking; paradoxically, game rules, procedures and obstructions can be liberating. If a starting frame is too open, we are less creative.

Creativity researcher Patricia Stokes also asserted that constraints can be viewed as 'barriers that lead to breakthroughs' (2005: 7). She examined constraints involved in structuring creativity-related problems as well as those that hinder novelty (Table 4.1).

Table 4.1   Kinds of constraints

Domain	Cognitive	Variability	Talent
Mastery of a specific knowledge area. Subdivided into *goal, subject* and *task* constraints.	This kind of constraint reflects physiological limitations on how many things our brains can process at one time.	This kind of constraint specifies how differently it must or should be done.	Talents are genetic – one either has it or not in a given area.

SOURCE Stokes (2005)

Deliberately setting up constraints that will lead to diverse perspectives and approaches to a problem is a core element of this line of thinking. Constraints are positive obstacles to work through or around, and they set the conditions for what can be achieved.

Reason 4: experiment and take risks in a constrained 'safe' space

Games create a temporary safe space for imagination and exploration that has been called 'a magic circle'. Salen and Zimmerman (2004: 96) explained this 'circle' as follows:

> Within the magic circle, special meanings accrue and cluster around objects and behaviours. In effect, a new reality is created defined by the rules of the game and inhabited by its players.

However, even though we, as game designers, sometimes feel like magicians after creating a great game and participants might experience a 'magical' and engaging session, there is really no magic in games. Therefore, we tend to call games what they are: *temporary ludic spaces*. They are places where participants – stakeholders or team representatives with diverse interests – can meet and explore ideas, scenarios, choices and future directions to identify potential consequences and discuss a range of possible futures in a structured way. Of course, a game cannot predict the future; we leave this to clairvoyants. However, they can function as the means by which stakeholders can explore alternative futures.

With games, a forum can be established in which we obtain strategic, organizational future directions through scenario exploration. Such exploration can be a starting point for development of a business portfolio with a range of opportunities to act on when the time seems right. A classic scenario-based game is the *kriegsspiel* (war game; see MacNab 2012), which was used by the Prussians during the 19th century. Considered one of the first examples of a war game, it was used to rehearse tactics for a military problem. Taking turns, the Prussians could play out specific orders and scenarios and then experience the responses of role-playing enemies. It was not intended to predict the future, but to prepare the Prussians for many possible events. The major strengths of scenario experimentation are that we develop more than one option (multiple futures), and we can evaluate scenarios against one another to explore potential benefits and consequences. A great scenario-based game challenges organizations' assumptions about the future.

Games can also work to explore roles, mindsets and working procedures, the necessary skill sets for teams and managers in the competitive landscape of the 21st century. The games described here do not aim to explore specific new strategic moves; rather, their purpose is to change the way we do things and, in doing so, build stakeholders' competencies regarding learning about innovation approaches and conditions in organizations.

A good organizational game will have certain constraints, obstructions or provocations to move beyond the status quo and challenge underlying assumptions. In-game feedback techniques lead to assumption testing, attempts at reframing and innovative design moves (Gudiksen, 2015). Surprises enabled by the game's feedback techniques can trigger changes in how we perceive things. There are many types of feedback techniques. Game designer and educator Marc LeBlanc (2006) stated that creating dramatic tension in games relies on two elements: uncertainty (when a pathway or outcome is unknown) and inevitability (a game activity that moves towards closure). A game will eventually reach closure, but dramatic parts rely on the ability to maintain tension until closure is achieved.

According to award-winning game designer Greg Costikyan (2013), *struggle* is at the centre of all games. Some might consider winning to be the event that defines a game, but competition is only one kind of struggle; struggles can be integrated through traps, barriers, puzzles, exploration, obstacles, changes in perspective and so on. Obstructions or constraints in games are created through these struggles; they are at the heart of what can be created to incorporate challenges and conflicts suitable for the organizational issue at hand.

Table 4.2   Quick recap of Challenge 4 and Reason 4

Challenge 4: Mitigating the clash between ongoing operations and innovation
Finding a balance between short term versus long term
Finding a balance between prediction versus uncertainty
No resources for experiments and testing
Reason 4: Experiment and take risks in a constrained 'safe' space
Creative constraints to support novel framing
Scenario exploration and comparison
Exploring working procedures and mindset

References

Costikyan, G (2013) *Uncertainty In Games*, MIT Press, Cambridge, MA

Govindarajan, V and Trimble, C (2010) *The Other Side of Innovation: Solving the execution challenge*, Harvard Business Press, Boston

Gudiksen, S (2015) Business model design games: rules and procedures to challenge assumptions and elicit surprises, *Creativity and Innovation Management*, **24** (2), pp 307–22

LeBlanc, M (2006) Tools for creating dramatic game dynamics, in *The Game Design Reader: A rules of play anthology*, ed K Salen and E Zimmerman, pp 438–59, MIT Press, Cambridge, MA

MacNab, I A (2012) Kriegsspiel and the sandtable: using tabletop wargames to teach tactics and exercise decision making in the classroom, Centre for Teaching Excellence, United States Military Academy, West Point, NY

McGrath, R G (2013) *The End of Competitive Advantage: How to keep your strategy moving as fast as your business*, Harvard Business Review Press, Boston

Munch, P (1999) The dogma doctor: interview with Mogens Rukov, *Politiken* (national Danish newspaper on Sunday), 14 March 1999

Salen, K and Zimmerman, E (2004) *Rules of Play: Game design fundamentals*, MIT Press, Cambridge, MA

Stokes, P D (2005) *Creativity from Constraints: The psychology of breakthrough*, Springer Publishing Company, London

5

Untangling complex problems

*And why games build the capacity for navigating complexity
and find pathways through the mist*

On occasion, there is uncertainty regarding organizational initiatives and a problem is perceived as *complex*, or *wicked* as they were called by Rittel and Webber in 1973. Wicked is to be understood as resistance to resolution and in opposition to *tame* problems where a solution can easier be found. When one stands with a wicked problem, alternatives and paths must be found that balance the requirements of the various stakeholders and that work to break down or around barriers. We see problems emerge that are highly complex and challenge conventional viewpoints on 'how' (tools and techniques), 'who' (stakeholders) and 'what' (criteria). The complex problems are dynamic and change over time. In addition, they are interconnected and interdependent on factors we cannot easily comprehend or foresee. Jeff Conklin (2005) argues that this type of problem seems to exist in all professional disciplines and further explains why the complexity only seems to increase in the years to come (Table 5.1):

> Fragmentation is a condition in which the stakeholders in a situation see themselves as more separate than united. The fragmented pieces are, in essence, the perspectives, understandings and intentions of the collaborators, all of whom are convinced that their version of the problem is correct.
> As we approach the end of the first decade of the new millennium, it is clear that the forces of fragmentation are increasing, challenging our ability to create coherence, and causing more and more projects to flounder and fail. The antidote to fragmentation is shared understanding and shared commitment.

Table 5.1 Complex problem characteristics in the 21st century

From Rittel and Webber (1973)	From Conklin (2005)
1 There is no definitive formulation of a wicked problem.	1 The problem is not understood until after the formulation of a solution.
2 Wicked problems have no stopping rule.	2 Wicked problems have no stopping rule.
3 Solutions to wicked problems are not true or false, but better or worse.	3 Solutions to wicked problems are not right or wrong.
4 There is no immediate and no ultimate test of a solution to a wicked problem.	4 Every wicked problem is essentially novel and unique.

(*continued*)

Table 5.1 *(Continued)*

From Rittel and Webber (1973)	From Conklin (2005)
5 Every solution to a wicked problem is a 'one-shot operation'; because there is no opportunity to learn by trial and error, every attempt counts significantly.	5 Every solution to a wicked problem is a 'one shot operation'.
6 Wicked problems do not have an enumerable (or an exhaustively describable) set of potential solutions, nor is there a well-described set of permissible operations that may be incorporated into the plan.	6 Wicked problems have no given alternative solutions.
7 Every wicked problem is essentially unique.	
8 Every wicked problem can be considered to be a symptom of another problem.	
9 The existence of a discrepancy representing a wicked problem can be explained in numerous ways. The choice of explanation determines the nature of the problem's resolution.	
10 The social planner has no right to be wrong (ie planners are liable for the consequences of the actions they generate).	

It goes without saying that because of this fragmentation, the need for activities that systematically invite and build shared understanding are sought after and in high demand. Influential design researcher Kees Dorst (2015) noted that the most important skill that sets well-known successful professional designers apart from other designers is the ability to *reframe* problems and situations by reframing their search for paradoxes, clues and paths beyond the initial framework and the seemingly limited ways forward. For this to happen, we need to view the situation, problem or opportunity from multiple perspectives.

Reason 5: build capacity for navigating uncertainty and complexity

Games are characterized by uncertainty in terms of their exploration of challenges, conflicts and choices. Once participants can effortlessly progress through a game, it loses all the meaning associated with it and becomes boring and irrelevant. When participants begin to master a game, playing it becomes trivial. One enjoys playing a game twice or more only if it is not predictable. In his major work *Man, Play and Games,* sociologist Roger Caillois (1961: 7) explained:

> An outcome known in advance, with no possibility of error or surprise, clearly leading to an inescapable result, is incompatible with the nature of play.

The uncertainty present in games enables us to search for pathways to follow in complex situations, thereby providing an opportunity to weigh our options. A contributor to this book, Ask Agger from Workz (Agger, 2016), states that the outcome of games is beneficial when situations are complicated:

> Games offer a unique possibility to address the challenge of high complexity and uncertainty. Games make it possible to simplify, categorize and structure the many factors, thereby creating clarity and providing strategic outlook.

Novel themes and perspectives also seem to rise out of this uncertainty. We are directed towards a variety of perspectives, with surprises occurring regularly and fresh ideas and perspectives constantly emerging.

Table 5.2   Quick recap of Challenge 5 and Reason 5

Challenge 5: Untangling complex problems
Unsolvable problems
Increasing stakeholder complexity
Framing problems from singular perspective
Reason 5: Build capacity for navigating uncertainty and complexity
Finding possible pathways in the mist
Novel ideas and radical framing
Framing problems from multiple perspectives

References

Agger, A (2016) [accessed 9 March 2018] Games in Strategy Development, Blogpost [Online] https://workz.dk/posts/games-strategy-development

Caillois, R (1961) *Man, Play and Games,* University of Illinois Press, Illinois

Conklin, J (2005) *Dialogue Mapping: Building shared understanding of wicked problems,* John Wiley & Sons, Chichester

Dorst, K (2015) *Frame Innovation: Create new thinking by design*, MIT Press, Cambridge, MA

Rittel, H W and Webber, M M (1973) Dilemmas in a general theory of planning, *Policy Sciences,* 4 (2), pp 155–69

6

Shaking up the roles we play

*And why games challenge participants
to suspend power relations*

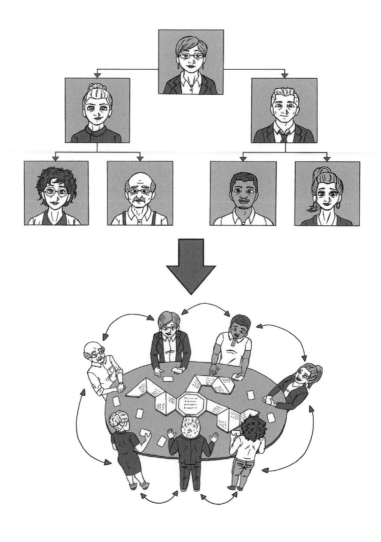

This challenge is by far the most complex and difficult to work with. It depends on the established power relations in organizations and points to the vertical–horizontal and internal–external silo issues. Who has decision-making power? What types of historical conflicts between actors lie underneath? What are the relationships between stakeholders? It can best be described as everyday organizational politics, which can stand in the way of real progress and crucial conversations.

Power is not to be considered corruptive in a Machiavellian sense of self-interest and personal gain (an influential viewpoint from the book *Il Principe* (*The Prince*) from Italian diplomat Niccolò Machiavelli). A more nuanced view is to view power relations in organizations through an understanding of patterns of mutual influence (Keltner, 2016). Social psychologist professor Dacher Keltner notes that:

> Defining power as altering others' states means that power permeates all
> relationships, in the family, among friends, and economic exchanges. (2016: 29)

There are many kinds of power issues to be found in group dynamics in organizations, and in general. According to a leader in the field of group facilitation Dale Hunter (see Hunter, Bailey and Taylor, 1995) five types of archetypical powers can be found at the outset (Table 6.1).

However, such power types are indeed dynamic and what can be seen in the titles does not account for the history, culture and similar events that have influenced work relations over time. Positive relations and empowering others lead to stronger group work and cross-function communication. Acknowledging the perspectives and experiences of other professional disciplines comes from a higher degree of social interactions in everyday work life.

To exemplify, the authors recently had a workshop session with an educational institution for a transport business with highly specialized employees

Table 6.1 Power types in groups derived from Hunter et al (1995)

Positional	Assigned	Knowledge	Personal	Factional
When a person in a group has a more powerful position (titles and rank).	When a group assigns a particular role to a group member.	When a group has specialist knowledge and experience in an area.	When a person, through personal skills and qualities, is looked to as a guide.	When several people within a group act together to influence.

who worked in silos all over the country (Denmark), and rarely met each other (down to, for instance, only one time per month). In a period of two hours, conflicts arose at a rapid pace, all of them leading back to the fact that they knew little about each other's work processes and conditions. In the final hour they eventually became more aware of the struggles and troubles that everyone seemed to be experiencing.

In our experience, such situations are common and it is remarkable how the act of meeting face to face outside of normal work patterns, and with somewhat systematized activities, can change relations for the better. Here, games have a role to play.

Reason 6: alter and level power relations to advance fresh perspectives

Games cannot eliminate power relations. Since they are a natural part of everyday work activities, their elimination is not our goal; however, these relations can be explored, shelved, or somewhat altered during play to make room for exploration of the challenge at hand. Ultimately, games can shed light on the roles participants play as well as how to organize these roles in the future for better results. To do so, the games maintain a careful balance between chosen game techniques for specific intents, combined with the right participation setup and support by the facilitator. When applying a game to an organizational challenge, success depends on the ability to balance already established power relations with the in-game techniques and participation setup, which are meant to shake up these roles and advance new perspectives and insights. Some are better than others to hold the seat as president, so the intention is not to remove *ranking* but to encourage more *linking*, with direct reference back to the concept of a boundaryless organization.

The concrete game setup depends on whether participants come from the same organization or from different organizations. Historical means and established power relations are impactful and can be barriers for the new perspectives, and subsequently for a change in practices. This often means that if you have a group of participants with no prior work history and coming from different organizations, you can delve deeper into everyday activities since participants are more willing to share. During play, some participants may experience new power or more power than they had before, while others will see a reduction, depending on the game format and how well they manage it. The games in general seek to alter these power relations during play in order to shed new light on the roles we play; this insight can be worked with afterwards, regardless of the game's intention to address real or fictitious cases.

Ultimately, being able to identify as many power relations as possible beforehand is key; however, it is rarely sufficient and there can be short time to develop a thorough understanding of these relations, while this also has a tendency to surface in the process rather than in pre-talks. A facilitator must have a good eye for the relations dominating the room in a business game workshop and be able to alter group settings if needed. In-game techniques can play a significant role in levelling the power relations. Some basic techniques include the following. *Turn-taking,* for instance, often makes use of a timer to ensure that all participants have the same amount of speaking time. Allowed in-game actions defined by rules and procedures can give participants the same resources to work with, thereby ensuring the same starting point for all. In the same vein, it is possible to address inequality by giving experienced managers fewer resources than inexperienced managers. In this way, games can alter and even level power relations based on the parameters at stake, that is, the types of power relations and mutual interdependence that influence the specific group dynamics.

Table 6.2 Quick recap of Challenge 6 and Reason 6

Challenge 6: Shaking up the roles we play
Everyday politics in the way of progress
Fixed power relations
History and culture prevents collaboration
Reason 6: Alter and level power relations to advance fresh perspectives
Alter relations to advance relations for the better
Exploring roles to understand perspectives and practices
Linking people rather than ranking

References

Hunter, D, Bailey, A and Taylor, B (1995) *The Art of Facilitation: How to create group synergy*, Da Capo Press, Cambridge, MA

Keltner, D (2016) *The Power Paradox: How we gain and lose influence*, Penguin, New York

7

Bolstering trustworthy relations

And why games connect people through social interactions

Customer-centric and employee-centric focus and, for some, human-centric focus in general are the main aspects that differentiate companies in a world in which competitors quickly rise and prices and costs are close. Service value propositions characterize larger, more established organizations. During the recent economic downturn, customers avoided brands to which they did not feel closely attached. It has been noted that one of the biggest challenges in becoming more human-centric is the fact that departments and teams neglect to share information across silos; this goes back to Challenge 1. A leftover from the Industrial Age, this is perhaps the hardest challenge for many companies to overcome – to move from employee tasks in teams and departments to a holistic, total understanding where humans in the organization help each other through trust-based relations to deliver totality and cohesive solutions.

Customers

Simply stated, if we do not aim for best-cost prices, we aim for trustees; developing relations is a competitive differentiator, both externally and internally. Influential service innovator Andy Polaine and colleagues (2013) explain the main problem for many organizations:

> Often, each bit of the service is well designed, but the service itself hasn't been designed. The problem is that customers don't just care about individual touchpoints. They experience services in totality and base their judgement on how well everything works together to provide them with value. (Polaine, Løvlie and Reason, 2013: 22)

It is necessary to experiment continuously with new service offerings and build customer relationships. Otherwise, a service risks being evaluated as average and being disrupted by companies that can offer a lower price for approximately the same service due to digital technology and a different organizational setup. Building relations will lead to more trustworthy endeavours internally (across teams) and a better, more cohesive service value proposition for customers, clients and partners, as well as a better cross-division employee experience.

Employees

Due to the increased attention given to the delivery of services to customers, organizational values and corporate culture have become increasingly important factors for recruiting and motivating employees. They are part of the decision-making pattern for customers and are therefore major concerns for management. Jeanne Meister (2017), an experienced Forbes contributor, argued:

> The next journey for HR leaders will be to apply a consumer and a digital lens to the HR function creating an employee experience that mirrors their best customer experience. (2017: 1)

This means the way forward appears to rely on supporting employees by giving them physical environments, tools and technologies, and providing favourable conditions for productivity. Such environments, tools and technologies need to take their point of departure as much in the individual as in a general management agenda. People have different working patterns that challenge how, when and where they are most productive. In addition, competencies, personalities and living conditions are factors that come into play in these human preferences. In their book *The Employee Experience Advantage*, Jacob Morgan and Marshall Goldsmith (2017) described the shift in focus from a 'need to turn up' to a 'want to turn up' at work.

In a recent talk, Simon Sinek (2016) described how millennials being hired by organizations today demand an impact on tasks, but also need to develop basic social coping mechanisms to leverage their talents and agendas, and to communicate and negotiate their way forward. From his perspective, organizations are forced to deal with this as an intentional, strategic focus of the work experience. However, this seems not be a generational consequence, but a technology and thereby culture change across ages.

On a similar note, Professor of Social Studies Sherry Turkle (2017) argued that we should reclaim conversations in a world filled with social media and interruptions in everyday work situations. Today, people are connected, but they converse without empathy. There is a lack of 'commitment to putting yourself in the other person's shoes' (Turkle, 2017). Turkle has seen this happening and has illustrated it with children's examples from the next generation. She has suggested 'sleepaway camps' or workshops that focus on conversation and understanding each other's perspectives and working procedures as a way forward. We could easily expand this to organizations, in which case managers would need to secure time for these camps. Week-long camps might not be feasible in an organization, but such concepts could be integrated into monthly practices.

Reason 7: connect people through social interactions

Games create a structure in which we can focus on the people at hand and their needs. They let us explore new ways to deliver service value propositions or, for instance, to align official managerial value sets with employees' experiences and changing customer needs. At the core of these games lie social interactions and multifaceted communications through which participants from the organizations can understand why we act as we do; that is, they discover the professional language and mindset we have through specific education and work experiences and how we might act in the future.

Through games, social interactions become more informal and more relevant to the participants' own experiences, viewpoints and prerequisites. Games call for participation and responsibility from all, rather than depending solely on the leader as the person who 'knows it all'. Through game rules and procedures, as well as the participation setup, new or renewed group constellations and interactions can be tried. Employees with diverse backgrounds or cross-disciplinary stakeholders can find a 'working language' and, to some extent, a common ground in the games. It is through these social interactions and changed work relations that the first sparks towards cultural and behavioural change can be observed.

The next time a specific organizational actor needs to go beyond the team or department to which he belongs, whether internal or external, chances are he will know who to contact and how to create better-aligned and smoother processes. This is in addition to the concrete output of the activities; the games become a vehicle for social and relational preparatory activities, rather than reactive or unprepared cross-unit contact that may be damaging. In this way, games function as innovative enablers that lead the way forward to more relevant, inclusive and productive dialogue, while also eliciting the cultural and social means that are vital for an organization to work with the agile methodology and deliver holistic, total experiences to clients, customers, employees, employers and stakeholders in general.

Table 7.1　Quick recap of Challenge 7 and Reason 7

Challenge 7: Bolstering trustworthy relations
Difficult to maintain relations in a fast-changing world
Pressure and technology makes one constantly available, interrupts authentic presence
Interruptions and no time for social interactions
Reason 7: Connect people through social interactions
Focus back on human relations
Relevant social interactions
Relevant, inclusive and productive dialogue

References

Meister, J (2017) The employee experience is the future of work: 10 HR trends for 2017, *Forbes*, 5 January

Morgan, J and Goldsmith, M (2017) *The Employee Experience Advantage: How to win the war for talent by giving employees the workspaces they want, the tools they need, and a culture they can celebrate*, Wiley, Chichester

Polaine, A, Løvlie, L and Reason, B (2013) *Service Design: From insight to inspiration*, Rosenfeld Media, New york

Sinek, S (2016) [accessed 9 March 2018] Millennials in the Workplace, *Inside Quest* [Online] https://www.youtube.com/watch?v=hER0Qp6QJNU&t=140s

Turkle, S (2017) *Alone Together: Why we expect more from technology and less from each other*, Hachette, London

PART TWO
A Series of Business Game Examples

Readers can choose to go directly for a subject matter closest to their current focus, or a target group they have in mind, by using either the 'What' cluster (Figure P2.1) or the 'Who' cluster (Figure P2.2).

Figure P2.1   'What' cluster

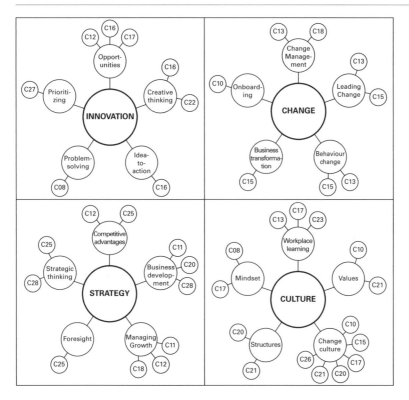

Figure P2.2   'Who' cluster

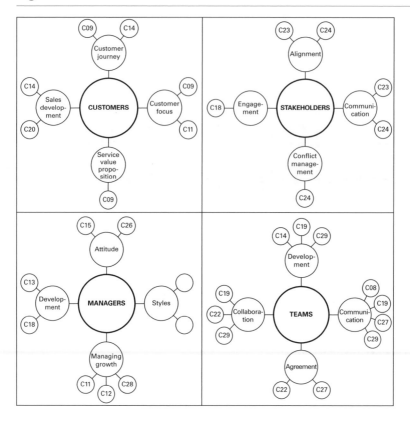

8
The Acid Test

An in-game demonstration of the learning cycle

CHRISTOPHER ELGOOD AND CHRISTINE ELGOOD,
Elgood Effective Learning

#TeamCommunication #TeamProblemSolving #TeamMindset

The Acid Test was designed for Rank Xerox to be used as part of a training course for sales staff. The company believed that staff placed too much emphasis on the number of sales calls made, irrespective of the outcome. The company thought that the number of actual sales would be improved by reflection on what happened during each sales call and how this information might be used to target the most likely prospects. The name Acid Test reflects the fact that each in-game decision provides information, like adding acid to a solution in chemistry and getting a yes/no answer (Figure 8.1).

Figure 8.1 The Acid Test at a size used for exhibitions

The challenge for Elgood was to design an activity that would be totally different from the rest of the course (which relied heavily on direct instruction), but where the post-game discussion would directly relate to the course objectives. It was agreed that the game needed to allow for immediate action, thus stimulating the instinctive need felt by many sales staff, having made one call, to rush on to the next with no time for reflection and analysis. It was also necessary that such immediate action should prove less satisfactory than careful examination of the problem and development of a coherent plan. The game message must demonstrate these processes, but do so by using a different scenario.

Gameplay

The Acid Test is based on excavation, such as in archaeology or mining, when one stratum gives way to another; practical experience suggests that when one type of rock is found, it is likely that a related type will be found below it. The game was created in the form of a puzzle that presents participants with 23 roofless silos, each showing a blue, yellow or green counter. The participants are told that each silo contains seven counters and that their task is to uncover 12 red counters by removing the layers one by one. The facilitator also provides them with a one-sentence verbal clue. The winning team is the one that finds 12 red counters by removing the lowest number of counters.

Initial development of the game was driven by the need to offer a credible allegory in a playable form that evoked an image of play rather than work. The guiding theory was that of experiential learning – the pragmatic process of learning through doing and reflecting. The Acid Test was based on experience and had no academic source, although the lessons regarding the sales process are essentially the same as those suggested by the Awareness, Interest, Desire, and Action (AIDA) model, where the first version is commonly attributed to sales pioneer Elias Lewis (see Lewis (1908) for an early version).

Inherent in the game is the strata of colours and the pattern of green, yellow, blue, red. Each decision to remove a blue, green or yellow counter (no reds are visible on the top row) is based on some theory about how the columns might have been planned. The removal of a counter supports the theory or casts doubt upon it. So, there is a sequence of theorizing, acting, discovering and reflecting. As more counters are removed, the evidence for the right theory builds, and players become confident that the next removal will reveal what they expect it to reveal.

Figure 8.2 Thought process the Acid Test is meant to promote

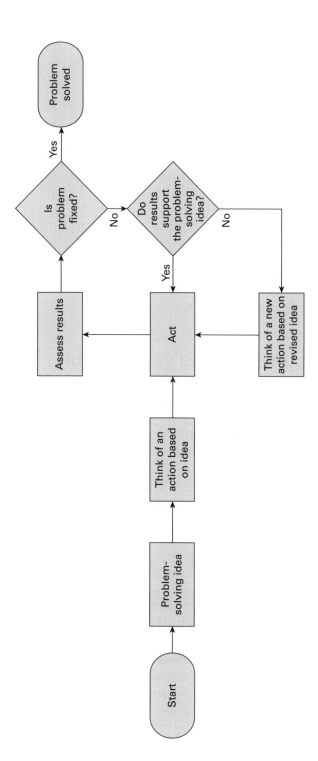

This means they will have improved their skill at building and testing theories and logically interpreting data (Figure 8.2). The Acid Test was deliberately created to demand this sequence of behaviours in a non-work environment. The abstract nature makes it very adaptable. One notable use of the game was at the Police Staff College (UK), where the coloured counters were perceived as clues leading to an arrest. The game does not require professional experience. The rapid action and immediate results are sufficient to arouse interest. In such cases, the principal lesson learnt is often about group effectiveness. Did members really listen to each other and try to understand conflicting theories?

The Acid Test is also a useful exercise for allowing participants to practise the discipline of an After Action Review (Scott 1983). This process, originally developed by the US Army, has been adopted by many organizations seeking to evaluate performance and initiate change. The simple process of asking the core questions of what happened, why it happened and how it can be done better can be very powerful.

Key gains that the game enables

Awareness of personal tendencies

Because this appears to be a simple task, there are always team members who fixate on a personal idea and act immediately and thoughtlessly, even pre-empting serious discussion. There are others who wish to assess the nature of the task before acting. Post-event discussion generally results in agreement about what ought to have been done and recognition of various mistakes that were made. The most frequent of such mistakes is failure to reach a common understanding of the nature of the task and what constitutes success. Discussions of this sort can lead to developing a general problem-solving discipline.

Attention to logic rather than prejudice

In the Acid Test, there is a logical way to interpret the clue and conduct experiments. It requires thought and often gives way to personal prejudice or reliance on some previous experience that was outwardly similar. Facilitators can ask the questions, 'Why did you choose that approach? Where did your idea come from?'

Valuing the review process

Once a project or activity is completed, there is a strong tendency in many organizations to move on to the next without reviewing performance. This tendency exists for both successful and unsuccessful projects. Reviewing the Acid Test encourages some familiarity with the concept in an easy application. In many organizations, review processes are not completed because they have become overly cumbersome and time-consuming.

Increased team skills

Success relies on good communication within the team. To achieve this, each team member needs to be able to express his or her own views, to listen actively and to understand the views of others. The initial clue for the game is ambiguous and is open to a variety of interpretations. So, for example, a salesperson might interpret the clue and activity in a very different manner from a police officer. Group members must work hard to understand one another. There is also the capacity for misunderstanding, in which two people think they have interpreted the clue in the same way, while another group member might see there was a difference between the two. Developing an understanding of one's own communication style and the potential barriers to good communication is a prerequisite for good teamwork.

About

Chris Elgood Associates Limited (Elgood Effective Learning) was created by Chris Elgood, MA, author of *The Handbook of Management Games and Simulations* (1997). The company's objective is to extend the use of games and simulations as an alternative to direct instruction. Christine Elgood, BA, MBA, took over in 1977 and has developed new material for the current environment and new methods that exploit up-to-date technology. The company's greatest strength remains treating each client as a special case.

References

Elgood, C, ed (1997) *The Handbook of Management Games and Simulations*, Gower Publishing Company, London

Lewis, E. St Elmo (1908) *Financial Advertising: The history of advertising*, Levey Brothers, United States

Scott, T D (1983) *Tactical Engagement Simulation after Action Review Guidebook* (No ARI-RP-83-13), Army Research Institute for the Behavioral and Social Sciences, Alexandria, VA

9
Add Value

Know Your Customer

CECILIE ELISABETH KALHØJ KOBBELGAARD, UCN act2learn

#ServiceValueProposition #CustomerJourney #CustomerFocus

The service industry continues to grow. We use services constantly. We check online banking on our mobile phones, use apps, order goods on the internet, go shopping, etc. In Denmark, the service industry accounts for a large part of the gross national product. Almost 70 per cent of all workers in the European Union (EU) carry out their functions within the tertiary sector (LearnEurope, 2017).

It is a huge market that keeps growing. This, together with the fact that customers are becoming ever more conscious consumers, mean that more is required from a service than ever before; this places greater demands on companies to meet their customers' needs.

Customer service often starts way before the customer has received the product. It could be on the company's homepage or webshop, through telephone calls, on the company's parking space, in the company's reception or entrance, etc. The customer experience does not stop when the product has been paid for. There might be complaints, customer clubs, newsletters, etc.

Depending on the type of customers a company has, the significance of the above will differ in respect to the customer's experience with the company. A good, effective service thus requires the organization to look at what experience it wants to provide or what difference it wants to make for its customers, based on their needs, because service and value are inseparable. Yale Information Technology Services (Yale University, 2017: 1) defines a service as 'A means of delivering value to customers by facilitating outcomes customers want to achieve without the ownership of specific costs and risks.'

But very few companies have this focus as part of the development and deliverance of the value proposition in their everyday business tasks. When the knowledge of the customer and the steps the customer takes in his or

Figure 9.1 A typical play situtation

her journey are integrated into the mindset of the company, their service is naturally improved. The Add Value game (Figure 9.1) helps companies to achieve this focus.

The Add Value game leads participants through all elements of the service experience. Participants learn which services to improve, whether the right services are offered, and which services can be discontinued since they do not create increased value for customers. During the game, participants review the entire customer service system and companies often make bold choices when playing. In this respect, the nature of a board game is important. Service and customer experience are aspects that are relevant throughout the company and therefore are often the subject of endless discussions. But the presentation in a game can level out this discussion and give everyone a voice. Often, those who do not participate in the endless discussions come up with the best ideas during the game and have the decisive voice. The board game creates an informal atmosphere that allows for more creative ideas, which pushes a company a long way in a short amount of time.

Gameplay

Add Value – Know Your Customer is divided into four parts, which take the customer on a tour of his or her meeting with the company. The points at which the customer meets with the company, such as reception, website

Figure 9.2   Personas and touchpoints

and so on, are called 'contact points' (Figure 9.2). Therefore, throughout the tour, the focus is on how the company can deliver good service to a specific customer at the individual contact points.

On the first game board, the players identify the company's customer. This customer is a central element during the rest of the game. In the second part of the game, the customer takes a tour of the company. On the way, the customer is given some challenges, and it is up to the players to play the part of the customer and to overcome the challenges that might arise. Following the tour, it is up to the players to prioritize the answers they received at the individual contact points. These priorities are then turned into actions in the last part of the game. Finally, participants develop three-star ideas that will give the company some insight into which contact points will make a difference to their customers.

Key gains that the game enables

Add Value has been played with many different Danish companies in recent years. To explain the gains earned in each phase of the game, we will use examples from these cases.

Part one – personas

In all its simplicity, the 'personas' phase of the game is about reaching common ground on which to understand the customer's needs. By knowing the customer's needs, the company can target its services directly at the customer and identify the contact points at which the customer meets the company (Nielsen, 2012).

In this phase, the players take turns to draw a personas question card to be answered. Each question focuses on specific knowledge about the customer. Together, the answers paint a picture of the customer and help the company to identify the customer's needs and possibilities to be aware of when designing its service.

Gains

The cases show us that companies gain more than just valuable knowledge about their customers. The discussion in this phase also eliminates and sometimes manifests the disagreements in the company's own understanding of the customers they serve. Furthermore, companies often discover areas of importance in their customer description of which they are not aware. After the game is finished, companies often have a better understanding of what they need to discover in detail in the future. This has been shown to be especially important for smaller companies, such as start-ups. Atnu, a Danish start-up that sells quality supplements for sport and a healthy lifestyle, explains their gains:

> For a start-up like Atnu, it is extremely important to be able to familiarize ourselves with our customers because time and resources are scarce. This means that we do not have many trials to meet the customer in the right way. Add Value has given us insight into our customers and how we need to address them and an overview of what we need to do. We now know how many factors we can work with and think about in our service. (Simon Hasbøg, National Sales Manager at Atnu, personal communication)

Part two – the user tour

The purpose of the user tour is to gain insight into the contact points at which the customer meets the company – before, during or after a physical meeting. At these contact points, it should be clear how the company approaches the specific customer at present, the value the contact point creates, and what the company can do to create added value for the customer.

Gains

The company is asked to find and prioritize the nine most important contact points at which there is a clear contact, either physically or electronically, between the company and the customer. The contact points must be placed in the natural order in which they occur. This gives the company a good understanding of the system the customers experience. There are numerous examples of companies that stop maintaining the various suboptimal contact points individually and start optimizing the service of the entire experience due to their newly gained overview. This has proven to be successful even in the most service-minded industries. The Danish hotel Comwell Sport Rebild has used Add Value to gain this perspective:

> We used the game to communicate across the different departments of the hotel. It made us talk about service within areas that are placed across the hotel and the journey of the customer – the services that can be extra hard to coordinate. (Jane Andersen, Hotel Manager at Comwell Sport Rebild, personal communication)

Throughout this phase, the company is challenged in how it interacts with the customer by drawing challenge cards. These cards introduce design-thinking methods, change the customer's needs, or change the environment in which the service is rendered. This forces the company to think differently about the way it usually performs services. After this phase, the company will have a better understanding of the customer's journey, what value is created at the different contact points, and have new ideas on how to develop the service in the future.

Part three – prioritizations

The purpose of the prioritization game is to reflect on which financial and customer values the specific contact points offer, as well as prioritize the most important contact points the company wants to continue working on. The participants are first asked to reduce the nine contact points to the five with the greatest potential for development. These are then assessed to discover the financial value the contact point creates for the company and the value it creates for the customer. Afterwards, the participants will vote for the best ideas on which to continue working.

Gains

Participants must have a focus for the development phase. Many companies have a tendency to assess all the possibilities and see all of them as equally important; accordingly, this round is often found to be very challenging.

Part four – the star round

The purpose of the star round is to describe concrete actions based on the contact points that the company has prioritized. The actions are described by each player. Next, all players discuss the actions together, which contributes to creating a common understanding and a basis on which to implement the company's actions.

Gains

In this round, the players create hands-on ideas that can be implemented immediately in the company. This ensures that the game has a tangible outcome. Several of the companies that have used Add Value have afterwards been able to change and optimize specific systems internally or externally, immediately after having played the game.

Kruse Vask, a Danish industrial laundry and textile service, played our game with a variety of employees to mix up the executive board with the production staff and the front-line staff with the closest contact to their customers:

> Add Value worked – across both functions, levels of education and presumptions and created a good and fun basis to talk in depth about our business and wishes for the future. This game really made sense for us! We ended up having very concrete modification possibilities for our daily business with the facilitation by UCN act2learn. (Sarah Kruse, Sales and Purchasing Director at Kruse Vask, personal communication)

Kruse Vask ended up implementing new procedures to deliver their products and internal changes to celebrate satisfied customers and positive feedback.

Service design as a differentiator

It is to a company's advantage to play the game several times, since it enables the company to become familiar with all elements of the customers' service experience. The company can also play the game with a focus on specific customers, to target services at their specific needs. The game can also be played at times when the company needs to be challenged about its service, and when management wants to evaluate the company. By using a board game to optimize and design the service, the company can address important subjects in just a matter of hours, even without substantial financial resources. Add Value takes participants briefly through all the steps of the design process. However, merely playing the game for a couple of hours is not sufficient. The company must then implement the lessons it has learnt.

Customer service must be a part of the company's DNA. For effective customer service, the company must have deep knowledge of its customers' wants and needs. The company must understand the customers' journey. To be able to change its customer service, employees must be able to speak freely within the organization, not just in board meetings and within the group of leaders. The company must hear about experiences and share in the knowledge gathered from all layers of the organization; it must incorporate all these aspects when it wants to make a change. A board game can create the informal atmosphere needed to kickstart this exchange of knowledge.

About

At UCN act2learn, companies receive tailor-made special and further education programmes with state-recognized qualifications at the Diploma Degree level or Academy Profession Degree level. In addition, UCN act2learn offers short- or long-term professional training courses, development processes and thematic one-day seminars. Our professional fields of expertise include education, health, technology, management and HR. We apply these both individually and as combined, interdisciplinary solutions.

References

LearnEurope (2017) [accessed 9 March 2017] The Service Sector [Online] http://www.learneurope.eu/index.php?cID=304

Nielsen, L (2012) Personas, in *The Encyclopedia of Human-Computer Interaction*, ed M Soegaard and R F Dam, Aarhus, Denmark

Yale University (2017) [accessed 9 March 2017] ITIL Foundations: What Is a Service? [Online] https://its.yale.edu/news/itil-foundations-what-service

10

Align

Implementing organizational values

THOMAS BENEDICT AND KARIN VRIJ, InContext Consultancy BV

#OrganizationalCulture #OrganizationalValues #Onboarding

Align is an online values game, aimed at introducing, exploring and understanding core values, as well as building enthusiasm and intrinsic motivation for participants to live their values in their daily work. Align is a game for 4–8 players, preferably working in the same family group. Participants receive challenges, events, chance cards and dilemmas. These game elements trigger discussion and reflection on values and key behaviours. Participants gain insights into how living their values every day helps themselves, their teams and, ultimately, their organization to be successful.

A different approach for implementing values

Our client is a fast-growing technical company working in different European countries. Initially, the business did not spend too much time on behaviour. Selling was easy and the growth was hardly manageable, since the company grew rapidly. Then three things happened: the company became so large that many employees became disconnected with the original founder's mentality and the excitement and drive that accompanied it. Large, multinational clients began to request a unified approach between different countries, triggering higher levels of interdependence and a need for more collaboration between various local entities. Multiple new players began to enter the market, which intensified competition and the need to improve employee and customer satisfaction.

New questions were asked: what is the common denominator in the organization? What makes us unique? Why do we all want to work here? How can we positively involve and align each employee? How do we tackle difficult challenges? When is a decision the right one? In asking these questions, it became clear there was a need to formulate a company identity. The exploration and definition of core values with an associated set of key behaviours was one outcome of this process. But merely defining values is not enough. Values that are not shared, lived and practised on a daily basis by all members of the organization have no effect. The Align game was designed to be a key part of the process of implementing core values. The dynamics of this game have been tried and tested in many different organizations to help people understand and live the desired behaviour. Align has taken this core to the next level: an easy-to-use, online, multilingual experience. Align was built in such a way that the game engine, the core of the system, can easily be reused to impact any organization, with different customers, products, employees, processes, dilemmas and core values. Only the contents need to be customized. The interface, logic and infrastructure remain the same.

Value: cornerstone of the company identity

Core values are a cornerstone of company vision. Together with its *core purpose,* which is the organization's fundamental reason for being, they define the company's *core identity.* Core values are an organization's essential and enduring tenets; they are the glue that holds a company together as it grows and changes, according to Collins and Porras in their influential article 'Building your company's vision' (Collins and Porras 1996). The company's core values shape its culture and reflect what it holds to be important. For decades, it has been recognized that organizational core values have a significant positive effect on the lives of employees as well as on their organization's performance (Posner, Kouzes and Schmidt 1985).

Every individual working in an organization is involved in making hundreds of decisions every day. The decisions we make are a reflection of our values and beliefs, and they are always directed towards a specific purpose. That purpose is the satisfaction of our individual or collective organizational needs. When we use our values to make decisions, we make a deliberate choice to focus on what is important to us. When values are shared, they build internal cohesion in a group (Barrett, 2010).

Many companies focus mainly on developing technical competencies, but often forget the underlying beliefs, the invisible 'oil', that make their companies run smoothly: core values. Establishing strong core values provides both internal and external advantages to the company: core values help companies in the decision-making process. They educate clients and potential customers about the company and clarify the company's identity (Fong, 2013).

To conclude, the core values of an organization shape its culture, give it an identity, and reflect what it holds to be important. It is the guideline when making difficult decisions and it drives employee fulfilment. Living the company's values in daily life improves the employees' as well as the organization's performance.

Objectives: Align game

The Align game was designed to be a key part of the core values implementation process – to introduce, explore and understand core values. The main objectives of the game are:

1 To help participants recognize the link between daily challenges, the core values and success.

2 To motivate employees to make decisions and act in accordance with the core values.

3 To experience behaviour aligned with the core values and learn to discuss and apply a combination of values in challenging daily activities.

4 To experience the (negative) impact of non-compliance on risks, customer satisfaction, quality and collaboration with colleagues.

This is not to be achieved by force, in a pedantic or manipulative way, but through exploration, interaction and dialogue.

Gameplay

The Align game is a digitalized board game in which, within two hours, players, will understand and experience the organizational values, accompanying behaviours and the effects in working thoroughly with these. Its aim is to generate the highest organizational score, working as one organization. During the game, players experience challenges, events, chance cards and dilemmas. Each player has an individual score on the core values and the

Figure 10.1 Dashboard of an individual player

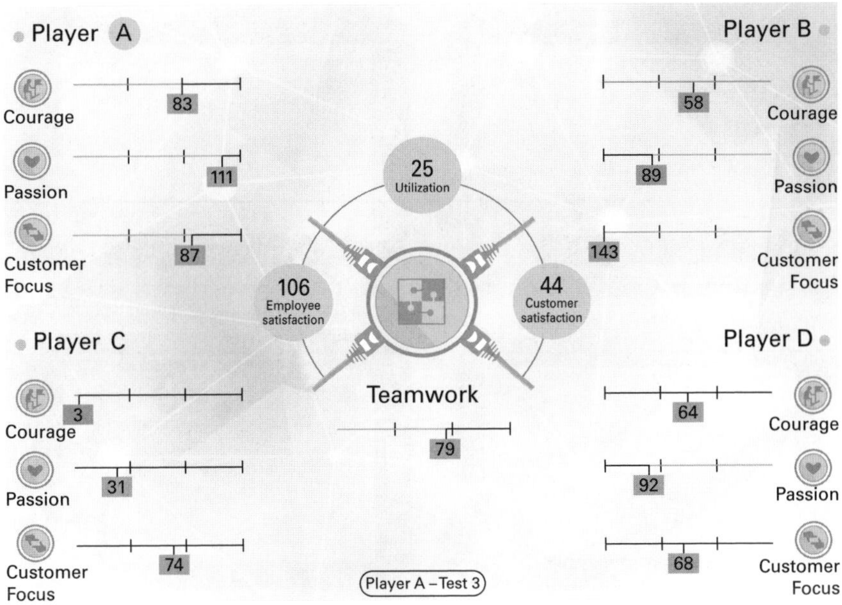

Player A – Test 3

three organizational result areas (employee satisfaction, customer satisfaction and total sales) to influence and monitor during the game. The game can be played repeatedly by all levels of the organization.

Start of the game

At the start, 4–8 players have their own tablet and sit around a central game board (Figure 10.1). There is a main leaderboard with the organizational score compared to other teams. One facilitator leads the game. He or she encourages and deepens discussions, confronts, clarifies insights and identifies key lessons.

Dilemmas, challenges, chance cards and events

Each player receives one of the four digital cards at random (Figure 10.2). A dilemma describes a scenario and a choice between two or three responses. The player is challenged to select the right response. A challenge describes a difficult situation, which the participant may choose to accept or not. A chance card contains a question or assignment. An event card describes events that one might encounter in a certain role during daily activities. Players are advised to keep the events they receive in mind during the game, since events are not generated at random, but as a consequence of choices made by each player.

Figure 10.2   Each player receives one of the four digital cards at random

Chance: Describes a question or assignment

Event: Describes events that you or the organization encounter(s) during daily activities

Challenge: Describes a challenging situation to accept or not

Dilemma: Describes a scenario with the choice between responses

Dialogue with different perspectives

The player reads the card out loud to the other players, before they decide upon their response. Often, a broad discussion takes place about why they should choose a certain direction. Independent of their own choice, they have already learnt from the dialogue between different points of view.

Karma: how you experience reality

The system records the choices the players make. The choices they make define how they experience reality. For example, a strong team player will have a different experience when he or she asks for help than an individualistic player. A strongly customer-focused sales person will get more results from his or her sales conversations. By tracking each participant's choices throughout the game, each player develops a profile. This profile, or 'karma', is not shared with participants openly, but drives which events the player will receive.

Short-term versus long-term results

Each player has an individual score on each of the core values. Through playing, it becomes clear that some decisions lead to more points on certain values, but fewer points on others. Participants are encouraged to discover that suitable events are generated based on their profile, which is represented by the combination of the scores on their values. In addition, the current profile determines what the best decision is for each new dilemma or challenge. Each time a decision is made, it in turn influences the profile and, through that, their events and opportunities for the rest of the game.

Individual versus common results

Another element in the game is the organizational result areas, which indicate how well the organization is doing. Every two rounds, participants can invest in either their individual values score or in their shared organizational result areas. During the game, participants learn that, next to a balanced investment in the organization, investing in living their own values accelerates organization results.

Key gains: living the values benefits organizational results

Making abstract core values come to life

During the game, players have discussed how to deal with difficult daily situations with the help of the core values. The effect of this is that the values, which started off as abstract sentences that someone else thought of, become loaded with meaning and emotions, so that they come alive in the minds of participants. Participants who have finished playing the Align game are deeply connected to the core values. They experience them as their own. They understand, discuss and think about how values could make a difference for themselves, their team and the organization as a whole. During the implementation process, the follow-up of the game consisted of the formulation of a team charter, in which participants defined how they would bring the values to life in their own work environment. This was always a lively and productive dialogue with very specific behavioural do's and don'ts related to daily practice.

Take responsibility for your experience

The choices participants make define how they experience reality. In the game, events do not just happen; rather, each player influences these events, even if this influence is indirect or unconscious. One of the key learnings of this game is that what happens to us is not solely driven by coincidence or the random acts of others, but to a large extent is the compounded effect of all the choices we have made up to that moment.

Working according to the values benefits organizational results

During the game, participants learn that living the organizational values accelerates success. Living the values, in balance, is the driver for exhibiting the most suitable behaviour and making the best decisions under difficult circumstances. The degree to which values are aligned has a positive impact on the results the organization achieves. Employees focusing on their values together become better at collaboration, more resilient, happier and more successful than others.

Reaction from participants

Players experience the added value of living the organizational values by playing the Align game. The values are not imposed on them, but players understand and explore the values and choose themselves to make a valuable contribution. One player reacted as follows:

> When I heard our core values for the first time, I thought this is, again, something made up by headquarters and not really relevant for me. After playing this game I really get why we have these core values and how I can apply this into my daily activities.

Next to this experience, the Align game provides a starting point and a context in which to reflect working methodology. After playing the game, players expressed this by saying:

> I really liked playing this game with my team and discussing together how to encounter challenges or respond to a dilemma aligned with our core values.

Players experience how their behaviour and choices can be of added value for themselves, their team and the organization as a whole. One player reached this conclusion by saying:

> I never realized that (not) acting according to these values would impact the overall performance of an organization. It really opened my eyes.

Align allows players to experiment and experience the results of their choices in an informal and positive way:

> During the game as a team we had so much fun figuring out all the questions and reaching for the highest score. Loved it!

Players look back on a pleasant learning experience and are enthusiastic about putting the lessons into practice. They reflect on and discuss behaviour and gain insight into how they can contribute to improving their personal, team and organizational results.

Origins of Align

Align is a concept that has evolved over the course of about 10 years. The first version was a board game that was developed as a general introduction instrument for an insurance company.

After this, the concept was adapted and used in different gaming solutions for clients in the banking, IT and high-tech industries. The current online version of Align is built in such a way that client-specific content is developed on top of the existing game engine. This greatly reduces development time and costs.

About

At InContext, strategic change in business and people come together. This is because InContext is at a crossroad between the business side (technology, processes, business models, marketing, sales, supply chain, finance, IT) and the people side (attitude, energy, skills, motivation, authenticity, connection, integrity). With this unique combination of knowledge and skills, we are able to place any intervention in the context of an organization and thus go directly to the heart of the problem. We link people to process, thereby creating impact and results.

References

Barrett, R (2010) [accessed 9 March 2017] The Importance of Values in Building a High Performance Culture [Online] https://www.valuescentre.com

Collins, J C and Porras J I (1996) Building Your Company's Vision, *Harvard Business Review*, **74** (5), p 65

Fong, W (2013) [accessed 9 March 2017] Company Core Values: Why to Have Them and How to Define Them [Online] https://7geese.com/benefits-of-having-core-values-and-how-to-set-them-in-your-organization

Posner, B Z, Kouzes, J M and Schmidt, W H (1985) Shared values make a difference: an empirical test of corporate culture, *Human Resource Management*, **24** (3), 293–309

11
Bizzbuilder

How to sustainably grow a professional services business

THOMAS BENEDICT, InContext Consultancy BV

#CustomerFocus #BusinessDevelopment #ManagingGrowth

Bizzbuilder is a digital game about growing a business in the professional services industry (Figure 11.1). Managers in these firms usually rise through the ranks and face the challenge of maintaining existing clients, developing new ones and keeping their professional teams happy. No wonder most of these firms invest seriously in developing their managers to be able to lead their businesses to success.

Figure 11.1   Bizzbuilder screens

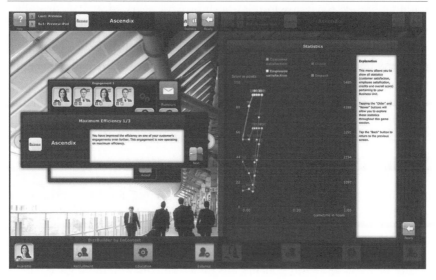

How to apply

Bizzbuilder is applicable for managers of consultants, lawyers, tax experts, accountants and other highly educated professionals who offer their services to large companies.

The hidden secrets of success

Participants experience a high-pressure simulated environment in which key tactical and operational decisions need to be made about maintaining focus, developing clients, building a strong and motivated team, and developing collaboration with other teams in the firm. The game allows participants to experience and understand the forces that govern the long-term success and growth of a professional services firm. Many of the hidden dynamics of these businesses can otherwise only be learnt the hard way, through trial and error, with years of experience. Bizzbuilder offers a safe, fast and challenging environment to learn together with colleagues what it takes to succeed.

Simply doing a good job does not give someone the edge to build a strong and sustainable business as a senior manager, director or partner in a large professional services firm. That requires consciously and actively investing in client relationships, developing and growing great people, and building high-trust, win-win relationships with peers within the firm. But delivering quality and investing in relationships at the same time is easier said than done. How does one put that into practice? Where does the company find the time? How can a manager inspire clients and colleagues to search for synergy together? The Bizzbuilder game was developed to let participants experience which choices and actions lead to sustainable growth and which ones lead to failure in the shorter or longer term.

Sustainable growth requires focus and balance

Bizzbuilder lets participants explore how to set the stage for sustainable growth without upsetting the fragile balance involving quality, customer satisfaction, new business opportunities, business focus, available resources and competences, team motivation, peer relationships and rate of growth. If any of these vital components are underestimated or misaligned, small issues start to arise. If these issues, in turn, are not dealt with effectively, a domino effect can occur that may ultimately put the business itself at risk.

Success depends on insight and counterintuitive behaviour

Bizzbuilder was originally developed for a large international accountancy, tax and organizational consultancy firm. This firm is structured around partners running their own business unit. Each partner is responsible for the profit and loss of his or her unit. As this structure is frequently used in large firms, it obviously has many benefits. One of the important downsides of this model is that each business unit tends towards protecting their own clients, instead of sharing them with other business units. Business units continue to serve clients even if the clients' needs surpass the specialization of the business unit. This means that the potential to serve clients optimally by utilizing all available specializations is generally not implemented. This causes client dissatisfaction and employee dissatisfaction; if it continues, it will ultimately cause growth to stagnate.

Understanding this essential downside of the organizational structure and the effects it has on individual decisions is the first step in making a fundamental change. In order to make the structure work and enable sustainable and profitable growth, each business unit must develop a realistic perspective on its area of expertise, as well as its limits. It is also essential that it develops trust between partners to share clients, so client satisfaction continues to be high, even when requests supersede the abilities of a single business unit. Understanding and dealing with these dynamics, and thus creating a basis for (further) growth, is the subject of Bizzbuilder.

Bizzbuilder game dynamics

Participants discover the positive effects of dealing with client relationships actively and selectively, collaborating with colleagues, and making client-specific investments in keeping with the business focus and available competencies. While playing the game, they discover how a proactive approach with existing clients can lead to more customer satisfaction, repeat business, information, and active referrals to potential new clients. After all the teams have input their decisions, the system gives them feedback about their total revenue, staff turnover and client information; it then provides a total impact score, comprising customer satisfaction, employee engagement, total sales and profit level. Based on this management information, teams can adjust their game strategy in order to improve their score. As the game proceeds and the chosen strategies are implemented, they can either gain or lose new clients and projects. In addition, each virtual team member evaluates his or her job satisfaction, leading to more or less engagement and productivity, as well as the decision of whether or not to remain on the team.

Systems thinking

Bizzbuilder was developed based on systems thinking, as explained by Peter Senge in his book *The Fifth Discipline* (Senge, 1990). Systems thinking helps us to understand the complex and non-linear relationship between cause and effect, so as to pinpoint learning disabilities in organizations. These learning disabilities can lead to an incorrect understanding of what is going on. For example, people who are themselves operating as part of the system find it hard to see the entire picture of mutual influence between parts of the system. Trying to solve business problems without understanding the entire system in operation usually causes unwanted outcomes. Examples of these outcomes could be that intended solutions have little or no effect, have unintended side effects or that short-term quick fixes have direct consequences for the health of the entire system in the longer term. All of these come to life while playing Bizzbuilder (Figure 11.2).

An example of a quick fix in the game is a participant who wants to grow his or her business fast and is given an opportunity to expand their services to a client. But in order to fulfil the assignments, they must ask their team to do work they are not trained to do. This means they must overstretch their abilities. This has two unwanted effects. First, the client will not be satisfied with the outcomes, and client satisfaction will therefore decline. With this, the client will be less inclined to offer new opportunities and the company's general reputation declines as well. Second, team members who are asked to do work for which they are not trained will be less productive and less happy. Their reduced happiness can lead to a decision to leave the team. So this quick-fix decision to grow the business will ultimately lead to a dissatisfied customer, a reduction in new opportunities, reduced productivity and a smaller team. Obviously, in the longer term, this quick fix will cause the opposite effect of the one intended.

Gameplay

Bizzbuilder is played with all participants in a meeting room, ideally with eight participants at each table. Each table represents a line of service and

Figure 11.2 System diagram for Bizzbuilder

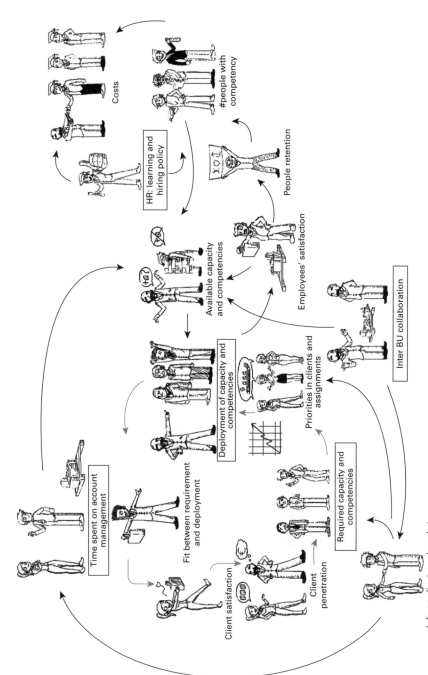

has four business units, with two players running each business unit on a specially designed tablet app that is connected to a central system. Each business unit makes its own decisions and faces its own consequences. In the course of the game, business units will need to collaborate in order to service larger clients, thereby achieving success in the game. Towards the end of the game, business units will even need to collaborate with other tables to reach the highest scores. The impact scores of all business units are projected, so that all participants can see how they are doing compared to their colleagues.

Key gains that the game enables

The impact of Bizzbuilder

By receiving clear, direct feedback, participants develop a straightforward, realistic impression of the consequences of their decisions. Are they winning new business, or losing clients? While playing the game, they develop strategies to better serve their clients. The results are shown in real time. This enables them to get hands-on experience about the effects of their choices on the success of their business. This experience can be transferred to building their business in real life. It helps them to understand the less visible, long-term dynamics that lead business units to success or failure.

Bizzbuilder helps participants to understand the dynamics of their business and see that many events, both positive and negative, can be linked to the decisions they made, instead of being caused by luck or coincidence. Participants learn that sustainable growth is only achievable if they truly understand and manage the entire system. Only balanced, well-thought-out actions will lead to long-term, positive outcomes. Bizzbuilder helps to build trust between important players in the organization in an area that is critical to success. It shows companies that collaboration reveals business opportunities that would otherwise remain hidden.

About

At InContext, people and strategic change in business come together. This is because InContext is at a crossroads between the business side (technology, processes, business models, marketing, sales, supply chain, finance, IT) and the people side (attitude, energy, skills, motivation, authenticity, connection, integrity). With this unique combination of knowledge and skills, we are able to place any intervention in the context of your organization, thereby going directly to the heart of your problem. We link people to process, thus creating impact and results.

Reference

Senge, P (1990) *The Fifth Discipline: The art and science of the learning organization*, Currency Doubleday, New York

12

Business Branching

Balancing ongoing operations and innovation initiatives

SUNE GUDIKSEN AND JAKE INLOVE, GameBridges

#CompetitiveAdvantage #InnovationOpportunities #ResourceAllocation

The innovation game Business Branching (Figure 12.1) deals with the difficult and complex challenge of balancing ongoing operations and new innovation-oriented activities. According to influential business thinker and researcher Rita McGrath (2013), companies can no longer expect sustainable competitive advantages and are forced to seek out temporary advantages on a regular basis in order to compete. Here, Rita McGrath (2013) asks the question: 'How do you reconfigure the organization to simultaneously disengage from the original advantage while moving resources into the next one?'

It is of vital importance for all companies to constantly work on finding this balance through resource allocation, competence development, and generally understanding the need for both parts of the dilemma to be present in everyday business situations.

Therefore, it is crucial for companies to build up a portfolio of business opportunities, so they can avoid significant declines in profit when specific markets are disrupted – or maybe even profit from seeking out business opportunities progressively. Consequently, leaders and managers need to learn how to balance the resource allocation between ongoing operations and innovation. The purpose of this game is to exercise the ability to allocate resources to launch and ramp up concrete new business branches, while also exploiting, reconfiguring and disengaging the old business branches.

A business paradox in play

It has been documented by business researchers that finding the balance between ongoing operations and new initiatives is key to successful operations on a leadership level (McGrath, 2013; Govindarajan and Trimble, 2010;

Figure 12.1 Business Branching game board

Govindarajan, 2016). For instance, Govindarajan and colleagues describe this as an inevitable paradox that businesses cannot avoid but rather need to find balancing strategies for. Ongoing operations are characterized by short-term thinking, repeatability and predictability, whereas innovation is based on long-term thinking, chaos, serendipity and unpredictability. The authors argue that:

> Organizations are not designed for innovation. Quite the contrary, they are designed for ongoing operations.

On a further note, Rita McGrath unfolds principles in moving from one business branch to another – from an existing advantage to a new one when the time is right – and timing is everything in this game. McGrath's principles are framed in the following themes: assets and competence allocation, and especially when to use what competencies. According to research from McGrath (2013), a transition from 'access to assets, not ownership of assets' can be observed as key success parameters in the 21st-century business markets.

With temporary, rather than sustainable, advantages being the new norm, the existing value model in companies will always come under pressure, suggesting the need for reconfiguration and renewal of advantages at a more rapid pace. Here it is important to prepare new business advantages ahead of time, rather than wait until economic decline.

Reconfiguration and exit decisions – ie closing one business to launch a new one – are vital. The move from one advantage to another is essential to continual profitability, which means that organizations need to master the transition of assets and competencies.

The business principles in play

Business Branching rests on three foundational business theories related to vital 21st-century challenges, and the game incorporates all three into a combined business game universe with systematic approaches.

Rita McGrath's business value cycles

Based on Rita McGrath's (2013: 13) extensive work on how to compete with temporary business advantages, Business Branching is about how to deploy the right resources in the five stages of a business branch, also called upstream flow in the game, which goes as shown in Table 12.1.

As one can imagine, each stage comes with its own challenges: 'launching' requires an entirely different set of competencies and resources than 'ramping up' or 'exploiting'. Here, the game offers some insights into the participating company on how the current business branches

Table 12.1 Value cycle stages derived from McGrath (2013)

1 Launch	This stage is all about exploring new opportunities and beginning to act on them.
2 Ramp up	This stage is about scaling up the business and trying to capture as many market segments as possible.
3 Exploit	This stage is the most profitable stage, where systems have been put in place and the company can enjoy continually delivering and developing an established and profitable service.
4 Reconfigure	This stage is when the established value proposition begins to be pressured by competing offers that steal market share and the company needs to reconfigure its assets and people to other advantages.
5 Disengage	This is the final stage of a business – when it's no longer profitable and the company needs to shut down that business branch and transition customers and partners to new value propositions.

are doing and how they can be managed. Many companies and leaders are competent in certain stages of the cycle but fall short when faced with the challenges of other stages. Some companies have been exploiting for so long that when faced by the need to reconfigure, they don't know how to launch new initiatives. Conversely, some companies are good at launching but fall short in their ramping-up efforts. Through tasks related to each upstream movement the participants create concrete initiatives to advance upstream movement and learn when to use what type of competencies.

Govindarajan and Trimble's strategy concept on balancing ongoing operations and innovation

The game framework builds on the argument that it is not enough to depict a single value cycle if the purpose is to be able to visualize the complete picture and move resources to new business branches. To move resources from one branch to the next and to develop the needed competencies, the participants need to operate between reconfiguring and closing down existing advantages while launching and ramping up new ones to create perfectly timed sidestep movement (Figure 12.2). Therefore, the first step of the game is to map the complete set of the company's business branches and mark which stage participants believe each branch is in – is it currently launching,

Figure 12.2   A single Business Branch illustrating a value cycle

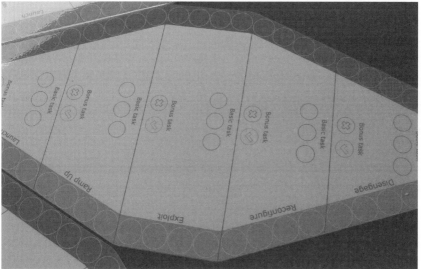

ramping up, exploiting, reconfiguring or disengaging? Furthermore, participants mark how the company's resources are currently allocated to the business branches.

Simon Sinek's golden circle concept

As participants have mapped their current business branches and resource allocation, they go straight to the base of the branches – the reason why the company exists, the big 'Why'. Here, participants examine the 'tree trunk' that holds different business branches together. It begins with the question Simon Sinek (2011) is famous for asking: 'Why does your organization exist?' Here, participants can explore the onset for potential business branches and examine their fit with the company's reason to exist, thereby either transforming the 'Why' or advancing new understandings and interpretations of it. Since business advantages are shorter lived, the 'Why' of a company becomes more flexible. Even though fundamental elements are intact – for instance, some values and core beliefs – new interpretations of the 'Why' are often inevitable.

Gameplay: moving upwards and sideways

The game consists of a centre board and up to eight possible branches. The centre board includes the 'Why' with a reference to Simon Sinek's golden circle (Sinek, 2011). Variations can be written into this 'Why', based on how new branches provoke new aspects of the 'Why'. The 'Why' of a company is always emerging when it comes to specific interpretations, either dealt with explicitly or as a movement forced by market changes. The branches illustrate value proposition cycles on a scale: 1) Launch, 2) Ramp up, 3) Exploit, 4) Reconfigure, and 5) Disengage. Participants are challenged both to move upstream and sideways. Challenges related to upstream movement relate to each stage in the value cycle. A variety of competencies, instantiations and strategies are needed for each stage. Participants have basic tasks to fulfil and bonus tasks that provide extra resources and movements in subsequent rounds.

Sideways movement marks transition from one branch to another. Here, the participants have to devise resources, but also place people either in the red zone (in need of competence development) or in the green zone (ready to fulfil tasks). As McGrath (2013) mentions, 'another factor in play in companies that can move from one set of advantages to another is that they consciously set out to educate and up-skill their people'.

The game lets groups of participants work with the basic tasks from minutes to hours, based on the time available, and then return to the board to discuss changes related to both the 'Why' of the company as well as the specific balance between ongoing operations and innovation. Based on McGrath's theory, Business Branching has a score algorithm that pressures participants to launch new branches before old branches die out or else they face the same destiny as companies in the real market – going bankrupt. This helps participants to look further into their future than their current business branches, while also letting them see that they should not launch new initiatives all the time. It strikes the balance between, on the one hand, being too overly enamoured with existing value propositions to launch something new, and on the other hand, launching too many new value propositions without having the necessary resources and the right competencies in place.

Marketing and promotion company case

In a case clearly illustrating the paradox between ongoing operations and innovation, we worked with a company that had years of success on their existing value proposition based on promotion and marketing. Now, they experienced the first declines and signs that reconfiguration and disengagement was not that far away, but they also found that maybe a scaling up on an existing business branch might lead to better times.

Based on this initial mapping of Business Branching, the team had identified existing value propositions and new potential business branches. Subsequently, the team was divided into two groups. One group focused on an existing business branch and how to scale this in a fierce competition (upstream movement on existing branch). The other group focused on a new value proposition of 'outdoor promotion events' (sidestep movement to a new branch). The groups went through a series of idea-generation activities to further unfold the potential of each branch, and then returned to discuss what these potential moves would mean for status-quo practices in the company.

Based on the game, the team concluded that they currently used all their energy on a declining business branch without advancing on new business branches. Resources were needed to experiment and test new business branches – and quickly, since they were currently falling behind competitors, in for instance, digital solution promotions. Also, employees had to quickly gain new competencies related to the new business branches, while there were still resources available and time to gain them.

In many ways, this case illustrates the paradox between ongoing operations (existing value propositions and practices) and innovation (identifying and launching new value propositions). It is not an either/or approach but rather a balancing activity for leaders and employees. For this reason, it is also of vital importance that this perspective is not geared only towards leaders but also employees, so that everyone understands that moving from one competitive advantage to another is happening at a rapid pace.

Game versions and layers

Business Branching can function as two game types. First, Business Branching can be a co-creation game, where its focus is on a concrete mapping of your company and figuring out how you can allocate resources in your company's current situation and ahead. Here, the game offers practical insights to launching, ramping up, exploiting, reconfiguring and disengaging your company's business branches. You co-create possible strategies to allocate resources and optimize your company's economic situation.

Second, Business Branching can be a learning game, where its focus is on helping managers learn how to handle the various problems with balancing innovation and ongoing operations. Here, the game is played with fictional, but relatable cases with a focus on the timing of resource allocation and a selection of built-in tasks.

We have played the game with both small and large companies. Based on this experience, we found that dealing with the problem of allocating resources to both ongoing operations and innovation is a dilemma that companies face regardless of their size. It is relevant for the entrepreneur who has launched, ramped up and exploited one business branch, but is hesitant to launch another. It is relevant for large companies, where middle management is too closely tied to a certain business branch and therefore hangs on to this branch for too long, even when critical numbers and decreasing signs tell them to launch something new. As McGrath (2013) states:

> Preventing resources from being held hostage by the leaders of a particular advantage will become more standard as firms become aware of the dangers of a leader hanging on to an old advantage for too long.

The same goes the other way around, as well. We have observed many strong managers and business developers having a big portfolio of strong ideas and potential new value propositions, however without the nerve and overview to choose only to launch and ramp-up the one with the most promise and follow this through.

Key gains that the game enables

The value of the game lies in the concrete action in upstream flows and side-stepping moves, as well as in learning about how to master this balance. The timing in the movement of resources and competence development is the key in the game and in developing temporary competitive advantages on a regular basis. Participants accelerate new insights on how to take action moves right after completing the activity based on the concrete situation they are in, and thus they learn how to manage the crucial balance. Since the game moves between concrete co-created action and advancement in overall understanding and learning, we can pinpoint the following outcomes:

Co-creation outcomes

- Concrete ideas on how to move upstream (advancing existing business advantages) and also when to leave them behind, including when to use what types of competencies and available resources.
- Concrete ideas on how to create strong sidestep moves, including moving resources and build-up competencies to support new potential advantages in a careful and optimal transition.
- Keeping the 'Why' flexible and advance new interpretations continuously in the fight to stay afloat and update business relevance.

Learning outcomes

- Learning how to overview a company's business branches and resource allocation, so one can spot weaknesses and pitfalls to be able to progressively handle them before economic crisis arises.
- Learning how to plan well-timed resource allocation and competence development, so one can diminish wasteful use of resources and resources held hostage to progressively build competitive advantages.
- Learning different strategies to handle each stage of a business branch, so one knows what to do when launching, ramping up, exploiting, reconfiguring and disengaging a business branch.

About

At GameBridges, we have an extensive overview of organizational tendencies, powerful theories and effective practices. We are future-focused in our approach, which enables us to identify upcoming millennial organizational challenges, and we encourage our collaborators to think ahead. Our games blend concrete innovative actions with powerful learning perspectives.

References

Govindarajan, V (2016) *The Three-Box Solution: A strategy for leading innovation*, Harvard Business Review Press, Boston

Govindarajan, V and Trimble, C (2010) *The Other Side of Innovation: Solving the execution challenge*, Harvard Business Press, Boston

McGrath, R G (2013) *The End of Competitive Advantage: How to keep your strategy moving as fast as your business*, Harvard Business Review Press, Boston

Sinek, S (2011) *Start With Why: How great leaders inspire everyone to take action*, Penguin, London

13

Changesetter

Leading change

**LEIF SØRENSEN, CAMILLA BOYHUS MADSEN AND
MAJA SPANGSBERG KROGSTRUP,** Actee

#WorkplaceLearning #ChangeManagement #LeadershipDevelopment

Changesetter is a game that addresses change management. Using the game, managers can practise leading changes in the workplace. Players face a wide array of challenges and dilemmas that they will recognize from everyday work scenarios. The players need to move 10 stakeholders, representing a team of employees or colleagues, through a change process over a period of time. This means players gain knowledge that can be directly applied the next time they need to introduce a change at the company. The game also provides a range of assets before and after the game has been played, to enable easy knowledge transfer from the game.

Gameplay

The game is played in groups (Figure 13.1). Each group is given a boat, which symbolizes the change project. The group must push the boat as far through the change as possible, spending only 100 hours. The result is measured by a calculation scheme in the game. Each choice creates a new situation, which the players have to take into consideration when choosing a new approach to solve the obstacles presented in the three sections. The game is typically played in teams of four to six or in larger groups of 15 to 30, with one consultant.

The sections of the game

The standard game case consists of three sections. Let's start the journey into Changesetter through the lens of these sections and through a content case

Figure 13.1 Floor board turn with Changesetter

called 'Destination CRM'. This case is about the changes involved in implementing a comprehensive customer relation management (CRM) system in the company. The player takes the role of middle manager in the company, with responsibility for implementation of the CRM system for a sales team, and goes through the following sections:

- Section one: initial actions.
- Section two: implementation.
- Section three: anchoring.

In section one, the sales company is ready with a newly aligned CRM system. The system will be rolled out throughout the organization. It is designed to collect all customer data in one shared database. The player has been told that the system change will be implemented in the team's work. Rollout will start in six weeks, and it will go live in 13 weeks. In this section, the player will struggle with an employee who will not go along with the change; this means he or she does not move forward on the game board either. Some choices will not have any effect until later in the game.

The player must spend 100 hours in each section. Each section contains a natural stopping point in order to examine the results created by the players.

This process provides an opportunity to draw players' everyday lives into the game. All choices and the phases in a conceptual cycle of change are built with a clear reference to a current theory. For example, if the player chooses option #4, that choice reflects prominent change management theorist John Kotter's (1996) step one, called 'Sense of Urgency'. First, this enables concrete, theory-based feedback. Second, the consultant has the opportunity to talk about experience and use the theory as a 'wall of qualification' of the everyday experience, while remaining open to other ways to solve the question of 'why' in a change. In section two, the installation of the IT solution is currently in progress. There is a range of technical installations that are much more challenging than expected, but overall, it looks like the system will be ready for use within the time frame.

The problems become clearer since it shows that the old system is structured in a way that makes it incompatible with the new solution. All in all, these delays mean that there is not really any progress in tasks such as customer segmentation, change of work processes or the like. The player will be exposed to a new situation and will be required to spend another 100 hours before the next board-game session.

In section three, the implementation process is almost finished, and the number of project activities is waning. The planned implementation process is coming to a close. In a week, the implementation project is officially over; after this phase, no further project activities have been planned. Technically, the system has been operational for a while now, and it works. The company has also finally succeeded in synchronizing most of the data with the original customer system, even though there was a small portion that had to be relinquished. But the system has proven to be very slow. It has also proven to be quite difficult to use. There are many hot keys and codes the employees in the game need to remember. The worries of the super-users about their colleagues' IT abilities have proven to be legitimate and many still use the system in a very limited way.

After the third section, the game is rounded up around the game board and the insights are anchored and reflected upon. This is an element in the game in which the players have an excellent opportunity to reflect on the game dilemmas and relate them to their own everyday working situation.

Other game cases and employee-level games

Some game scenarios, tailored for the employee level, are made to be played by employees and can be facilitated by team managers. This allows the game to be anchored at all levels in the organization, where it will be applied to everyday working situations. In this way, the game works as a supplemental tool to the overall learning value for the company.

The game can take from one hour, using the employee game, to more than four days, using the full version; the full version includes assets attached to the game, such as a gap analysis tool, analysis of choices, working directly on the different phases in the change using Changesetter Live, and looking into leadership and change.

Important effects and learning value

The game is designed over Kolb's (1984) learning circle. The player will go through the learning circle every time a choice is made. To explain this, imagine the player is observing a specific business situation in which he must consider the status of the stakeholders and the boat (representing the change) before acting. In relation to Kolb (1984), this would be the stages of analysis (experience) and reflection (reflection on that experience). From this point, the group takes specific action by using the game choices. Making a choice is complicated, since the choices are divided into management and leadership sections that make the players reflect on their own experiences. At the same time, the players need to have an understanding of leadership and the resources available before making their choice. This takes time and needs to be discussed among the groups. If the players are from the same company, they will naturally use their own organization as a basis to discuss preferences and use the theory as their guide and, as mentioned above, as a 'wall of qualification' (solution based on experience and reflection). Once the choice is implemented in the game, the player gets feedback; this is the most exciting moment in all games. Two types of feedback are given:

1 A text, which reflects the theory upon which the choice is built.

2 Graphics, showing the movement among the stakeholders (employees), which the players are trying to move forward in the change.

This is the testing period in Kolb (1984) (testing the new approach). This process repeats itself approximately 30 times in the general long-version game, less in the short versions, and only six times in the employee version.

Expected outcomes and effects

When considering using a game, the most important question to be answered is: what is the expected outcome? What is it the game needs to help with? Here are some obvious benefits:

- It's fun and it energizes the participants. The game is frequently used as an energizer during the last few days of programmes.

- The learning outcome can be concrete and effective.

- The case can be targeted at a specific situation such as a merger, a new sales approach, a tech transformation, a reorganization, etc.

A game can be provided in different ways and have different formats (employee version, paper version, physical materials, only online, etc). If we look at the overall value for the company using Changesetter, it provides a high impact throughout the organization because the company can play the game in different formats in different settings in the organization. The IT department can play one scenario, and the retail department can play another. A short version can be played with employees and another with managers. In some situations, the game is facilitated by consultants, but the game design is also made for internal facilitators within the company or organization, to drive their own processes. Thus, the value outcome is very much dependent on the distribution design (Figure 13.2).

Regarding the outcome, the higher the number of employees exposed to Changesetter and additional tools explaining the model, the greater the value to the company. This means that it is not only the game that has an impact. Tools, such as the mapping tool called Changesetter Live, or the Changesetter App, support the impact of the learning. Changesetter can therefore be used in all settings. It has been used in relation to mergers across the globe, and there are more than 1,500 facilitators around the world. It has been used by very small companies, just as a tool to create an inspirational day. It is also a tool used by single consultants in their work, as a way of talking about change and helping companies in transformation processes. The overall frame for Changesetter is *change* and *creating transformation*, but under these, more specific themes and topics can be added. Here are some examples: leadership, mergers and acquisitions, co-creation, sales, reorganization, cultural change, system implementation, onboarding, etc.

Figure 13.2   Digital part of Changesetter

Game purpose

Changesetter is a game concept developed for understanding and managing change. The Changesetter simulation cases are especially designed to increase awareness about the change process and the organizational dynamics that follow any change for a team, a company or an institution. The following are some of the theoretical perspectives incorporated into the Changesetter concept.

The management model

The management choices in the case are constructed according to a systematic approach, which is visualized in the model below. The origin of the model is mainly Leavitt's (1965) diamond model, which consists of four interactive components: people, task, structure and technology.

The leadership model

The model describes John Kotter's (1996) eight-step process for implementing a successful transformation, which has become the basics of a 'recipe for change' for many leaders around the world. In Changesetter, the steps represent the leadership tools that the change manager uses through the cycle of change.

The cycle of change and resistance to change

The 'cycle of change' is a model developed by change management expert Rick Maurer (1996). The cycle of change is a tool to heighten our insight into and reflections about how we react to changes. Rick Maurer has described the close coupling between resistance to change and the cyclic nature of changes. According to Maurer's studies, resistance is a reactive defensive action (passive or active) towards a change that appears threatening.

Key learning from Changesetter

In the case scenario 'Destination CRM' the player has the chance to train a team in managing, leading and handling the implementation process of a new CRM system in a sales company with proud traditions and independent employees. The participant plays the middle-level manager who must ensure that the new CRM system functions as expected and is implemented and anchored in the company. The facilitator of the game can train the participants to motivate and lead experienced employees who are independent and used to structuring their own work. Some of the employees have developed the existing CRM system and have a great deal of professional pride invested in it.

At the same time, the participants learn to drive a change and implementation process through a series of leadership and management choices, as well as leadership-style choices. They also learn to handle the frustrations that are bound to arise when the system unexpectedly breaks down. A Changesetter case can be tailored to any organization's specific needs. It is a business process in which the case development is written in close collaboration with the company and Actee. Thus, the following example should be further adjusted around the change concept of Changesetter in order to fulfil a company's specific requirements in regard to change considerations and challenges. This will elevate the learning, since the process focuses on relevance and transfer of learning for the player, both at the specific level (specific change tool) and at a more general level of transferring learning insights.

What does a Changesetter case contain?

As Changesetter encompasses various elements, there are no immediate limitations to how it can be applied. The elements upon which Changesetter are based include:

- a theoretical foundation that embraces the 10 major change management theories;
- physical and interactive models and materials;
- an online case simulation;
- Changesetter Live and a change-coaching technology.

In short, Changesetter has the flexibility to be used as a change management simulation, but also as an analytical tool. This means that a company can modify the process to fit its specific needs and opportunities. With regard to the learning method, it is important to ask the question: who will use Changesetter? To answer this, a company should refer to its organizational chart. Here are some examples of potential target groups in an organization:

- employees affected by the change on all organizational levels and divisions;
- managers at all hierarchical levels or project managers, who have been introduced to and have worked with the Changesetter concept;
- internal consultants and trainers, who have been introduced to the concept and want to be certified in the use of Changesetter;
- external consultants and trainers, who want a tool for driving change;
- HR department personnel, responsible for content on training programmes within the field of change management.

Changesetter holds some great learning advantages as a game. But let's take a critical look at some key arguments for using a game for organizational development.

The engagement argument

Gaming is fun and engaging. This is the best point of departure when something new must be learnt. One valuable advantage of using the Changesetter concept for learning is that it creates a frame around the discussions, through which reflection and perspective sparks. Using a game, the process and the player's experience can be controlled. It is no longer limited to a person delivering the process alone. But the consultant must also feel included in the process design, mainly for reasons of personal motivation. The quality and focus of the dialogue with regard to going through the game sections are very much dependent on the consultant. Therefore, the consultant's role is a very important part of the design. It is also an area Actee supports as much as it can.

The reinforcement argument

If the game is considered without facilitation, the learning outcome might be less rich. But a high outcome supporting the overall learning goal can still be achieved. When it comes to reinforcement of learning, the learning industry has a challenge. The trainer's support ceases when the players leave the workshop. This is a challenge we take seriously in Changesetter.

Game example without workshop

Playing the game even without a full workshop can be a very powerful experience. One Actee customer, an international company, had employees who played the game 3,500 times across seven countries. In the game session, the employees scored 4.86 out of 5. This is more than most evaluations from workshops on the same scale. This is an example of how Changesetter has been a great, usable game tool for development within a large-scale global organization. Changesetter and the operational learning design were applied to business units and departments across country borders by providing a platform for managers in which they could use the knowledge they gained from workshops directly in their own working environment. If this had to be done as a regular process, it would be very costly. Just multiply the 3,500 employees with 20 people x day rates on consultant fees. Another argument is the context of the players. Here we have the player in his or her own context and the discussion facilitated by the manager. This will naturally lead to a dialogue about the player's real situation and perhaps also a quest for solutions to the everyday practice dilemmas.

A client case

In another case, the client comes from the telecom industry. It has a Nordic head office in Norway, but controls brands around the world, including Asia, China, India, Thailand, etc. They have used Changesetter more than 2,000 times per year now over the last couple of years and have put almost 20 per cent of their managers through a Changesetter workshop. The telecom industry, by nature, is often disrupted by technical changes. Therefore, the company needs to develop the capacity for rapid change; at the same time, because they operate all over the world, they need to cope with different cultures and understandings of leadership and management. The Organization Development Manager in the telecom company explains why they have made great use of the Changesetter concept:

> Gradually, more and more of our business units are using the change management concept. Overall, we use Changesetter to make people aware of change in our organization and to identify the real issues with people not succeeding in change initiatives. Thus, we have used the simulator to make people in our organization aware of different kinds of change models, to understand the cycle of change and resistance to change. This has received very positive feedback across the group business units. We use Changesetter as a global theme for change. We have experienced that the concept with its tools and methodologies work very well in Scandinavia, Central and Eastern Europe (CEE) and Asia. Thailand, as an example, has really embraced Changesetter, where they use a customized version with theories related to change agents suited for their work culture. It has been good learning to see that one concept can work really well in different settings across our global organization.

Analyses of game info

Does analysis of game choices prove learning has occurred? One great advantage of game-based learning is the possibility of analysing the choices made in the game. Figure 13.3 illustrates the choices made in the game between sections one and two in a company case within the telecom industry. These four choices are measured against the same four choices made by all players in the same case, but outside of the company. This allows us to see the difference in focus between companies and the average player of Changesetter. Since the four choices represent four different approaches in making a compelling change case or creating a sense of urgency, it is possible to see which approach is the preferred one.

These four choices enable seeing the development over time in the specific company with regard to the creation of a sense of urgency (a phase attached to the beginning of the change). The value for any company using

Figure 13.3 Changesetter simulator

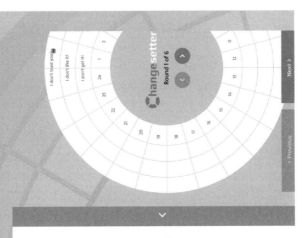

First meeting with the change – how do the colleagues react? (Choose one situation)

1 Visions and Results

The colleagues are gathered for a meeting where it is announced that the new business system, called Optimus Prime, is about to be rolled out in the department. They get information about visions and results, but no further concrete details about why this system has been chosen. On right side of the screen you see the Cycle of Change. The boat tells you where the change is at this point in the process. Click on the

2 Have You Heard?

Some of the colleagues have heard talking in the corridors about a new cutting edge business system, which will replace the existing system, but their manager has not unveiled anything about it yet. Choose this situation to see the colleagues' reactions and learn how it will affect their positions in the change process.

3 An Informal Talk

The manager enters the shared office space to have an informal talk with the group of colleagues. She tells them that she will be there for them throughout the process and that they are always welcome to air their feelings of frustration or doubts to her. Choose this situation to see the colleagues' reactions and learn how it will affect their positions in the change process.

4 No Information Yet

Everything is as usual in Omni Channel. The colleagues are using the IT-system they have had for a long time. Some of the colleagues sense that something is up, but they have not heard anything from their manager yet. Choose this situation to see the colleagues' reactions and learn how it will affect their positions in the change process.

Changesetter can be a proof of the direction the company is taking, with regard to creating a sense of urgency. Figure 13.3 can also serve to illustrate the status, to see the results of the change work. When Changesetter is used as a learning game, a very important question regarding the lessons and outcomes from an organization's change work can be answered: are we spurring any development among our people, when they are exposed to our change efforts? Can we see the results of our change work?

Only by looking at the four choices can we conclude that the company, over the past three years, has moved from a see–feel–change approach to an analyse–think–change approach. Great advantages common to both these approaches are that they focus on activating a deeply felt wish to act on the challenge. Both approaches are often a source of a true sense of urgency, which has the potential to be a very positive and focused driver for change.

On the other hand, the analyse–think–change approach, unfortunately, has the weakness that even though it might appeal to the rational, intellectual side of the stakeholders' minds, it will rarely be able to win their emotions with an impact that will truly raise the sense of urgency. This means that this specific company needs to put more focus on the emotional side of the change work. They might want to support managers who are in need of additional communication material, with a focus on supporting emotions and feelings about the future state of the change. But the overall picture of the game is that the company is getting results, and they are moving people in a direction with more focus on creating the business model before moving ahead. This seems like a great result in an environment of rapid change, with a need for innovative, design-oriented thinking.

We are able to analyse the rest of the choices in the same manner. By examining the two most frequently selected choices and the two most rarely selected ones in each section, we can put together a general picture of the most common trends and methods by which leaders are working, along with their preferences in the daily change work. The major benefit here is that we can gather the data from the cases across the platform, to support a variety of business focuses.

About

Actee brings joy, excitement and curiosity to everyday learning. We advise, teach and coach organizations and companies on how to use games as a part of developing their workplace. We operate in the professional field of organizational development, change management and leadership development, where we have developed innovative educational game solutions for organizations, corporations and companies from around the world. We use games to give companies new knowledge about organizational development and change management. In both our board games and online games, players are presented with realistic dilemmas and challenges, and will gain knowledge that can be applied directly to their daily work life.

References

Kolb, D A (1984) *Experiential Learning*, Prentice Hall, Englewood Cliffs, NJ

Kotter, J P (1996) *Leading Change*, Harvard Business Press, Boston

Leavitt, H J (1965) Applied organizational change in industry: structural, technical and humanistic approaches, in *Handbook of Organizations*, ed J G March, pp 1144–70, Rand McNally, Chicago

Maurer, R (1996) *Beyond the Wall of Resistance: Unconventional strategies that build support for change*, Bard, Austin

14

Changeskills

*Implementation of change through
a game of guiding questions*

SAMI SARÉN, KARI MALINEN AND HILTRUD KINNUNEN,
Muutostaito Oy

#TeamDevelopment #SalesDevelopment #CustomerJourney

The foundations of Muutostaito's game format were laid at the start of the 1990s. A gamified intervention tool named Team Game was developed to improve the work of teams; the tool was based on a library of questions covering every essential aspect of team development (Hackman, 1990). The game was developed at the Helsinki University of Technology; in conjunction with this development work, several studies were conducted on how the game could be applied (Jaakola, Ruohomöki and Teikari, 1999).

Unlike many existing board games used for training, an essential feature of this game was that it was not used to teach teamwork. It was more of an intervention tool to speed up development of the team as a group. The questions in the game guided the team towards discussing important matters in terms of the team's development, and working together to resolve and agree upon any matters that arose. The questions had no right or wrong answers. The game was played on a game board, and players could choose which type of question they would like to address by moving around the board. The questions were divided into three different themes: ground rules for teamwork, problems, and knowing other people. The game was an individual competition in which points were awarded for factors such as being on the side of the majority when players decided on their stance on a particular question theme. The winner was the first player to reach the specified number of points on all three question themes.

As such, this game was primarily an intervention tool for organizational developers rather than an educational game. The game was played at more than 100 organizations, where it helped to achieve verifiably good results in terms of team development and promoting interaction within organizations.

Developing the concept into a group game

The Team Game was a workable concept, but it could only be played by a maximum of eight people in a session with a single game facilitator. In addition, the point-scoring mechanism required improvements to make it more flexible in relation to the duration of the game. At that stage, the library of questions was also strictly limited to themes related to teamwork.

Based on the principles of the Team Game, the Change Creators game concept was developed in the late 1990s for groups of 16–25 people. In this game, players gave their views on the game questions in teams rather than as individuals. The theme of this game was change management. Almost 200 game questions were printed on ready-made playing cards, covering various areas of change management and focusing on practical implementation. At that stage, the game could also be played using a game board affixed to a wall.

Developing the game concept into its present form

The Changeskills game format has been developed from 2010 onwards. Muutostaito acquired the rights to the game format developed in the late 1990s. This was then adapted and developed to make its elements work better. The content themes have also been expanded to cover all the essential areas of organizational development and requirements of business life. The Changeskills game format was developed by using some key elements from the Team Game and transforming it into a facilitation tool for large group workshops (Figure 14.1).

The key change was to strengthen the role of the game facilitator. Now, games are always run by a facilitator from Muutostaito itself or a facilitator certified by Muutostaito. This allows for more rules and more complexity, to ensure that the game has a sufficient number of alternatives and is not too easy or too difficult. The trained facilitator explains the necessary rules at the relevant time (Figure 14.2). This enables players to feel that they have sufficient control over the game during each phase, and there is a suitable amount of new content to come as the game progresses. The trained facilitator is also able to plan the game's dynamic in advance on a case-by-case basis, taking into consideration each customer's goals and the composition of the group.

Figure 14.1   Group settings in the Changeskills game

Figure 14.2   Drawing of the tables and groups

The group dynamic is actively steered during the game workshop itself. The facilitator can add gameplay elements if the group dynamic so requires. For example, the number of points available for each game round can be doubled. The number of gameplay elements can also be reduced by actively guiding the directions in which playing pieces can be moved. Muutostaito's game format worked better than the previous model, and the way in which the game was conducted began to develop with increasing rapidity after the game had been played several times.

Flexible game concept

An essential aspect of the Changeskills game format is that the questions have no predetermined correct answers. The teams score points for their answers based on joint discussion. The game design process focuses more on discussing the right questions than precisely identifying the right answers.

Content design was improved and the process of implementing the game was made more efficient by deploying an information system that contained all of the previously used game questions. This boosts the efficiency of design and facilitates the selection of appropriate questions for each theme and situation. Questions are continually produced in accordance with customer needs. Muutostaito currently has more than 2,500 game questions in its question library. The Changeskills game format can be used with several different types of game boards that are marked with the key headings related to the game board's theme. Custom game boards can also be designed specifically for organizations, even if they are only used for a single game workshop.

Nowadays, the majority of game implementations feature questions and a game board designed specifically for the customer. This ensures that the customer's brand is incorporated into the game and its contents. In addition, the customer is part of the co-creation process, where Muutostaito's game format and the ability to create suitable questions are combined with the customer's business substance and experience.

Game purpose and effect

The purpose of Muutostaito's game format is to create a structure in which participants produce interpretations, insights and solutions for predesigned questions and topics with the help of the game. The discussion that takes place during the game is created by the players themselves and solutions arise through such discussion. The participants bring their own interpretations, tacit knowledge and wealth of experience to bear on the game topic. The participants are motivated to engage in discussion when the topics are directly connected to their own work. The game involves taking a stance on the questions and answer alternatives, first in small groups and then in a larger group. The answer alternatives are designed to elicit a range of important perspectives on the question.

Open atmosphere of mutual trust

The basic philosophy of the Changeskills game format is that discussions involve all participants and all viewpoints are valued. This leads to an open atmosphere of mutual trust around the game. Even participants who do not usually engage in training events find it easier to participate because the questions are directly related to their own work and the answers do not allow the possibility of failure.

Putting effort into answers and listening to others

A key element of the Changeskills game format is listening to and understanding other teams' positions. In addition, the teams are required to make joint decisions in a limited time in such a way that a group consensus is reached without voting. The game motivates and encourages players to give reasoned and high-quality answers because the format involves evaluating the other teams' responses and every team is evaluated in turn. As the format involves evaluating the other teams' responses, they become more interesting; listening to other teams' viewpoints is a natural part of the workshop that increases the intensity of the game even further. This combination of making an effort to create answers and intensively listening to others, together with the limited time available, gives rise to an intensity and working atmosphere that is unlike a normal group work.

A game of feelings

In the Changeskills game, feelings are mainly created through the dynamics between the players rather than the interaction between the player and the game content. Games based on the Changeskills game format are clearly not entertainment games, but the competitive setting and differing interpretations of questions and words arising during the game create funny moments and the space for humour. The game facilitator's professional skill enables this dimension to be fine-tuned and, if necessary, the atmosphere to be lifted or the focus to be shifted back towards work.

The Changeskills game brings feelings to the fore more readily than normal because the players know each other and give each other feedback during the game, either in the form of points or verbal comments. Because there are no correct answers in the game, this feedback is based on the subjective views of each person or team, as well as the interpretation of the question. Various emotions arise in situations in the game in which players are required to accept views that differ from their own. Players may be surprised that rewards in the form of points may not be received because another team has considered the issue in a different way. However, the thrill of success can easily be experienced when the neighbouring team has thought about the issue in the same way; the outcome of this can be seen on the scoreboard.

Incorporating feelings into the game is an absolutely essential part of the dynamic of the Changeskills game format. It enables the discussion to become deeper and more relevant to the players, as they are required to see things from other perspectives. For this reason, the discussions during the game are usually more memorable than those of ordinary training days. It is also important to activate feelings when, at the end of the game, the participants prepare their own plans for how they intend to work differently in the future.

Equal dialogue

The game's structure is instrumental in ensuring that all the players are equal within the game, regardless of the participants' roles or positions. Similarly, the game's structure and schedule contribute to ensuring that all the planned topics receive the planned amount of time for discussion and that socially active personalities do not dominate the discussion.

Strong questions are essential

The formulation and selection of questions is the most important aspect in terms of the game's results. The game should guide the discussion in the intended direction and give rise to a clear need to change the status quo to head towards the target. However, the topics and arrangement of questions play a very important role in determining the extent to which a solution-oriented, unifying atmosphere is created within the workshop, as well as the extent to which the discussions lead to practical measures and changes in the future.

When selecting subject areas, it is important to ensure that the game features questions that are important to all the participants and that as many participants as possible can influence. The questions must also be formulated so as to avoid an outcome of illusory democracy, in which the question appears to promote discussion of a matter but the decision is ultimately made by someone else. For this reason, questions do not usually involve considering strategic or operational options. Instead, they focus more on how the selected policy could be put into practice within the organization.

A further perspective on discussion and question setting is the static or dynamic point of view. The game is about change, so questions are set in such a way that they highlight the tensions between the target state and the status quo; the discussion is guided towards ways of getting from the status quo to the target state in the area in question. The game format itself encourages players to understand differences and varying viewpoints and tolerate different interpretations of the same matter. In this regard, the facilitator aims to ensure that the game does not get bogged down in semantic or linguistic details, and that the focus of discussion is practical action rather than theoretical differences of opinion.

Implementing change using Muutostaito's game process

In recent years, in addition to the Changeskills game format itself, Muutostaito has also developed its game design process, ie the way the Changeskills game format is applied to a specific situation with a specific game. In the early phases, this game design process was developed to ensure that customer-specific game content could be included in an agile manner, in a short time if necessary. As a result, an increasingly large proportion of games are related to a theme of current significance to the customer's organization. In most cases, the aim is to use the game to make a start on an important process of change for the organization, or to drive such a process forward.

In this context, the term 'process of change' can be understood very broadly. It can refer to the implementation of strategy or a programme of cultural change on a large scale. On a smaller scale, it can refer to the desire to encourage the group participating in the game process to behave or do things differently in relation to certain matters in the future. Such games include the Customer Game, the Leadership Game and the Well-Being at Work Game.

The design process focuses on identifying the question areas where real change is desired. A second, parallel approach to preparing the game questions is to ensure that the questions cover the essential perspectives of 'why', 'what' and 'how' in terms of change management. In practice, this means that the game involves discussing why changes are essential, in addition to talking about what will change.

Post-game process

The game concept incorporates both joint and individual responsibility. In practice, this means promotion of individual responsibility by ensuring that game workshop participants always leave with a tangible plan, activity or commitment that they intend to bring to fruition after the workshop. This is based on the philosophy that we consider the game to be a tool for implementing change rather than an educational game. As such, it is not sufficient for the game workshop to result only in participants gaining new insights or learning something. We want all participants to immediately incorporate something from the game workshop into their everyday work.

Over the last two years, Muutostaito has developed a process for following up on the plans made during the game and evaluating implementation. This post-game process typically takes three to five months, so from the participants' perspective the game process now takes several months, rather than just a single day. In terms of enacting change, the process helps to create and maintain internal motivation for the change among the participants. The process provides participants with the autonomy to decide for themselves which change they would like to implement in their everyday work. When the plans and commitments are public, the process supports social commitment and learning from others. The post-game activities at the end of the process reinforce the feeling of success and provide participants with good public feedback when they have made progress towards bringing their own plans to fruition. Successes are noticed and brought to the fore.

Case example: Finnish Bookstore chain

The Finnish Bookstore is the biggest bookstore chain in Finland, with around 450 employees, turnover of more than €100 million, and 60 bookstores throughout Finland. The company was founded in 1912 and is part of the Finnish graphic communications concern, Otava Ltd. The Finnish Bookstore has invested in customer service training for its employees in various ways for more than 10 years. In 2014, the company began looking for a new way to refresh its commitment to provide active, expert and cheerful customer service.

After experiencing a game demo, Muutostaito's Customer Game was chosen to become the next method for training personnel in customer service. It was also decided immediately that Finnish Bookstore wanted a unique game board, tailored specifically for the company. Finnish Bookstore had prior experience of Muutostaito's generic Well-Being at Work Game, having played it in 2012 and 2013. Back then, some of the bookshops' sales personnel took part in half-day game workshops arranged by mother company Otava Ltd on the topic of occupational well-being.

Planning the game project

A project group was set up to plan the company-specific Customer Game. The project group was tasked with planning the content of the game, along with the graphical elements and slogans for the game board. The content of Finnish Bookstore's Customer Game consisted of various questions related to customer service situations in shops. The target was to identify situations that are challenging for sales personnel, in which the sales personnel might have different approaches. The situations were connected with the themes relating, for example, to the customer experience, different issues concerning the actual customer-facing situation, and interacting with challenging customers. The game board was designed accordingly. The slogan 'We help the customer to buy' became the name of the game. This is an apt description of the game's targets: to increase the rate of additional sales as well as the way in which additional sales are made at Finnish Bookstore – by helping customers to buy products. The game was created from the objectives of offering Finnish Bookstore customers the best multichannel shopping experience and continuously delivering on the customer service commitment with consistently high quality.

The game's content and functionality was tested in a pilot game. The steering group received permission to confirm the timetables for a total of 23 games during spring 2016. The second key purpose of the pilot game was to involve sales personnel, managers and personnel in positions of responsibility from different shops in the forthcoming process, in advance. When the participants in the pilot game had experienced the game and gained information about the forthcoming project and its targets, they were able to take this information back to their own shops and get people involved in the project in advance.

Executing the game project

When the game commenced, the dice began to roll and the playing pieces moved around the giant game board. Almost all 450 employees of Finnish Bookstore took part in game workshops held all over Finland; however, the company's new sales personnel played the game towards the end of

2016. Each game was played by about 20 people from different parts of the company. Participants in Muutostaito's games are always divided into teams, which roll the dice to move around the game board and compete against each other. One of the teams wins the game and receives a prize. This gamification brings a certain intensity and quality to the day's discussions. The game involves competing to see how groups solve tangible, everyday challenges: how can I analyse a customer's needs? How can I have a positive effect on the customer's experience? How should I interact with challenging customers?

The game and its events also provide players with an opportunity to exchange ideas and experiences with people from other shops and to learn from each other. This is no small thing. In Finland, people are often located far from one another. Settling down for a day of discussing and working on questions related to sales work is considered important, by employees as well as managers. The game forces people to participate. Many of the personnel had previously worked in groups in which some people talked while others held back. In small groups, everyone is able to speak and everyone is listened to. The game brought up a totally different way of participating. The game has a jury, which listens to the teams' reasoning and awards points. Teams can also earn points from other teams and from the game board. At the end of the day, the winning team receives awards, as well as a basket of fruit to share.

The personal promises are followed up transparently in everyday work

After the game is over, an even more important step begins. Each player thinks about which aspects of his or her customer service they would like to improve, and he or she formulates a tangible promise or pledge. While everyone makes their own personal promises, everyday work in shops involves taking action together after the game.

This activity will be maintained using a gamified follow-up process jointly developed by Muutostaito and Finnish Bookstore. The objective of the follow-up process is to realize actions that develop operations and a positive buzz. Above all, it should draw attention to successes and how participants have succeeded in developing themselves in terms of the targets created during the 'We help the customer to buy' part of the game. Development should be transparent so that everyone can evaluate and verify it. Promises and pledges made during the game workshops have been kept, with an average certainty of more than 85 per cent with the help of this follow-up monitoring and feedback process. The promises and pledges are everyday actions that lead to changes in everyday work.

When the follow-up process also includes a playful competition between shops on aspects that can be monitored using indicators, it adds something extra – positive pressure for development – because everyone wants to be the best. Shop-specific successes are brought to the fore in the shops' weekly letters, and the best examples are included in the company's internal monthly letter. Successes matter and they are noted.

When all the shops had played the game, the decision was made to arrange a game day for personnel in the head office of Finnish Bookstore in autumn 2016, along with a subsequent follow-up process. The content of the game was redesigned so that the game focused on enhancing internal cooperation. The following themes were developed for the game: feedback, cooperation, appreciation, utilization of expertise, development of operations, the flow of information, sufficient quality, enthusiasm and time management. Some staff members in the head office were already familiar with the method, as they had also, in some capacity, taken part in the game events for shops.

The game immediately creates a freer atmosphere, even if the players do not know each other. There are no right or wrong answers; the main thing is to use strong reasoning for answers in order to get points for them. A competitive spirit guarantees that the answers are well thought out. The head office aims to create the same culture and positive buzz that has arisen in the shops.

Results

Thanks to the game projects, Finnish Bookstore has created an even greater atmosphere of mutual encouragement, both in its shops and in its head office. Although personal successes are still rewarded, a stronger culture of working together has arisen in the chain. This culture contributes to success at work, effectiveness and occupational well-being. Customers have also noticed a positive change in the operations of Finnish Bookstore. Regularly monitored customer feedback reveals that operations have improved, and sales figures show that sales work has been successful.

The game and the post-game activities have provided supervisors with good tools. In some shops, very good, new promises and pledges were made; everyone understood the goal. Successes have also begun to accumulate at a gratifying rate. Finns often find it hard to talk about their successes, but now they are actively sought out. It is precisely these things that make work enjoyable and keep people in good spirits all year round. This has created a positive buzz.

Enthusiasm is born of success

Sini Kortelainen, a salesperson in a Finnish Bookstore shop, comments on the game workshop:

> The day was really rewarding and relaxed. We went through some customer interactions, operating methods and putting the values into action in practical work. There was a lot of discussion throughout the day and everyone was listened to. We learnt from the more experienced personnel and gained some new perspectives. It was also motivating to notice that I had something to give to the newest employees. The day gave me more enthusiasm and motivation, and it provided a clearer basis for continuing my work in the shop. (Sini Kortelainen, personal communication)

Katja Roth, shop manager, summarizes the game day like this:

> None of the sales assistants said that the game day was a waste of time. This is quite good. Such a major investment in developing the professional skills of sales assistants shows that we are valued. And it is worth it: when we are good at our jobs, work becomes more enjoyable. (Katja Roth, personal communication)

Marje Stolpe, area sales manager, adds to this:

> The game project has been really good for the atmosphere. When the starting point is to get people to experience success, it has a positive impact, both in terms of employee satisfaction and the customer experience. (Marje Stolpe, personal communication)

The game projects have led to a desire for a better understanding of other people's work, which in turn has created a desire to provide better service. For example, employees from the head office have visited shops to work as sales assistants for a day. This has been an eye-opening experience for many people, and many have found it inspiring. In addition, the service culture within the head office has improved. It has been streamlined, thanks to familiarity with and a better understanding of other people's work. Finnish Bookstore understands the importance of continuous development, a good basis on which to continue moving forward. The tools and methods are now in order, so it is easier to keep this matter on the agenda.

About

Muutostaito is Finland's leading company in using a wide variety of gamified methods to promote change implementation and learning. We are focused on business development projects and training that excites, motivates and engages managers and people at all levels of the organization. Our consulting and training processes always aim at everyday change of behaviour and renewal. We believe that successful change starts with common understanding, commitment and participation.

References

Hackman, J R (1990) *Groups that Work (and Those that Don't): Creating conditions for effective teamwork*, Jossey Bass, San Francisco

Jaakola, M, Ruohomöki, V and Teikari, V (1999) *Project Report: Team game as a team development tool*, Helsinki University of Technology, Helsinki

15

Exploring Change

Mastering change and transformation

WOLFGANG KARRLEIN AND LARS KRONE, Canmas GmbH

#LeadingChange #BusinessTransformation #LeadershipAttitude

Change is a social process, not just a project. It is experience driven, iterative, and often requires taking unforeseen turns. In a transformation project, we use CELEMI Exploring change™ as a key element to create this experience and develop a common understanding and language.

Strengthening change leadership and corporate identity

Initial situation and assignment

Our client is an IT professional service company. Its business currently yields several hundred million euros. The company has grown in recent decades by acquiring smaller start-ups and competitors. Technological development makes new services possible. To tackle the challenges emerging from its market conditions, the company's strategy focuses strongly on innovation and developing new services that require heavy investments.

In this situation, a growth programme was initiated, accompanied by reorganization in some areas. It turned out that the fast growth by acquiring smaller companies lacked deeper integration; this led to different identities and information silos. It also resulted in friction in the new organizational set-up, which hampered the development of a new, unified culture. The goal of the project was to bring together the managers in order to create a common understanding and a positive attitude towards making the new set-up a success and put them in the driver's seat to plan how this could be achieved. If they were convinced about the course of the company, living their conviction in everyday life, it would have an impact throughout the organization. Creating momentum with a clearly future-oriented organizational identity, to be developed by the managers, seemed to be a good investment. However, in recent years, this angle of corporate culture has been placed at the bottom of the to-do list.

The game concept

This project was conceived in three phases. In the first phase, interviews were conducted with many of the affected managers. These interviews were based on two intentions:

1 We learned much about the individual perceptions of the people, their personal point of view on the past, and especially on the latest developments. In addition, we wanted to learn their thoughts about the future of the company and what they thought of their role in it.

2 We also received valuable information on their ideas and expectations on the forthcoming change programme. This input helped us to tailor the next steps, in terms of both methodology and content, to the mindset and expectations of those participating.

Lacking the feeling that they had been heard or involved in the reorganization process, it turned out that most of them had hardly any deeper or systematic notion about either the challenges and pitfalls or the levers and methods of the change processes that they were expected to promote and live. For the second phase, we therefore chose to apply a tailored, extended version of Celemi's Experience Change Power Dialogue. The goals of this phase, comprising several power dialogue workshops with subgroups, were twofold:

1 Participants would be exposed to, discuss and learn about change processes and their special features. They would develop a common idea and language about what they would be facing and why.

2 Participants would then lay the foundation for the third phase, in which workshops (conceived as organizational conferences with a large number of participants) would be held.

The third phase would build upon the input from the interviews, plus the preparatory work and ideas from the second phase.

The role of Celemi Exploring Change

The two intentions that we chose from Celemi Exploring Change are described above. This power dialogue provides a safe setting in which to experience the challenges of change processes in a structured, powerful framework for learning, discussion and building insight. It also involves a close-to-reality case of a fictitious company. The participants can discuss the events they learn about by meeting several people during the change process. As it is a fictitious company, it facilitates discussion of what happens in a less emotional, political manner than if the participants were to discuss their own company from the outset.

With regard to learning about change, Celemi Exploring Change provides the condition to be introduced and introduces some valuable, practical models about phases within change processes. Even though Celemi Exploring Change is not a simulation in the strict sense, it incorporates the basic learning principles of Power of Learning by Klas Mellander, described elsewhere in this book (see Chapter 26). We will next introduce Celemi Exploring Change. Then we describe our extension of the game, which transfers people's new insights on change into their company's real situation. We conclude with key learnings from the extended, tailored version of Celemi Exploring Change.

Celemi Exploring Change at work

Background – why change is even more constant

We live in a world filled with volatility, uncertainty, complexity and ambiguity (VUCA), which result from an unprecedented increase of interconnectedness in the (business) world. For companies, this means a paradigm shift for leading and managing organizations, planning, loyalty and job certainty, as well as balance between stability and change (see Table 15.1). It means dealing with three key shifts (Kruse, 2014).

Inside Celemi Exploring Change

Adaptability and agility are keys to flourishing in the markets. Leaders must gain and strengthen their ability to engage employees in change; this is one key to business success. Therefore, leaders and change agents need a clear

Table 15.1   Paradigm shifts leading to change pressure

Trend 1: Trap of complexity	
From a linear or slow-moving environment →	to a dynamic or non-linear environment
Actions are planned and pursued to reach goals. They are planned and guided by defined strategies. Belief: the more you know the better you can predict and plan.	Complexity can best be mustered and reduced by recognizing patterns (note: details often kills the ability to recognize patterns; not to see the wood for the trees.
Management is based on knowledge, what and how goals can be reached.	Leadership needs to create a frame to reduce complexity by involving many (diverse) people.
Knowledge means to know, which actions are effective and productive.	Knowledge means to decide on and form the frame for orientation.
Trend 2: Industrial democracy	
From a linear or slow-moving environment →	to a dynamic or non-linear environment
Organizations work by positions and structures, which define the power over decisions.	Shaping an organization and preparing decisions are feasible by achieving resonance with members of the organization.
Management means thinking ahead, giving instructions, and acting as supervisory authority to control implementation.	Leadership means sharing the conviction to be member of the system and being accountable to stimulate the resonance.
Hierarchy is the governing pattern for managing organization long-term.	Autonomy, accountability, and ownership are key for organizational development
Trend 3: Meltdown of working relationships	
From a linear or slow-moving environment →	to a dynamic or non-linear environment
Security and identity are mediated by affiliation of individuals to organizations.	Affiliation changes to become steps in the career paths of individuals.
Management is a role model and based on authority.	Leadership acts as companion and mentor along the career paths.
Loyalty based on formal and especially an informal job contract (loyalty in exchange to job security) constitutes the long-term job relationship.	Attractiveness replaces loyalty; job relationships are determined by meaning, comprehension, and significance of the joint activities and goals.

understanding of which factors are involved in change processes. Only then will they have the navigational skills to choose the appropriate actions and create adequate resonance with their people.

Celemi Exploring Change provides a structured, powerful dialogue that highlights four key success factors that can fast-track change in an organization. Specifically, it emphasizes the human dimension of change. During the dialogue and discussions, it provides valuable insights to help leaders drive change and mobilize people to actively join in. Celemi Exploring Change comprises three phases, covering the following key concepts:

- organizational resistance to change;
- communicating the greater picture;
- emotional responses to change;
- building shared ownership;
- aligning internal conditions (structures and processes) to motivate employees.

Phase 1 In the first phase of the dialogue, the participants are provided with frequently heard characteristic statements from people affected by change initiatives. Working in teams, the participants discuss issues triggered by various aspects of the statements. For instance:

- Does the issue sound familiar in their environment?
- If so, what influence will the underlying motives have on the success of the change?

Have any of them experienced a situation in which these aspects were handled successfully, and what was the difference engendered by this success?

The statements are grouped to highlight the above-mentioned key concepts. During the interactive debriefings, meaningful models and conceptions are introduced. The main purpose lies less on the theoretical foundations, but provides a mental framework to think about (human or emotional) change effects and create a common language among the participants to talk about their own change situation. The modes involved are (but are not limited to):

- the eight-step process of leading change, developed by John P Kotter (1996);
- the change curve, based on the five stages of grief proposed by Elisabeth Kübler-Ross (Kübler-Ross and Kessler, 2014);

- the house of change, developed by Claes Janssen (1996);
- the adoption curve, developed by Everett M Rogers (2003) and Bohlen and Beal (1957).

Phase 2 In the second part, the participants are faced with a change endeavour in a fictitious company. They meet with four employees in different departments, roles and positions. The meetings take place at different times within the first six months of the change process. These individuals are faced with the different situations they describe. In their view, these situations may hamper the success of the change. They ponder what would be the best way to handle what they perceive and fear. The participants' job is to understand and discuss the viewpoints of these four people, their considerations and how they might deal with the case. In a structured process, the teams record their opinions and take notes regarding their conclusions on a specific work mat.

Phase 3 The last phase focuses on transferring their common understanding and lessons from the power dialogue into their own reality in their organization. This phase depends very much on the specific situation of the client.

Experience-based perspectives in the game

To link Celemi Exploring Change even more strongly with the challenges of change and the approaches to handling it, we added and expanded the following:

- We integrated the four key success factors into a larger picture of what might happen during a change process, thereby creating our change navigator.
- We developed a card game to create and deepen participants' common view on their organization, what they do well, and where they must take action to increase the chance for success.

The change navigator

Change does not proceed in the same manner as a technical project. The process of change is challenging because it triggers the emotions of the people affected by it. Therefore, it is hardly a linear process but will require iterations, repetitions, loops, and a lot of communication (which should not be mistaken for providing information). It is therefore important to have a kind of 'map', or navigational instrument, to help people orient themselves to the phase of the change in which they find themselves (see Figure 15.1).

At its centre is 'Communication'. Organizations exist because people communicate with each other in many different ways, with the aim of achieving a common goal. It is no different for a change process. Communication is key; without communication, there is no change. To the north, it is about creating a vision of where the change should lead. A vision is a (mental) picture of the future state. Its purpose is to provide direction and convey meaning. To create meaning, people must see (be aware) of what is happening. This ties into creating and communicating the big picture.

To the east, meaning is the source for raising people's (intrinsic) motivation. It is about initiating the wish to act. To support this, one must

Figure 15.1   Change navigator

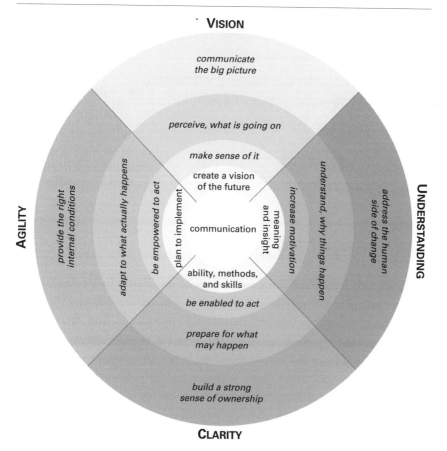

understand why things develop as they do. The key success factor in addressing the human side of change ties into this phase, as meaning and understanding are connected to emotions.

To the south, it is about developing and strengthening the ability, competence and skills to act. The goal is to ensure people have the tools, methods, knowhow and so on that are required to drive initiatives that prepare the organization for the future development. It is also the basis to create a broad, strong sense of ownership.

To the west, it is about planning and implementation, along with the freedom to actually take on responsibility. Removing internal barriers is also important, as is adapting to changing conditions; sticking tightly to a plan may become less effective due to changes, such as those that might take place in the environment. It is about giving trust to the people in the organization who are willing to make the change successful. This ties into the key success factor of providing the right internal conditions.

The outer rim of the Change Navigator is vision – understanding – clarity – agility, or VUCA. The various aspects in the four sectors support this meaning of VUCA. As Bob Johansen (2012) suggests:

- vision helps in dealing with volatility;
- understanding helps in dealing with uncertainty;
- clarity helps in dealing with complexity;
- agility helps in dealing with ambiguity.

The Change Navigator is a simple image to support orientation in change. The following card game is very valuable to linking Celemi Exploring Change to developing a change road map in the participants' own organization.

The change card game

The rationale to expand the transfer portion of Celemi Exploring Change was to prepare and strengthen the link of the power dialogue with the subsequent workshops and organizational conferences. Our goal was to trigger a discussion about communication patterns, ways of dealing with others within a team and across divisions, or whether existing cultural rules prevail. Participants might agree the organization is doing well with some topics. They might agree other topics need attention or require improvement in light of the change process and goals. To trigger the discussion, we prepared a set of 40+ statements, falling into five categories:

- organizational set-up;
- communication patterns;
- openness and dealing with change;
- vision, guiding principles, mission statement;
- goal orientation and management.

Each card comprises an 'OK' side (a statement and comment are phrased in a positive manner) and a 'Warning' side (a statement and comment are phrased in a critical way).

Step 1: discuss and identify both critical and positive statements

The participants read both sides of each card and discuss their perception of their organization. They then form two piles. One pile contains statements they agree to be predominantly OK for their organization. The other pile contains statements they deem to be predominantly critical. The latter are aspects that participants agree need to be addressed somehow to make the change successful.

Step 2: run through an 'idea processor'

This is a special work mat. For each card from the Warning pile, the teams review the question-and-answer scheme on the work mat. Depending on the answers, a card may end at the exit saying: OK you must live with it. The team members agree this pattern is something that cannot be changed or addressed for some reason, yet will influence the smoothness or success of the change and its initiatives. The team must therefore be vigilant about it. There are several alternative paths, including one saying 'Just do it', at the bottom of the work mat. Cards that end up here show patterns about which the team members think they can actively do something. The cards and their statements cover typical situations from various change programmes and organizational development projects. However, we encourage the teams to write additional cards and statements, when they think of something that better suits their experience or to supplement the preset cards. There are several advantages related to this card discussion game:

- It dovetails neatly with the power dialogue provided with Celemi Exploring Change.
- It provides the participants with situations that may be relevant to their organization or their specific change endeavour.

- The discussion about which card to be added to one pile or the other establishes a common view among the participants about their organization.

- Based on this common view, it creates awareness of what the organization is doing well and where they see areas for improvement.

- The idea generator helps to think and exchange the different opinions about what to do with the Warning topics; it provides a prioritized list of topics, including an initial idea about what can be done.

- Running through the idea-generator steps creates a sense of ownership among the participants.

In summary, this process with the cards and idea generator addresses important success factors (seeing the big picture, having a sense of ownership and establishing a basis for creating the necessary internal conditions), which were presented in the first phase of Celemi Exploring Change. Finally, in the case of our customer, the result of running Celemi Exploring Change was very valuable input for the subsequent series of workshops and organization conferences.

Key gains the game enables

Specifically, Celemi Exploring Change provides a lively and proven platform for dialogue and discussion about key elements in a change process (which is why it is called a 'power dialogue'). The platform supports leaders and change agents to:

- share individual experience from change processes;

- support tailoring and operationalize theoretical models on change to specific needs;

- deepen understanding of the significant difference of a change to a usual subject-specific project, the 'human side' of change.

At the same time, almost going unnoticed, the lively exchange aligns individual views, creates common ground for understanding and establishes a shared language. A larger view on what will happen in and during a change endeavour and organizational transformation process is gained when transforming the insights into the reality of one's own organization. Celemi Exploring Change establishes the foundation to grasp that kicking off and driving the real change process requires monitoring many facets. Neglecting one may lead to different, unintentional effects, as summarized in Figure 15.2.

Figure 15.2 Change topics and effects in case of disregarding them

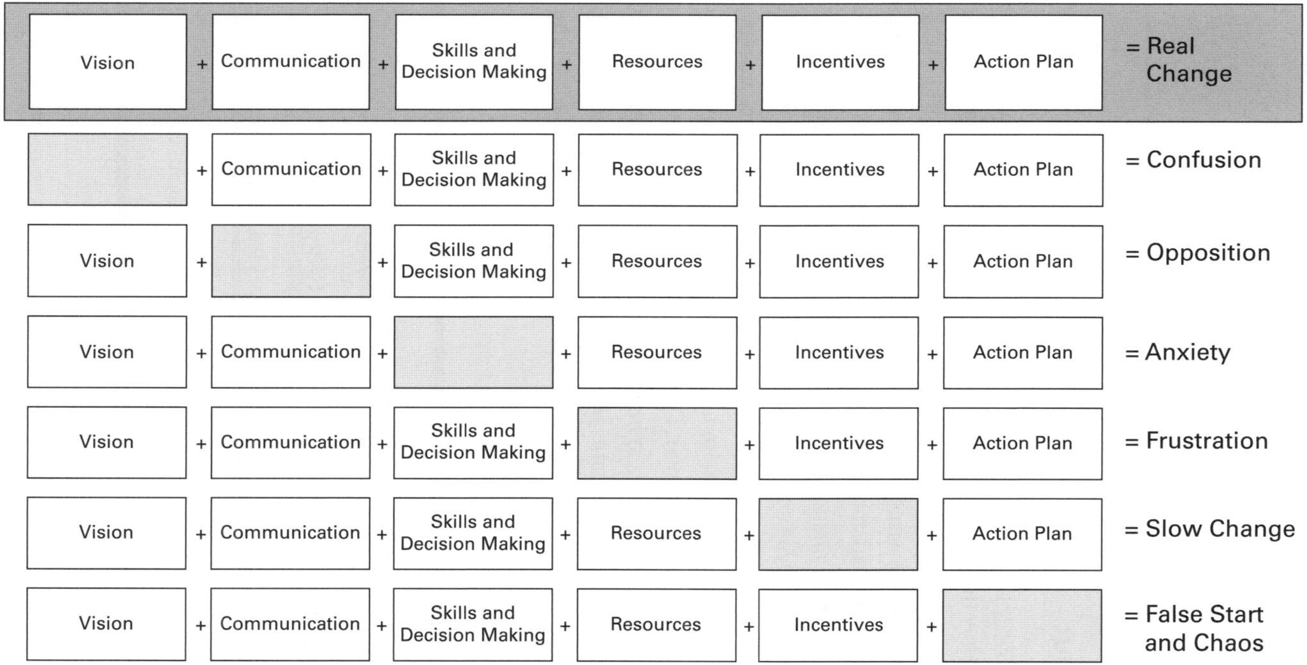

Vision	+	Communication	+	Skills and Decision Making	+	Resources	+	Incentives	+	Action Plan	= Real Change
	+	Communication	+	Skills and Decision Making	+	Resources	+	Incentives	+	Action Plan	= Confusion
Vision	+		+	Skills and Decision Making	+	Resources	+	Incentives	+	Action Plan	= Opposition
Vision	+	Communication	+		+	Resources	+	Incentives	+	Action Plan	= Anxiety
Vision	+	Communication	+	Skills and Decision Making	+		+	Incentives	+	Action Plan	= Frustration
Vision	+	Communication	+	Skills and Decision Making	+	Resources	+		+	Action Plan	= Slow Change
Vision	+	Communication	+	Skills and Decision Making	+	Resources	+	Incentives	+		= False Start and Chaos

The Change Navigator integrates the phases, goals, benefits and means by which the change will be implemented into one picture. Methods like the Change Statements card game can serve to identify areas in which the company and its people are doing well concerning the change ahead, as well as those that must be addressed, improved or changed. It helps to focus on the right things and do everything right.

About

Canmas – Business Learning and Consulting Ltd is a change facilitation company that provides proven customer-tailored methods to mobilize leaders, change agents and employees in business organizations. Our clients are mid-sized and large corporations who have the challenge to change and transform their business. We provide support to activate people for the change as facilitators, act as pilots for substantiating change initiatives and programmes, and as partner when it comes to mobilizing the organization as a whole. Our facilitators have gained their experience over more than 20 years in various leadership roles in international companies. Celemi is a strategic partner to us whose business simulations have been globally successful for more than 30 years in making corporate learning more effective. We share the same understanding concerning the key success factors for effective change.

References

Bohlen, J M and Beal, G M (1957) The Diffusion Process, *Special Report No 18*, Agriculture Extension Service, Iowa State College, pp 56–77

Janssen, C (1996) *Förändringens fyra rum* (The Four Rooms of Change), Wahlström and Widstrand, Stockholm

Johansen, B (2012) *Leaders Make the Future: Ten new leadership skills for an uncertain world*, 2nd rev edn, Berrett-Koehler, Oakland, CA

Kotter, J P (1996) *Leading Change*, Harvard Business School Press, Boston

Kruse, P (2014) [accessed 9 March 2018] Zukunft Der Führung: Kompetent, Kollektiv Oder Katastrophal? [Online] http://www.forum-gute-fuehrung. de/zukunft-von-f%C3%BChrung-%E2%80%93-kompetent-kollektiv-oder-katastrophal

Kübler-Ross, E and Kessler, D (2014) *On Grief and Grieving: Finding the meaning of grief through the five stages of loss*, Simon and Schuster, New York

Rogers, E M (2003) *Diffusion of Innovation*, 5th edn, Free Press, New York

16
Innovate or Dinosaur
A collaborative innovation game

TAMARA EBERLE, Traction Strategy

#InnovationOpportunities #CreativeThinking #Idea-To-Action

Innovate or Dinosaur is an award-winning, collaborative innovation game that helps teams, businesses and organizations think creatively and critically, generate new ideas for real work opportunities and challenges, and put these ideas into action. The game offers a different kind of innovation experience and builds participants' capacity to innovate every day. It is framed around the following metaphor – innovate or dinosaur – described in this comment from Eric J Romero (Romero, 2012: 1):

> Don't be a dinosaur... evolve and innovate! While changing is not easy, becoming an unconventional thinker is worth the effort. It can help you become open to new ideas, creative, flexible and willing to take the risks necessary to innovate and win.

The challenge of innovation and case example

The business challenge: scarce resources and tough competition

Innovate or die. Do more with less. This is what individuals and teams are being pushed to do if they want their business to survive and thrive. This challenge is not new to people in countries with scarce resources, as argued by Radjou and Prabhu (2015), but businesses in resource-rich countries have experienced the rise of the frugal economy over the last decade:

> The insatiable demand for ever higher-quality products will continue to rise while at the same time the availability of the resources needed to satisfy that demand will remain constrained.

Being innovative and creative in this context is more important than ever for differentiating oneself. As Edward de Bono (2008), the guru of lateral thinking, puts it:

> Creativity has become essential. This is because everything else has become a commodity available to everyone... There is nothing you can do to prevent your competitors also becoming competent... That leaves creating new value as the basis for competition.

This was the case for four large retail-based properties in North America that are part of an international property management and development company. In an effort to continuously stay ahead of the competition, the company issued a challenge to all their asset classes to be better, faster and cheaper.

Feeling stuck

For these retail properties, this challenge put more pressure on the teams to increase performance and output, use resources differently and improve quality of service at the same time. These already high-performing teams wanted to rise to the occasion but felt tapped out of new ideas. They, like many other business teams, were continually asked to 'go forth and innovate', but became stuck and frustrated when they did not have the time or tools to do it.

Getting unstuck: playing, rewiring our brains and being uncomfortable

To help these ideation-weary retail teams, multiple *Innovate or Dinosaur* game events were held at each site with representatives from every department. These innovation game events were a welcome departure for the teams. While the teams were all too familiar with facilitated planning and brainstorming events, it was a refreshing change to use a game-based process to fuel their participation. For example, a maintenance supervisor who had been through dozens of ideation sessions and felt the lustre of the process had worn off a bit, found that:

> The board game was very innovative in itself and created a great atmosphere and a logical framework for innovation. It was very easy to enjoy the session. (personal communication)

But it is not just using a different process that is motivating. The key motivator is the opportunity for playfulness that a game provides. While playfulness is an important factor in innovation (as described later in this section), it has also surpassed 'having a sense of purpose' and 'building on potential' to become the number one direct motivator for work (Doshi and McGregor, 2015). Once the group was engaged with the game, the main hurdle was helping the participants break out of their fixed thinking and gain some new perspective, new energy and innovative ideas. Even those with the best intentions can become fixed in their thinking. Neuroscientist Donald Hebb was the first to introduce the idea that when we learn or think in a particular way for a long time, our neural pathways become 'wired' in that way. This causes us to automatically ignore information that does not fit our 'set mind' (Hebb, [1949] 2005).

The good news is we can create new neural pathways surprisingly quickly and come up with new ideas that we have not thought of before. In the first part of the *Innovate or Dinosaur* game, Explore (Figure 16.1), participants are invited to open up their thinking and shift their mindset by applying six different tried-and-true creative-thinking techniques to their work opportunities and challenges, and generate ideas that are both new and possible.

One Director of Operations, who was sceptical that the game would help him and his team come up with something new, said: 'I was in awe of the

Figure 16.1 Image of the Explore board in action

speed with which we began generating ideas. I had my doubts. But, within minutes our team was right in there coming up with innovative solutions' (personal communication).

While most people find being creative fun, this part of the game can actually be a struggle for some who have a hard time letting go of their initial ideas, trusting the process and building off the ideas of others in the group. Interestingly, these people are sometimes the ones who are considered to be the creatives in the organization, as they are confident that their thinking is already creative enough.

As one participating security manager noted: 'This really makes you collaborate outside of your comfort zone!' (personal communication). The great thing is that working with people outside your sphere and being a bit uncomfortable is good for creativity, as it helps you see things from another perspective (Degsell, 2016). During the Explore part of the game, different teams chose different strategies for winning. While most teams were highly motivated by the competitive nature of the game, and worked hard to get around the board the fastest to maximize their time and learning experience, some teams did deep dives on a particular opportunity or challenge and aimed to succeed in generating the best idea possible.

Ideas are not enough

For the participants of these events, it was important to have a meaningful experience and net ideas that would *actually* move to implementation and not just stay in the room after the game was over. One-off brainstorm workshops and innovation labs are a great way to get some traction, but often stop short at creative ideation, and ideas alone are not enough. Critical thinking is the other side of the innovation coin and the key to driving the ideas to action. In fact, the hit rate on innovation failure can be as high as 80–90 per cent if the organization does not spend time on organizational readiness, according to professional market researcher Lee Jacobson:

> For many companies, no matter how much they claim to embrace the concept and understand its importance, new ideas can be a virus that is attacked by 'antibodies' within the organization. Organizations that are continually successful with implementing new ideas spend a lot of time on preparing their process and the support systems. (personal communication)

To increase the chance of success, the second part of the *Innovate or Dinosaur* game event, Evolve (Figure 16.2), gave the participants from these retail

Figure 16.2 Image of the Evolve board in action

properties the opportunity to refine their ideas, prepare them for implementation and nurture a sense of responsibility to put them into action.

By applying a series of critical-thinking questions about organizational readiness and using the Evolve board to plot the outcomes on an 'effort' scale (measuring how much effort it would take to be ready), the teams were able to clearly see what it was really going to take to bring their idea to reality. The positive outcomes were not lost on the participants. One operations team member was 'astonished' at the number of actionable ideas that were put into motion. He commented that:

> Not only did we walk away from this session with a framework that outlines
> an innovative thought process, but we also left with several great projects
> that can really bring our customer experience to the next level. (personal
> communication)

It is important to clarify that this step is NOT about dismissing or accepting ideas as 'good' or 'bad'; rather, it is about examining the feasibility of the idea and figuring out the actions that are needed to make it happen. This includes looking at factors such as the extent to which it aligns with organizational goals, the benefits and consequences, the strengths of the team, market forces and the stakeholder interests. To close the innovation event, each team made a creative presentation of one of their great ideas, using the Pitch Posters that were provided. Prizes were given for the team that was fastest around the board, as well as the one that had the best idea (as voted on by the rest of the participants).

Outcomes with impact

Playing *Innovate or Dinosaur* with these retail property teams netted tangible outcomes, and this series of game events won a Platinum Facilitation Impact Award (IAF-FIA) recognizing this achievement. Specifically, the project ideas that were generated were so well thought out by participants that 90 per cent of them received full funding or approval within a few weeks of presenting them to the leadership team; some ideas developed into projects that will have a 100 per cent return on investment (ROI) over a few years; others resulted in waste diversion initiatives that will keep significant amounts of construction waste out of landfills; and still others resulted in months of time saved on HR negotiations.

Game design and application

Game framework

To be effective, *Innovate or Dinosaur* is designed based on some of the key ingredients for innovation identified by Nobel Prize winners (Tobias Degsell, founder of Combiner and former curator at the Nobel Museum in Stockholm, conducted a survey of living Nobel Prize winners to understand what they believe to be the conditions and elements of innovation) – the most highly recognized innovators in the world. These are:

- *Collaboration*: participants work in teams to apply innovation–thinking techniques to real workplace activities and services.
- *Competence*: participants learn multiple creative and critical tools and techniques that they can easily apply in any situation in which they want to be more innovative.
- *Communication*: the game requires effective communication between the team members to get the best results, and provides an opportunity for building understanding of work activities and services that can be improved.

- *Vision*: this game can connect to an organization's strategic vision or goals as well as inspire ideas for where the company could be headed.

- *Playfulness*: *Innovate or Dinosaur* allows people the space to be open and let go of judgements and mental constraints. The gaming and competitive elements allow participants to have fun while doing it.

- *Work*: innovation is not all fun and games. Participants must apply themselves and make an effort. While this is a game, it does require commitment to collaborate, opening one's mind to new thinking and active participation.

Diversity and collaboration is key

Having a diverse range of roles and perspectives at each game table is a key to success, as it enables the group to examine an opportunity or challenge from multiple perspectives, experiences and knowledge. Tangentially, collaboration is central to the success of this game. If participants play *Innovate or Dinosaur* competitively, team members *must* collaborate to win. This is not just about sharing ideas or getting through a task together; it is about tapping into the 'collective intelligence' of the group to generate something greater than the sum of the individual parts. Juanita Brown describes the potential of collaboration in her book on the World Café process. She says that collaboration:

> Holds the promise of providing one intentional way not only to engage the fascinating network dynamics of emergence but also to access the unique relationship between the individual and the collective that enables a special type of mutual intelligence to emerge. (Brown, 2005)

Especially in the Explore part of the game, teams play around with creative techniques together to see if they can come up with an idea that is fresh and different. Like a sports team that 'finds its groove', when a group has found their collective intelligence groove, there is a burst of energy and excitement as they realize they have done something unique together. This can boost morale and ultimately leads to an increase in the team's capacity to work better together.

Applications for the game

Innovate or Dinosaur is not just for big, one-off innovation events. There are many occasions on which the game, in whole or in part, can be used to help teams be creative and get to action. Table 16.1 describes 10 possible applications.

Table 16.1   Innovate or Dinosaur game – potential applications

1	Generate new ideas or solve a problem when the team has idea-generation fatigue.
2	Feed the team's innovation pipeline or find ways to be different, better or more competitive.
3	Turn market research opportunities into innovative ideas that are strategic and actionable.
4	Advance a particular aspect of the company's business, such as customer service, an operational system or sales development.
5	Brainstorm, solve problems and think a little more creatively in informal settings, such as around the lunchroom table.
6	Incorporate the game into strategic planning or business development processes.
7	Engage people in collaborative, innovative thinking around general opportunities or a specific topic at the next industry or internal conference or team retreat.
8	Use individually to get unstuck creatively or test whether an idea is worth pursuing.
9	Engage employees in sharing their ideas and provide a fun opportunity for them to collaborate and develop cross-team/cross-function understanding.
10	Get out from under a pile of ideas and get something implemented.

Additionally, the game is highly flexible and adaptable and offers several modes: quick play can be used by individuals and small groups, single-team competitive play can be used by groups of four to six players, and multiteam play can be used by groups of 6–600 who are looking for a fuller innovation lab experience.

Summary of benefits

The game nurtures collaboration and provides an opportunity for cross-functional engagement:

> Power to the people to find solutions together! (National Retail Director, personal communication)

It teaches new creative and critical thinking skills and helps to break through stuck thinking:

This was a great way for my team to gain valuable creative problem-solving skills while still having fun. (General Manager, Retail, personal communication)

It drives ideas to action and cultivates ownership over the implementation of the ideas:

The problem we were working with wasn't even my problem. But by the end of the game I became very committed to the solution. (Guest Services team member, personal communication)

It is inclusive and allows for participation by all types of people:

I like the game format personally. As an introvert, it invites people like myself the ability to offer ideas – people who otherwise might be too shy or reserved to share thoughts and feelings. It gives each person a turn to feel valued. (Marketing Director, personal communication)

It is a 'sticky-note-free experience' that engages people in an unconventional and unexpected way:

This was very inspiring, creative and fun! (Administration team member, personal communication)

Finally, this game will not only help generate new ideas and forge a path to their implementation, but will also build participants' capacity to innovate every day. After all, the measure of success is not what happens during the game workshop. What matters is what happens outside the workshop room, when the team has to overcome the organizational barriers to innovation and bring their awesome ideas to life. As such, participants are encouraged to put the creative and critical thinking techniques in their back pocket and pull them out any time they need a creative jolt or a sober second thought on an idea. The ongoing, everyday use of these thinking skills will build the organization's strength for continuous improvement, differentiate it from competitors and prevent it from being left behind.

About

Traction Strategy is a multi-award-winning consulting company providing certified professional facilitation, training and organizational game design in the areas of innovation, creative problem solving, strategy, change and stakeholder engagement. We help you get together, get a grip and get going with collaborative and engaging events and tools that ignite your thinking and activate your ideas.

References

Brown, J (2005) *The World Café: Shaping our futures through conversations that matter*, Berrett-Koehler Publishers, San Francisco

De Bono, E (2008) *Creativity Workout: 62 exercises to unlock your most creative ideas*, Ulysses Press, Berkeley

Degsell, T (2016) [accessed 9 March 2018] Spark of Creativity [Online] http://passet2015.blogspot.dk/2015/04/keynote-speaker-tobias-degsell-spark-of.html

Doshi, N and McGregor, L (2015) *Primed to Perform: How to build the highest performing cultures through the science of total motivation*, Harper Collins, New York

Hebb, D O ([1949] 2005) *The Organization of Behavior: A neuropsychological theory*, Psychology Press, New York

Radjou, N and Prabhu, J (2015) Frugal innovation: how to do more with less, *The Economist*, London

Romero, E J (2012) [accessed 9 March 2018] 8 Tips For Becoming An Unconventional Thinker That Beats The Competition [Online] http://ifawebnews.com/2012/02/20/8-tips-for-becoming-an-unconventional-thinker-that-beats-the-competition/?mobile_switch=desktop

17

Innovation Diamond Learning Game

Creating an innovative mindset

JONAS SPROGØE, Brilliant Innovation

#InnovativeMindset #InnovationOpportunities #InnovationCulture

The Innovation Diamond Learning Game enables developing and acquiring four leadership roles associated with the early stages of an innovation process; namely, the knowledge detective, the jester, the conceptualizer and the gardener. By working with 16 different tasks, the players gain hands-on experience with the four leadership roles. Throughout the game, the players are prompted to reflect on individual and organizational learning (Figure 17.1).

Figure 17.1 A play situation in the Innovation Diamond Learning Game

Case or application description

The Innovation Diamond Learning Game is played around a fictitious but realistic innovative focal point. The innovative focal point can be defined by the group itself. It can be based on a real-life issue, or the group can choose from among a number of predefined innovative focal points, such as: 'It has been a long time since you launched a new product'; 'Two departments are merging into one'; 'Organizational restructuring is affecting cohesion and unity within teams'. Sixteen different tasks, four for each leadership role, are played. The tasks enable exploring, recognizing nuance, developing and qualifying the understanding of the innovative focal point. The leadership roles and the four associated tasks for each role are described in Table 17.1.

Table 17.1   Jester, knowledge detective, gardener, conceptualizer

The jester	The four tasks associated with the jester are:
	• 'Questions' – a task in which the players are trained in questioning techniques and explore what is not necessarily known about the innovative focal point.
	• 'Have you thought of…?' – a task in which the players are trained in association techniques and improvisation.
	• 'What If?' – a task in which the players are trained in powerful questioning and the ability to see new angles and perspectives in the innovative focal point.
	• 'Think like a child' – a task in which the players are trained in the ability to change perspective.
The knowledge detective	The four tasks associated with the knowledge detective are:
	• 'Network' – a task in which the players learn to map out their access to valuable knowledge.
	• 'SPAC analysis' – a task in which the players learn to systematize their collective knowledge base and map out Strengths, Possibilities, Attention points, and Challenges in relation to the innovative focal point.
	• 'Dig deeper' – a task in which the players learn to map out and discuss underlying assumptions of the innovative focal point.
	• 'See the obvious' – a task in which the players are trained in the use of a mind map to reach a common understanding of the underlying assumptions of the innovative focal point.

(continued)

Table 17.1 *(Continued)*

The gardener	The four tasks associated with the gardener are:
	• 'Power play' – a task in which the players talk about power relations in groups and the relevance of body language.
	• 'Slack lining' – a task in which the players are trained in creativity and focus, and stimulate positive relations.
	• 'Coat of arms' – a task in which the players get to know more about each other and learn about others' competencies.
	• 'Mingle' – a task that builds group relations and creates a more energetic atmosphere.
The conceptualizer	The tasks associated with the conceptualizer are:
	• 'Our story' – a task in which the group creates a common understanding of concepts and the players gain insight about others' thoughts and priorities in relation to the innovative focal point.
	• 'Metaphors' – a task that trains the players to see new relationships and develop new, unexpected thoughts in relation to the innovative focal point.
	• 'Give Shape' – a task in which players are trained in the ability to give physical shape to thoughts and develop a common understanding of concepts.
	• 'Haiku' – a task in which players are trained in alternative ways of communicating and the systematizing of thoughts.

Artefacts such as picture cards, templates, coloured pencils and play dough are used in the various tasks to stimulate reflection and learning. The game also contains four Reflection cards to facilitate and enhance learning and reflection throughout the game. The Reflection cards contribute to individual and collective learning about how the various roles offer differing approaches in engaging with the innovative focal point. The Reflection cards are designed progressively and ask the players to reflect on the following:

• What are the similarities and differences of the four leadership roles?

• What are the pros and cons of the four leadership roles?

• What roles are the players most comfortable in and what leadership roles does the organization have the most of?

• What are the overall learning points from playing the game and how can the insights be used going forward?

Applied case examples

The game is used by organizations who wish to strengthen their innovative culture by enhancing their employees' ability to innovate. One example is a Danish secondary school. The high school had initiated a year-long process of developing a more innovative and collaborative organizational culture. The Innovation Diamond Learning Game was used at the kick-off seminar, with two goals. First, the Innovation Diamond Learning Game was played to develop and train an innovative mindset. Employees and managers played the game together, familiarizing themselves with the four different leadership roles, through solving the tasks and reflecting together on the individual and collective lessons from the game. Second, the tasks were used to develop participants' own ideas about working towards an innovative, collaborative organizational culture; some examples include giving shape to the various conceptualizations of such culture, asking wild questions about what such culture might entail, and discussing in greater depth the concrete actions that must be taken, and by whom, in order to achieve an innovative, collaborative culture.

The game was facilitated by expert facilitators to ensure flow and learning, and was documented by a graphic designer in order to collect and maintain important points in a creative and thought-provoking manner. The Innovation Diamond Learning Game was used as an informal initiator for a longer organizational development process. The game provided a fun way to create a common language of innovation, as well as a common frame of reference in relation to wishes, challenges, tasks and roles for the journey ahead. By playing the Innovation Diamond Learning Game, management also gained two other important things: a crucial commitment to the organizational development project through the development of a common understanding of the project, and competence development for employees in relation to innovation.

Game purpose

The purpose of the Innovation Diamond Learning Game is to develop and train four essential leadership roles associated with the early stages of an innovation process. Research shows that the early stages of innovation processes, what is labelled the *pre-ject*, can be improved dramatically if teams continually shift between different modes of inquiry to clarify expectations and visions for the project, are open to different types of knowledge, and are able to create a common understanding of the process.

Darsø (2011) developed four distinct roles for supporting innovation processes. These are: the knowledge detective, who helps create a sound body of knowledge about the proposed innovation; the jester, who challenges existing knowledge and stimulates divergent thinking; the conceptualizer, who creates a common understanding and frame of reference about the proposed innovation; and the gardener, who facilitates and stimulates a productive, supporting learning environment. Each role can be assigned to one person, or the group can take on the leadership roles together. There is no set time for being in a particular role.

The Innovation Diamond Learning Game is a learning game rather than an innovation game or process. This means its primary aim is to enable participants to learn about these roles and acquire hands-on experience of how they work rather than on innovating a particular product, process or procedure. Thus, the game is designed to maintain optimal focus on the roles. Henriksen (2010; 2012) pointed out a number of pitfalls in designing learning games, namely fun and competitiveness, realism, content richness and lack of reflection, and holding only post-experience debriefing (Henriksen and Lainema 2010). If a game is too entertaining and competitive, playing and winning become ends in themselves, leaving only little incentive for exploring other areas. If a game is too realistic and builds on actual organizational problems or refers to real characters, the players might avoid potential conflicts and difficult discussions. Finally, if a game is too content-rich, it might become complex and confusing rather than enlightening and easy to engage in. The Innovation Diamond Learning Game avoids these pitfalls by maintaining a constant learning focus in the design.

First, the tasks of the game are centred around a fictitious, yet realistic innovative focal point. The tasks tied to the four roles are played out in relation to a common point of reference throughout the game. Players can develop their own innovative focal point or they can choose from a number of preprinted focal points in the game. The innovative focal point is fictitious, to ensure players do not go into problem-solving mode; at the same time, it is realistic enough to enhance motivation and engagement. Second, the tasks are time-bound and simple. Each task is set to last approximately eight minutes, which includes a couple of minutes for reflection. The time limit creates a flow in the game and ensures that the group does not lose itself in one particular task, thereby missing the opportunity to try out the other roles. The tasks are easy to engage in, such as creating a mind map, asking what-if questions and creating a play-doh model. Third, each round of the game finishes with a reflection card, which enables players to reflect on their individual and collective learning from playing the round.

Figure 17.2   The difference between learning game and innovation process

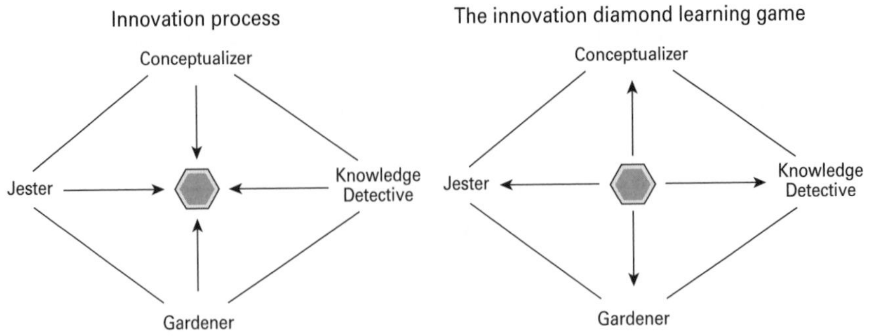

In the Innovation Diamond Learning Game, the topic or innovative focal point is used to guide the acquisition and training of the roles by practising a number of tasks. Learning the roles is the purpose of the game. However, once familiar with the leadership roles, participants can transcend the learning aspects of the game and use their competence for innovation. In an innovation process, the four leadership roles are used for innovating a particular topic through the application of a number of tasks, ie the tools provided in the game. Thus, the roles are then the means to an end. The difference between the learning game and an innovation process is conceptualized in Figure 17.2.

The game is graphically and aesthetically designed to encourage the players to engage interactively in playing. Creating an aesthetic game is important, as aesthetics can support learning by representing particular ways of experiencing, communicating about, perceiving and engaging in the world (Brodersen, 2015). Different colours are used to visually emphasize the various leadership roles (the gardener tasks are green, the jester tasks are red, etc). The game consists of sturdy wooden pieces that can be arranged in various geometrical forms. In addition, there is no fixed way to set up the game, which allows for constant debate around rearranging the pieces. Thus, together with materials such as templates and other items, the design lets the players engage in the continuous creation and innovation of the game.

Gameplay

1: Introduction

The game master explains the purpose of the game and introduces the procedures and rules. If necessary, the game master explains the theory behind the innovation diamond and the four associated roles.

2: Practice round

First, the group chooses a timekeeper to keep track of time and ensure momentum in the game. The group then decides on an innovative focal point. It can either be defined by the group itself or it can be chosen from a number of predefined innovative focal points found in the game box. The five tasks, 'slack lining', 'questions', 'give shape', 'see the obvious' and 'reflection #1' are laid out from the innovative focal point (see Figure 17.1). One player reads the task aloud and the group solves it (six minutes). When the task is solved, the group reflects briefly on it. The round is finished when the group has solved all four tasks and answered the questions on the Reflection card.

3: Subsequent rounds

The group chooses four new tasks, one for each of the four roles. It lays them out in any desired order, with reflection #2 (and, subsequently, #3 and #4) finishing off each round. The game continues as one player reads the task aloud and the group solves it (six minutes) and briefly reflects on it (two minutes). The round is finished when the group has solved all four tasks and answered the question on the Reflection card.

4: Outro

At the end of the game, the game master can facilitate a round of reflection on such game elements as the importance of the order of tasks, strengths and weaknesses in the four roles, how to utilize the roles in future innovation processes, group dynamics or other learning points relevant to the group.

What makes this a great learning game?

The game is self-explanatory. The group can play the game and learn the roles by following the instructions on the tasks and the Reflection cards. The game master can enhance and facilitate learning by pointing to group dynamics, individual preferences among players, organizational perspectives, etc. The game is designed with multiple learning opportunities.

First, the players develop an innovative mindset, by learning and experiencing how the different roles work. This process is facilitated by Reflection cards throughout the game. Second, the players develop a common language about important aspects of the innovation process, as well as a common understanding of crucial roles for innovation. Third, the players must choose the order of the tasks and thus discuss how best to engage in innovative processes. For example, they must decide whether it is better to begin an innovative process by asking wild and explorative questions as a jester, or by creating a common frame of reference as a conceptualizer. Fourth, the game initiates reflections on team composition and dynamics, for example, are there any roles that must be downplayed or enhanced in order to create more effective innovation processes? Fifth, the game has a rapid pace with multiple tasks that last only around eight minutes; this enables the players to test and try several process tools and role perspectives within a limited time frame, yet remain in the constantly playful atmosphere of a learning game.

Key learning from the game

First, taking on and rehearsing the four leadership roles are specifically important in the early phases of innovation processes. Darsø (2010) labels the early phase of the innovation process *PRE-ject*. This refers to the phase of problem identification, goal seeking, knowledge creation, crystallization, developing an innovative climate, etc: 'The pre-ject phase is important because it is where the seeds of innovation are sown and cultivated' (Darsø 2010: 44). Learning to navigate through this chaotic, divergent, goal-seeking phase is fundamental for the quality of the innovation process as a whole. Through its design, the game provides a framework for learning to navigate and handle the complexity of the pre-ject phase.

Second, the Innovation Diamond Learning Game provides personal experience with the four leadership roles and facilitates reflection on personal and organizational preferences. Gaining hands-on experience with the four leadership roles enhances the likelihood of applying the knowledge and approaches later on in the innovation process, which makes the subsequent processes far more effective. Feeling and sensing the effects of the different leadership roles on individuals and groups promotes a common understanding of what approach is needed where and when in the process. These points can be illustrated by the following quote from a participant: 'We actually get the chance to be a jester – crazy – that is normally not something we dare. It allows us to see new possibilities, not to limit ourselves, and to try new things and perspectives' (Nielsen, Sprogøe and Nygaard, 2013).

Thirdly, the Innovation Diamond Learning Game is designed to collectively – and in a playful, aesthetic and stimulating way – uncover actual knowledge and underlying assumptions regarding a specific area. Thus, the game qualifies the decision-making process by allowing different perspectives, nuances, ideas and assumptions to be discussed and renegotiated. In addition, the game is designed to stimulate relation building and both internal and external communication through a number of creative methods that enhance the participant's thinking skills (De Bono, 2010).

Fourth, the Innovation Diamond Learning Game creates a common language to conceptualize complex innovation processes through the continual discussion of the four leadership roles. This is described by one participant as: 'We actually created real development, talked innovation and also improved our relations to each other. It was fantastic; fun and done very quickly... We could have used two to three hours more without any problems' (Nielsen, Sprogøe and Nygaard, 2013). A positive side-effect of the game is the demystification of rather difficult processes; it becomes clear that innovation is not reserved for a few creative and divergently thinking developers, but is something that everyone in the organization can be part of and contribute to.

Finally, and perhaps most importantly, the game's learning outcomes are applicable to other development areas. After acquiring the leadership roles and the associated tasks, participants can apply the skills and competencies in other settings, where new perspectives, nuances, idea generation and common conceptualization are needed. Thus, the game contributes to developing a learning culture, where the value of problem identification and knowledge creation is seen as a prerequisite for problem solving and knowledge sharing.

About

Brilliant Innovation ApS. was established in 2014 with the goal of creating and developing learning games that teach and train innovative leadership roles in a practical, playful and efficient way.

References

Brodersen, P (2015) Oplevelse, fordybelse og virkelyst – et æstetisk perspektiv på undervisning (Experience, contemplation and enthusiasm – an aesthetic perspective on teaching) in *Oplevelse, fordybelse og virkelyst*, ed P Brodersen, T I Hansen and T Ziehe, Hans Reitzels Forlag, Copenhagen

Darsø, L (2010) *Innovation in the Making*, Samfundslitteratur, Frederiksberg

Darsø, L (2011) *Innovationspædagogik: Kunsten at fremelske innovationskompetence (Innovation Pedagogics: The art of fostering innovation competence)*, Samfundslitteratur, Frederiksberg

De Bono, E (2010) *Thinking Course: Powerful tools to transform your thinking*, BBC Active, London

Henriksen, T D (2010) Mindre spil og mere læring, tak (Less games and more learning, please), *Asterisk*, 50, pp 24–28

Henriksen, T D (2012) Læringsspil i organisationsudviklingen (Learning games in organizational development), *Erhvervspsykologi*, 4, pp 2–9

Henriksen, T D and Lainema, T (2010) Didactic design for business games, paper presented at the 4th European Conference on Games Based Learning, Copenhagen, pp 55–62

Nielsen, L H, Sprogøe, J and Nygaard, S (2013) The Effect of Playing the Innovation Diamond Game, written report, Master in Leadership and Innovation in Complex Systems, Aarhus University

18
Leadership development simulations

From the best of intentions to real-life balance

ASK AGGER AND MAX MØLLER, Workz A/S

#BehaviourChange #ChangeManagement #StakeholderEngagement
#LeadershipStyles

Most managers have a fairly clear idea of what good leadership looks like. They have read the leadership books, they have participated in various training programmes, and they have been through profiling tests and 360-degree surveys. The real challenge comes when all the good intentions must come alive in daily behaviour. For most of us, the best intentions end like most New Year's resolutions – after an initial effort, we return to our old routines and behaviour.

In this chapter, we explore how game-based tools for leadership development can help managers be the leaders they aspire to be. With inspiration from behavioural design and the *kriegsspiel* (war games) of the Prussian Army, we use cases and experiences to look at how gamification can be utilized to support real-life changes in leadership behaviour. We describe three leadership simulations: *Wallbreakers*, *Gamechangers* and *Bridgebuilders*. These simulations can work together as a whole in a series of sessions or alone in single-day workshops.

From leadership training to new behaviour

B J Fogg's (2009) behavioural model highlights the three factors that must be met to anchor new behaviour. The model asserts that for a target behavior to happen, a person must have sufficient motivation, sufficient ability and an effective trigger. All three factors must be present at the same instant for the behavior to occur. The first factor is motivation. If motivation is lacking, most people will revert to old, familiar behaviour. Motivation can either be a stick or a carrot – from compelling vision and positive incentives to feelings of necessity and urgency. We design our leadership simulations so that they motivate the participants to change their leadership behaviour. They will experience the frustration of making mistakes in the game, which will emphasize the need to change leadership approaches, and they will enjoy success and encouragement when they are able to succeed by adjusting their leadership priorities, based on their failures.

The second factor is ability. Even with high motivation, we stick to our old behaviours if changing behaviour seems difficult. It is necessary to make the new approaches appear easy. In our game design, we spend a lot of time on ability training. Participants become familiar with new leadership concepts and tools in a safe environment, in which it is OK to make mistakes and talk about failures.

The third factor for changing behaviour is triggers. Triggers are situations in our daily work life in which we are afforded opportunities to exercise the new behaviour. These range from subtle reminders and nudges to deadlines and customer demands. Leadership development often lacks a sufficient link to everyday triggers. Leaders have a good deal of inspiration, knowledge and skills, but may lack the right occasions to apply the new training in real life.

Our leadership simulations are designed so that the lessons and insights are easy to transfer to real-life leadership behaviour afterwards. We especially ensure that the key elements of the game, often the game board itself, can be used in real life as mapping and planning tools. In addition, the key terminologies of the games are designed to give the participants a shared language they can use to discuss real-world challenges, long after playing the game.

Conservative by design

Nature created the human mind and body with an integrated optimization consultant, known as evolution. Throughout history, we have continually upgraded to improve our chance of survival, to stay in the game. This is the reason why we lost our tails, developed thumbs, and reap the benefits of long-term investments in a big brain that is great at language, empathy and sudoku.

But evolution is a slow learner and adapter by modern standards. In fact, our latest 'patch' from evolution is approximately 45,000 years old – we are still optimized to the lives that our forefathers lived as hunter-gatherers in the Stone Age. Back then, it was a great idea to eat fruit when it was ripe, which is why we still have a sweet tooth and cannot be trusted to behave responsibly when there is a sweet jar nearby (Jensen, 2017).

In recent decades, the emerging research fields of behavioural economics and behavioural design have helped us to understand our irrationalities and biases. The naive idea of '*homo economicus*', humans as rational and profit-optimizing actors, is still dominant in many parts of society; however, we are slowly starting to acknowledge that even when we have the best of intentions, it is still difficult for most of us to live our lives as we intend.

A key insight from behavioural economics is that humans are conservative by nature. We are designed to stick to the habits that have ensured our survival in the past (Kahneman, 2011). Repeating what works is no doubt a solid strategy in many aspects of life, but when working with learning, leadership development and change, it is counterproductive. In the end, all learning and training is about changing behaviour; therefore, our organizational training efforts are often an uphill battle.

Leadership simulations as a safe practice field

A professional soccer coach about to send his team to the World Cup prioritizes optimal preparation. He selects the team, refines the interplay and combinations on the training grounds, and reveals critical errors through test games against other teams. To put it simply, the coach will do his utmost to ensure that the players are in the best possible position to act as a team when it really counts. Anything else would be unprofessional.

In the same vein, how does one roll out a new strategy or initiate an important project in a modern organization? How often does one select the team and fine-tune and rehearse before the implementation? Unfortunately, it is the rule rather than the exception that we start off with little or no preparation or training. This is equivalent to waiting until the day of the big match to select the team, and then afterwards wondering why the game lacked finesse and why so many misunderstandings occurred between the players.

Like practice fields, simulations and games offer a safe playground in which participants can test various scenarios and make educational mistakes without facing any real-world consequences. This has multiple benefits when it comes to anchoring learning in real-life behavioural changes. Let's look at a few of them.

Handling high complexity

Leadership entails facing high complexity and making decisions based on limited information. Numerous experiments in behavioural science have documented how we all have a limited capacity to reflect and make rational decisions when facing high levels of complexity. We rapidly grow mentally tired and succumb to the autopilot of our traditional approaches and habits (Kahneman, 2011). This is a problem when one is trying to teach complicated subjects, like most leadership issues. The benefit of game-based training is that a well-designed game enables us to decrease the complexity of an important issue by filtering out irrelevant details, while at the same time providing an environment in which we dare to try different options and make mistakes. In short, games can heighten our mental ability for rational reflection on difficult topics.

Repetition

Repetition accelerates retention and long-term memory. Doing something multiple times is a way of telling the brain that the thing is important and should be remembered. This insight, that there is a substantial benefit from a small number of repetitions compared to just training at something once, goes all the way back to ancient Greece. To quote Aristotle: '[i]t is frequent repetition that produces a natural tendency' (Ross, 1906). A leadership simulation enables us to perform rapid iterations and learn through trial and error. In a few hours, we can immerse ourselves in change processes and leadership circumstances that would take weeks or months in real life.

Excitement

Games are fun and engaging. We become engrossed in tough decisions and difficult dilemmas, and before we know it, hours have passed without our notice. Excitement is motivating, but it also helps us to learn and remember by increasing levels of hormones such as adrenalin, dopamine and oxytocin. Simply put, high levels of these hormones in our bloodstream are a way of telling our cave-dweller brain that something important is going on that should be remembered (Lieberoth, 2013).

Leadership simulations with Prussian inspiration

Workz offers a portfolio of leadership simulations that have been developed and refined over the course of a decade. These award-winning simulations address different leadership themes and capabilities – from change leadership and stakeholder engagement to project management and team performance – and have been used by more than 40,000 managers across the globe by industry leaders from multiple sectors. They are available in eight different languages.

All these simulations are inspired by the Prussian tradition of '*kriegsspiel*'. In the middle of the 19th century, the Prussian army underwent a radical transformation centred on a new leadership doctrine called '*auftragstaktik*' (mission command), which called for a very high degree of front-line autonomy and empowerment (Bungay, 2011). To train the officers in the new doctrine, the Prussians used a combination of intensive field exercises (summer training) and elaborate board games, so-called *kriegsspiel* (winter training) (Hilgers, 2000).

The board games simulated the complexity of battle and trained the officers in understanding and acting in changing circumstances. The point was not to learn how to make the perfect plan or to predict the outcome of a battle; instead, it was about building what modern-day researchers call 'scenario awareness', the ability to cope with high levels of complexity (Hanghøj, 2011). In the same way, the leadership simulations provided by Workz are designed to help modern-day managers develop a deep understanding of how different leadership approaches and actions can be used efficiently under highly complex circumstances. The simulations normally form the core of a one- or two-day training workshop and are used for three different training purposes:

To sharpen personal leadership skills

In these cases, the simulations are used as part of corporate academy programmes or talent development, in which the purpose is to sharpen individual leadership skills. The simulations are often supplemented by relevant profile and assessment tools, and all reflections during and after the game are focused on how the participants can improve their own practice as leaders.

To support a specific project or change

The simulations can also be used to support the handling of a specific and immediate challenge, such as establishing a new international team, the roll-out of a lean project at a big site or the implementation of a strategic change project. All reflections during, and especially after, the game are used to help the participants make better decisions in their immediate challenges. This is very much just-in-time training.

To inspire organizational development

Finally, the simulations can also assist with organizational development in a broader sense. In these cases, the simulations are used by internal management teams to inspire discussions about issues such as cross-silo collaboration, diversity, corporate culture, strategy execution and project management practices.

Even though the simulations are separate games with different learning objectives, they all share some core design principles:

Physical representation

Our leadership simulations are all board game-style physical solutions. We see games as 'conversation pieces' and game design as a way of designing meaningful conversations. There is a risk of losing something important when the conversations must be facilitated through a screen.

Strong metaphors and visual representation

We try to design simulations with strong metaphors and visual elements that function as a shared reference and language among the participants. One example is our change management simulation, Wallbreakers, in which we use a bus with passengers to represent a department with different team members. During the game, when a team member exhibits resistance against change, he or she 'falls off the bus' and is moved to a pavement next to the road.

Fictional cases

All the simulations use fictional scenarios inspired by real-life cases. We try to design relevant and credible scenarios with the right balance between not playing too close to home but also not playing someone too exotic and far-fetched. It is often harder to learn if players must play themselves; a slight change of perspective can add important new insights and reflections.

Theoretical foundation

When we develop a leadership simulation, we try to include the most widely used and recognized theories and models in the game design. The theories are built into the game 'engine' and help to determine the outcome of the players' decisions and priorities. In some situations, such as when our leadership simulations are used at university MBA programmes, we use the games to explain and discuss the theories in depth; in other situations, the simulations are used with a more pragmatic focus and we spend less time on the theoretical and academic aspects.

Anchoring

We strive to design the core game elements so that they can be used to support the anchoring of new leadership behaviour long after the game session has ended. In many cases, the game board functions as a highly efficient mapping tool that will help people map their key stakeholders and employees and understand their real-life challenges and leadership options. This leverages the benefits of the simulations as talking and thinking pieces.

Scaffolding

We try to develop the games with a high degree of scaffolding to ensure that key discussions and learning points can be introduced and addressed separately. We design the simulations with a gradual increase in complexity, slowly adding new decision factors and elements.

Balanced competition

Too much competition often has a negative impact on the learning outcome. Competition can be highly motivational and engaging, but it should be used in moderation. It is important that the participants focus on learning from the game and each other, not just on winning the game. Now let's take a closer look at the three simulations.

Wallbreakers – change leadership

Wallbreakers is designed to train implementation and anchoring of organizational change. The game (Figure 18.1) is about the leadership side of change management – transforming resistance towards change into understanding, acceptance and support. The simulation focuses on how to motivate employees to take part in the desired change, and how the different phases of change processes require different forms of leadership.

Wallbreakers is built around a fictional business case about a merger between two IT companies. The participants work in groups of three to six, and each group plays a team leader who has to help a team of diverse employees navigate a three-phase change process. The players must consider change intensity, prioritizing of resources, and handling various personality types and individual needs among the employees.

The game is divided into three rounds, each focusing on a different phase of the change project: start-up, implementation and anchoring. The game board is a very large round circle placed on the floor. The circle is similarly divided into three sections, representing the three phases of the game. A number of small model buses are placed on the game board, each representing a team, with the employees as passengers. In each round, players choose the pace of change by selecting one of four 'gear' cards. They balance the pace of change with the focus on the department's daily tasks.

Figure 18.1   Wallbreakers in action

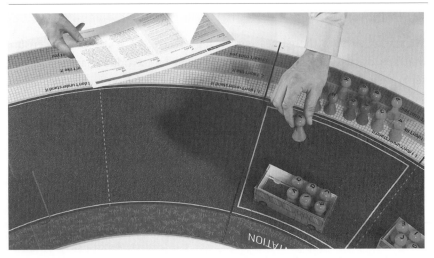

The employees on the fictional team have different profiles and preferences, and react differently to change. The employees are modelled on well-known personality models such as the Myers–Briggs Type Indicator (Myers, McCaulley and Most, 1985) and the DiSC model (De Jonge and Dormann, 2003). The different personalities react differently in the three phases. Some personality profiles will prefer a quick pace at the beginning but lose interest in the change when it becomes part of the daily routine. Others will be wary of the change at the beginning but get on board with the strategy when they begin to see results and become impatient if the change does not pick up pace. Yet others' reaction will depend on the reactions of the people around them.

When employees react negatively to the change, they drop off the bus and are left behind by the rest of the department. This is a strong metaphor, which becomes part of the shared language about change in the organization long after playing the game. The employees can also resist the change in different ways. The pavement on the game board represents the three levels of change posited by Rick Maurer (1996):

Resistance Level 1: The Informational Level
- 'I don't understand it. It doesn't make sense to me.'

Resistance Level 2: The Emotional Level
- 'I don't like it. I need to feel more secure.'

Resistance Level 3: The Level of Trust
- 'I don't trust you. I have to see it to believe it.'

Players handle employees' resistance using leadership action cards that target the different resistance levels. Of course, different employees have different preferences in leadership styles, and participants must also take this into consideration. The leadership actions run the gamut of leadership styles, from a commanding style (for example, by setting clear expectations for the department during the change) over a relational or democratic style (for example, by getting all the employees together to talk about the change), to a coaching style (for example, by giving employees a chance to voice their concerns in one-on-one conversations).

The leadership actions represent the managers' time and focus. Participants have only so much time, so they must carefully choose who to engage and how. In each round, participants choose four leadership action cards from a selection of 12. Each action card affects the selected employees differently. Their effects often depend on certain conditions. This makes the participants' choices particularly difficult as they need to take many parameters into account. If the game were simply a linear representation of one theory, in which the prescribed action produced the expected result, it would be easy to figure out the game and it would quickly become tedious. The interplay of theories and a realistic case with conditioned effects, depending on specific game states, gives participants a much more developed understanding of the applicability of the embedded theories. It also makes the game's case memorable and full of stories. A few reflections from some of the many organizations that use Wallbreakers:

> At Arla we use the leadership simulation Wallbreakers to work with changes in the company in an educational way and with great effect. The pace of change, and resistance to it, are difficult to handle, and the managers need to be prepared for the different aspects of resistance and change. Many more learning channels are activated by using a game than if the employees just sit down and passively receive information. In the game, managers play different roles and have a limited number of choices. How do you utilize the options you have in the best way? You get more engaged and you can relate. (Pernille Graesdal Beck, Senior Manager, Arla Foods, personal communication)

> Wallbreakers works as a perfect frame for understanding the dynamics at play in change processes and the importance of a management that cares for the human dimension. The balance between activating the competitive element and the serious dialogue and idea exchange that are built into the game are particularly efficient. (Torben Pedersen, former senior HR Consultant at Danfoss A/S, personal communication)

Wallbreakers is based on a series of acknowledged and well-established theories on personality types, management, organizational culture and change processes, including those of Edgar Schein (2010), John Kotter (1996), Rick Maurer (1996) and Daniel Goleman (2006).

Gamechangers – strategy execution

Gamechangers is an award-winning leadership simulation about strategy execution and influence in complex organizations. The game (Figure 18.2) focuses on how to engage stakeholders in carrying out a strategic initiative throughout the organization. Implementing lean, rolling out sustainability or building up a new sales platform can be the obvious choice for a corporation. Yet the execution often fails. This is because cross-organizational strategic initiatives are often so extensive that it becomes necessary to fundamentally change the way people work and the way a department collaborates with other departments. This requires a leader who is able to

Figure 18.2 Gamechangers in action

build coalitions and create trust in the strategy, in the future and in himself or herself as a leader. In Gamechangers, the participants are trained in using various influence styles and models for conflict resolution. They learn to ensure momentum by identifying, understanding and engaging the people who are necessary as ambassadors and active co-players.

The participants are given the responsibility of implementing the new Green Shores strategy in a fictional organization. They have to engage colleagues with different motives and key performance indicators (KPIs) to work in the interest of the strategy. Their ability to create results and support are measured throughout the game. The game is divided into two sections, each comprising two rounds. The first part of the game focuses on building and utilizing networks within the organization by communicating and engaging with the important stakeholders. The second part focuses on realizing the benefits of the initiative, maintaining momentum, and integrating the initiative into the systems and daily life of the organization. Each part can be played alone or in combination, to experience a strategic project from its inception until it is part of daily work.

The central representation is the Move board, which represents stakeholders' positions towards the strategy. There are two dimensions to their position: for/against the strategy and active/passive. Stakeholders can, for instance, be passively supportive of the strategy. These are the stakeholders who will express their support for the strategy at meetings but fail to actually get anything done. Stakeholders can also actively ignore the strategy. These are the stakeholders who never answer the phone when the manager calls. This is an important learning point in the game. It is not enough that the majority of the organization has a positive attitude towards the strategy. The manager requires active support from a strong coalition of key stakeholders to actually get things done, not just the creation of positive buzz around the strategy. Players need to carefully select the most important stakeholders. They cannot get all stakeholders on board with the strategy.

At the start of the game, only a few stakeholders are placed on the board. At the outset, players do not know how most of the organization feels about the new initiative so they must spend time exploring the organizational landscape. Players act by choosing leadership action cards in each round. Actions represent time and focus; they range from initial meetings with stakeholders to different negotiation tactics. Actions can make the stakeholder feel more positive towards the strategy; however, this frequently requires removing obstacles first. These can be organizational obstacles, such as aligning sales KPIs with the new strategy. Obstacles can also be based on previous experiences with the management of the company, such as the employee who is worried that the strategy is just a front for layoffs. This sort of resistance can be won over by building personal rapport.

Personal relationships with stakeholders are also an important part of the game. Personal relationships are represented by green and red tokens, which are placed beneath the stakeholder on the Move board. Personal relationships can be leveraged to influence other stakeholders through informal networks. But players must ensure their ambassador understands and supports the project before he or she is sent out to represent the interests of specific players.

Of course, the relation can also be negative. The stakeholder's reason for working against the strategy might not have anything to do with the strategy. The negativity might in fact be directed at the player; this personal issue needs to be resolved before the stakeholder can support the strategy wholeheartedly. Gamechangers uses matchbox car racing as a metaphor to track the progress of the different teams in the game. Each team is assigned a model of a sailing ship. During the game, they place small stickers on their model to represent different achievements that will move them forward and help them to implement the new strategy successfully. If they make mistakes, the teams can also be assigned anchors that will slow down their progress. A reflection from one of the organizations that uses Gamechangers:

> Gamechangers will for sure increase the awareness and understanding for our leaders to work and manage internal stakeholder relationships. To achieve results in a company like Arla it is not enough only to focus on your own tasks and activities in your team – but also fully to understand how others in Arla

can help you in creating performance. Having organizational understanding and proactively building positive relationships are core competencies for leaders in Arla. Gamechangers helps leaders to understand and strengthen these competencies in an effective and fun way. (Thomas Schou Høj, Arla Foods amba, Global HR Services, Learning and Development, personal communication)

Gamechangers is based on well-established theories and models regarding negotiation, conflict resolution, influence styles and change leadership, including theories by John Kotter (1996) and Stephen Bungay (2011).

Bridgebuilders – global leadership

Bridgebuilders is an engaging tool used to train leadership of globally distributed teams. The game (Figure 18.3) teaches leaders how to form well-functioning global teams and run them through good times and bad. Bridgebuilders focuses on how to build efficient, cohesive teams across distances and cultures, while creating and maintaining good stakeholder relations and adhering to the fundamentals of good leadership.

The participants play the role of a leader of a newly formed global team with corporate responsibilities. The players must build a high-performing team that can deliver quality output in an environment occupied by sometimes sceptical stakeholders with their own agendas. In the first round of the game, the participants face the challenges of establishing the team, from

Figure 18.3 Bridgebuilders in action

forming relationships and building trust to securing alignment on goals and responsibilities. In the second round, a new global client increases the workload and raises expectations for the team. Now the players have to show that they can lead the team from good to great. Cultural differences and local autonomy create challenges. In the third and final round of the game, a crisis occurs. Now the players must demonstrate that they can create results under tough conditions, in which stakeholder relations are stressed by mistrust and internal politics.

A key element in Bridgebuilders is working with balancing the needs for alignment and autonomy. To have a high-performing team, the employees must be empowered and motivated to act locally, with a high degree of autonomy; at the same time, there is a need for alignment on strategic direction and core processes. This balance is visualized directly on the game board, on which each fictional team member is represented by a game piece that moves in a matrix based on alignment and autonomy. Sometimes the players must prioritize leadership actions that decrease local autonomy in an effort to boost alignment; at other times, the key to winning the game is to boost local autonomy through empowerment and delegation.

Another central element is leading across distance and time zones. In the game, the players must prioritize their limited travel budget and time, and make tough choices about when there is a need to meet face to face and when it can be done through digital platforms such as Skype or Yammer. A key point in the game is that building trust across distance is hard, and that highly relationship-oriented employees appreciate leaders who are willing to invest in informal socializing and face-to-face interaction.

Cultural differences are also a core aspect of Bridgebuilders. In the game, we describe cultural and personal traits based on four themes: motivation and collaboration, leadership and decision making, communication and conflict, and planning and workflow. All stakeholders and employees in the game have a unique set of traits. During gameplay, the consequences of the players' leadership actions are adjusted by the cultural traits of the affected people. Leadership actions might be appreciated by some, while they might be met with indifference or even resentment by others.

The game is designed with a high degree of flexibility, so the facilitator can build different scenarios depending on which cultural differences are most relevant. A case can be created in which the team leader is located in the United States at the company headquarters, but the rest of the team works in South America and Europe. Or a scenario can be set up in which a team leader based in Asia struggles to align colleagues located in Europe and the Middle East.

A reflection from one of the organizations who use Bridgebuilders:

> In Autoneum, a global leader in acoustic and thermal management with operations in more than 20 countries, Bridgebuilders is used to train collaboration and leadership across distance and cultures in our global organization. The simulation accomplishes exactly what we are looking for by creating awareness of issues in global leadership and provokes some really interesting discussions and learnings on issues such as alignment, autonomy and trust in a matrix-organization. (Marianne Fischer-Rasmussen, Autoneum, Head of Global People Development, personal communication)

Bridgebuilders is based on acknowledged theories on management, virtual teams and cultural traits, including those of Daniel Goleman (2006) and Stephen Bungay (2011).

The end goal

In the end, all our learning, development and change activities are about changing behaviour. If new meaning, knowledge, wisdom and skills do not translate into ordinary workday behaviour, they are a lost investment. It only matters what we actually do and get done. Changing behaviour is hard. We are designed by nature to stick to our habits and what we know best. In facing these challenges within leadership development, game-based learning offers a unique training ground that allows us to address all three aspects of anchoring new behaviour – motivation, ability and triggers. While games may not

About

Workz is a Copenhagen-based change agency. We specialize in change management, leadership development, learning, and the design of game-based tools for involvement and training. Our multidisciplinary team helps our clients communicate a clear strategic direction, build commitment and ownership, and enable action by providing the right competencies, tools and structures. Our consultancy services and award-winning tools are used globally by industry leaders in a number of sectors, including finance, service, pharmaceuticals, biotech, food, IT, energy, engineering and shipping. Ask Agger is the author of Adfaerd på Spil (Behaviour at odds) (2017).

be a sure recipe for success, when designed and utilized well they offer a very efficient tool kit for accelerating learning, change and new behaviour.

References

Agger, A (2017) Adfaerd på Spil (Behaviour at odds), in *Adfærdsdesign*, ed T Dahlsgaard, A Lieberoth and N Jensen, Plurafutura Publishing, Risskov, Denmark

Bungay, S (2011) *The Art of Action*, Nicholas Brealey Publishing, London

De Jonge, J and Dormann, C (2003) The DISC model: demand-induced strain compensation mechanisms in job stress, in *Occupational Stress in the Service Professions*, ed M F Dollard, A H Winefield and H R Winefield, pp 43–74, Taylor and Francis, London

Fogg, B J (2009) A behaviour model for persuasive design, *Proceedings of the 4th International Conference on Persuasive Technology*, p 40, ACM

Goleman, D (2006) *Emotional intelligence*, Bantam, New York

Hanghøj, T (2011) *Playful Knowledge: An explorative study of educational gaming*, Lambert Academic Publishing, Saarbrücken

Hilgers, P (2000) 'Eine anleitung zur anleitung: das taktische kriegsspiel 1812–1824', *Board Games Studies*, 3, pp 59–77

Jensen, N H (2017) 'Hjernens evolutionære design', in *Adfærdsdesign*, ed T Dahlsgaard, A Lieberoth and N Jensen, Plurafutura Publishing Risskov, Denmark

Kahneman, D (2011) *Thinking, Fast and Slow*, Penguin Books, London

Kotter, J P (1996) *Leading Change*, Harvard Business Press, Boston

Lieberoth, A (2013) Hukommelsessystemer og oplevelseslæring: hvordan forvandler hjernen episoder til semantisk viden? (Memory systems and experience learning: how the brain transforms episodes of semantic knowledge), *Cursiv*, **11**, DPU, Aarhus University

Maurer, R (1996) *Beyond the Wall of Resistance: Unconventional strategies that build support for change*, Bard, Austin

Myers, I B, McCaulley, M H and Most, R (1985) *Manual, A Guide to the Development and Use of the Myers-Briggs type indicator*, Consulting Psychologists Press, Palo Alto, CA

Ross, G R T (ed) (1906) *'De sensu' and 'De memoria'*, Cambridge University Press, Cambridge

Schein, E H (2010) *Organizational Culture and Leadership*, vol 2, John Wiley & Sons, Chichester

19

Linkxs

Team collaboration simulation

THOMAS BENEDICT, InContext Consultancy BV

#TeamDevelopment #TeamBuilding #TeamCollaboration

InContext Consultancy Group designed Linkxs to allow teams to practise self-organization, communication and collaboration. Linkxs first holds up a mirror to participants by offering a team challenge that stimulates individualistic, non-collaborative behaviour. The game (Figure 19.1) shows the team the undesirable compounded effects of this behaviour. Subsequently, the team embarks on a journey to optimize team performance and complete the game successfully. Teams of participants discover insights for their daily work, which allows the game to function not only as a mirror, but also as a window onto more effective collaboration behaviour.

Figure 19.1   Playing the Linkxs game

How it can be applied

Linkxs is meant to be played by teams of participants who work together in daily life. It has been used extensively from operational teams to leadership teams of global organizations in more than 30 different countries around the world, including China, Japan and Korea. Linkxs is an easy-to-use simulation, so many facilitators like to use it as a high-energy booster in all sorts of sessions. If the participants do not work together as a team normally, the value of the simulation is limited to a high-energy experience, personal insights and general tips on team collaboration.

Linkxs can be used by groups with different levels of education. A higher level of education does not necessarily correlate with a better simulation result. Groups of participants with a technical background do marginally better than non-technical groups. While Linkxs may be utilized at various moments, for example as part of a larger programme, it also lends itself well to being played by teams as an eye-opener in its own right.

Experience-based perspectives in the game

Linkxs aims at allowing a team of participants to experience and solve the following challenges:

- how to balance individual goals with team goals and goals of others;
- how to help each other to succeed;
- how to optimize team productivity;
- how to avoid unnecessary competition;
- how to deal with conflict.

With increasing frequency, individuals and teams within organizations are given the space to organize their work independently, which is not always easy. Not only do tasks have to be carried out, they have to be planned and managed in conjunction with others. In constructions like these, people need to communicate with each other extensively, to balance their own objectives with the objectives of others and optimize the productivity of the whole team (Deshon et al, 2004). When a team is working under pressure, unproductive behaviour, even by only one or two people, can seriously obstruct the progress of the entire team.

We originally developed Linkxs for teams of managers working together in the Dutch post office organization. A big problem for this organization was that individual managers were attempting to reach their own goals without recognizing their interdependence or opportunities to synergize their individual efforts. In fact, they were focusing so much on their individual goals that they unwittingly created a system that made it more difficult to reach these goals. Bringing this process to light was the original trigger for developing the game. We later recognized that individuals throughout the many organizations in which we subsequently tested and delivered the game all have the tendency to focus on individual goals under pressure, even if this is obviously not a successful strategy. The combination of unsatisfactory results and the lack of a successful strategy to improve them causes frustration and laying blame on others, which further reduce performance.

Recognizing this process as it happens is difficult. Participants find it hard to participate in the simulation and reflect on their own performance at the same time. Observers, who are randomly selected from the group of participants but who do not actively participate in the game, can both recognize the process of suboptimization and link it to examples in real life. Using observers from the group of participants has therefore developed into a best practice when delivering Linkxs.

Facilitation insights

Simplification

Over the years, Linkxs has been played many times and in many variations. The game developed from a relatively complex set with many different puzzles and building materials, to a handy set of pop-out cardboard-based boards that hold both the puzzles and the construction materials. This has some significant facilitation benefits. First, it is easy to set up the game, which is especially important when Linkxs is used as part of a larger workshop or training. In addition, players can be sure that all the correct pieces are in their correct places at the start of the game, as this is often challenged by highly energized participants at some point during play. A third benefit is that the parts do not need to be retrieved from all over the training room at the end of the session. Because Linkxs is so simple and straightforward, there is no need for participants to undergo long presentations or preparations at the beginning. The game has a one-minute introduction, another minute of reading the rules, and then GO.

Empowering observers

As stated above, we like to use observers from the group of participants because they know the players and can link what they see to reality. In facilitating Linkxs, it helps to point the observers towards hot spots in the game, where they are likely to see interesting things happen. In addition, it helps to give the observers insight into the working of the game and various collaboration strategies, so that they can put their observations into context. An open, collaborative, helping and transparent approach to observers gives the best results.

Frustration and attribution

Participants can become tense and frustrated if there is little progress, especially during the first half-hour of play. They may react to this by apportioning blame towards the game or other participants. A certain level of conflict between participants is valuable, but this can escalate to non-productive levels, especially in groups who experience negative tension in their daily work. A facilitator can help a heated-up participant to calm down by listening to him or her express emotions. The facilitator can redirect non-productive communication between participants by positioning himself or herself as the centre of communication, which means that the participants talk to the facilitator instead of directly to each other. He or she can stress the importance of finding a way through the puzzle together as a journey and an experience. If this does not work, a facilitator can choose to actively help the emotional participant to get through the roadblock and then discuss what happened when the participant has calmed down.

Daily work

Linkxs is built in such a way that participants bring elements of their daily work experience into the game. They recognize patterns, behaviours and processes from their normal work experience. It is useful if they do this, because they will be able to link the game learning directly to their daily work. It is not productive for participants to initiate this discussion while the game is still running, however, because it becomes very confusing. In addition, observers might have an instant, massive insight that they want to start sharing immediately, while the participants are still trying to understand the puzzles. To avoid this, we stop daily work conversations during the game and ask people to write down their points and save them for the evaluation.

Experience success

Most groups can finish the simulation within 60 to 90 minutes. Depending on the allotted time, the participants' practical abilities and the level of collaboration in the team, it can take longer. Towards the end of the game, it is important for all participants to experience success. The facilitator may therefore have to coach or even help some participants to solve their puzzles and build their construction. A group that has experienced success at the end of Linkxs is much more likely to enter into a constructive evaluation with high take-home value.

Gameplay

Linkxs groups are divided into four subgroups. Each subgroup has an assignment and a table to work on. Each subgroup receives a number of cardboard boards containing puzzle pieces and construction elements. The objective for each subgroup is to solve the puzzle and finish the construction as soon as possible. One important rule is that participants are not allowed to visit each other's table. There is a designated table for communication and exchange of pieces, usually just outside the training room. This is done to simulate the fact that teams are not always in close proximity when working together and cannot always be reached for consultation.

Key gains enabled by the game

Understanding the counterintuitive elements of teamwork

At the beginning of the game, participants tend to compete with each other. They focus too much on their own work, as they want to do better than others; this is usually unintentional. As participants are confronted with their behaviour, they are able to recognize it and can take more responsibility for their own actions.

Reach goals by helping others to reach theirs

Participants exercise with the magnetic effects of their behaviour. They gain awareness of the impact of their (un)collaborative behaviour on other participants and learn to make conscious decisions regarding their own actions. On the positive side, this leads to a virtuous circle of high trust and cooperation. However, it can also lead to a vicious circle in which self-interest is leading and mutual trust diminishes.

Seek to understand before seeking to be understood

The high pressure of the game means many individuals may want to make their point simultaneously or have their individual needs tended to. There are generally far too many speakers and too few listeners in workplaces. Participants have the opportunity to practise techniques to truly listen to each other, improving general communication and decision making. Participants learn they should seek to understand before seeking to be understood (Covey, 1989). Fulfilling their individual interests is encouraged by helping others to achieve their goals (Figure 19.2).

Think before running

As playing Linkxs is a high-pressure challenge, participants tend to hit the ground running instead of taking a moment to analyse the task. The game is such a complicated challenge that thinking through the process and making a joint decision on an approach will accelerate finishing the game.

Participant learning

Teams of Linkxs players, especially if they are a team or family group in real life, consistently report that Linkxs was a strong learning experience with real meaning for their team behaviour. Linkxs is the kind of experience

Figure 19.2   Balance system

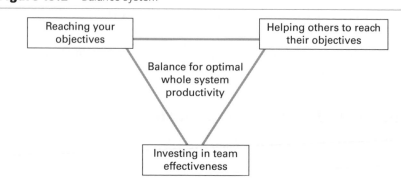

that people remember for a long time, due to the combination of intensity, confrontation and fun. One participant, who later became a game developer herself, said it was best when participants experienced the frustration of non-collaborative behaviour at the start of the game:

> Everyone had their own ideas about how to improve the exchange process, people shouting and snatching pieces of puzzle out of one another's hands. We all wanted to get the puzzle done as quickly as possible. I had a couple of pieces wrenched from my hands. (personal communication)

Eventually, the group starts to understand what is needed:

> Within an hour it became painfully clear that we didn't really have any conflicts of interest.

The game ends with the participants experiencing effective collaboration:

> Now I've seen and experienced firsthand – via serious gaming – what behaviour is like when colleagues work together.

The beauty of Linkxs

Linkxs is by far the most played and most loved game that InContext has ever built. Our facilitators usually have a couple of Linkxs boxes in the car, just in case they might need them. Linkxs is about generic issues that arise in any organization and is therefore universally recognizable. The immense energy generated, the confrontation and the steep learning curve are not caused by an advanced system, loads of detail or complex rules. It is just a little box with some cardboard inside.

About

At InContext, strategic change in business and people come together. This is because InContext is at a crossroad between the business side (technology, processes, business models, marketing, sales, supply chain, finance, IT) and the people side (attitude, energy, skills, motivation, authenticity, connection, integrity). With this unique combination of knowledge and skills, we are able to place any intervention in the context of an organization and thus go directly to the heart of the problem. We link people to process, thereby creating impact and results.

References

Covey, S R (1989) *The 7 Habits of Highly Effective People*, Simon & Schuster, New York

Deshon, R, Kozlowski, S, Schmidt, A, Milner, K and Wiechmann, D (2004) A multiple-goal, multilevel model of feedback effects on the regulation of individual and team performance, *Journal of Applied Psychology*, **89** (6), 1035–56

20
Managing Your Sales Business
Improve results through effective management of your team

CHRISTINE ELGOOD AND PETER MACNAUGHTAN,
Elgood Effective Learning

#SalesManagement #TerritoryPlanning #OrganizationalCulture

Managing your Sales Business (MySB) is a business game originally designed for the Oracle EMEA Sales Readiness department to improve the effectiveness of sales managers. The market within which the company operates was changing and senior management felt there was a need to reorganize the way the sales force was structured, put best practices among sales managers into effect, and ensure common standards across regions and countries. There was also the recognition, common in many other organizations, that successful salespeople were too frequently promoted to a sales management role without adequate training. Good salespeople were promoted, given a territory to work in, allocated some staff and then expected to replicate the success they had achieved as an individual salesperson. This, despite having little experience in managing a team or working at a more strategic level in the organization.

The impetus for the project came from the top, with the Executive Vice President (VP) for the EMEA region placing responsibility in the hands of the VP for Organizational Development, a person with significant experience in all aspects of change management. In the business simulation, game participants work in teams. Each time they represent the sales manager of a territory. The team must manage the demand generation process to ensure there are sufficient leads and opportunities in their pipeline and coach their team so there are enough man hours available to convert the pipeline into sales won. One participant offered this comment:

> Business simulation – so real to life! – has given me a great way of approaching opportunity management positively and constructively!
> (personal communication)

Teams compete over eight periods to see which one can generate the most sales and weighted pipeline. Each team's success is determined by its own actions and the decisions of one team do not affect those of another. However, there is plenty of competition between the teams. This was crucial for gaining engagement from the audience for whom the product was designed.

Gameplay

At the start of the activity, each team is seated around a table with a playing mat (Figure 20.1). The mat depicts a visual and physical flow that demonstrates the flow of a demand generation initiative through to leads, opportunities and, finally, a sale.

Each team is given a limited number of bespoke counters that signify a scarce resource (marketing capability). These counters are used to invest in demand-generation activities; however, the players do not know which activities will be released as the game progresses. This means they must manage an unknown. This mirrored the real world at Oracle, in which a central team prepared all the material for demand-generation activities and the sales manager did not know which campaigns would be available in the future. There is a short PowerPoint introduction to the activity, explaining its purpose and what the teams need to do. This is accompanied by a two-page player brief. The activity involves a series of linked activities to show

Figure 20.1   The MySB playing mat in action

where support could be most appropriately given to a sales representative. There are two different but related phases of the game, each of them with four subphases (Figure 20.2).

Phase 1 has four planning phases, each lasting 30 minutes. This section is all about the planning activities in which a successful sales manager must engage. The activities revolve around a simplified version of a territory management tool that was being introduced at Oracle across the region. The team must review a series of plans simulating the types of material a salesperson might bring to a review meeting.

Figure 20.2   The route map for the sessions

THE BUSINESS GAME ROUTE MAP

STAGE		ACTIVITY	TIME	TOTAL SESSION
INTRODUCTION			15	
PHASE 1	PERIOD 1	Territory Plan and Demand Generation	30	45 MINUTES
PHASE 1	PERIOD 2	Territory Plan and Demand Generation	30	
PHASE 1	PERIOD 3	Territory Plan and Demand Generation	30	1 HOUR 30 MINUTES
PHASE 1	PERIOD 4	Influence and Discovery map and Demand Generation	30	
REFLECTION			30	
INTRODUCTION			15	
PHASE 2	PERIOD 5		30	
PHASE 2	PERIOD 6	Opportunity Management and Demand Generation	30	2 HOURS AND 15 MINUTES
PHASE 2	PERIOD 7		30	
PHASE 2	PERIOD 8		30	
REVIEW AND RESULTS			30	30 MINUTES

These include:

- account segmentation;
- product strategy;
- channel strategy;
- identification of gaps in knowledge about the customer and their pain (influence and discovery map).

As an example we can describe the account segmentation activity. The material for these activities is printed on large paper, so the entire team can gather around it. The methodology used for determining the right strategy for an account – Invest, Milk or Hit – is based on proprietary material. However, the actions associated with the agreed classification are underpinned by the Boston Consumer Grid matrix (Henderson, 1998), which categorizes customers to enable companies to understand where their revenue comes from and what might need to be done in the future. The methodology in the product strategy activity is informed by the Ansoff matrix (Ansoff, 1957), which helps assess the risk associated with a mix between old and new products, and old and new markets.

The scoring for the territory planning activity also calls for the facilitators to judge the coaching questions that the teams formulate. The scoring is based on the extent to which the coaching question encourages the salesperson to think, rather than elicit a yes/no response. In each of these periods, the teams must also decide whether they want to invest in a demand-generation activity and complete a planning activity. For each of these actions, they receive some leads and opportunities (from the demand-generation decision) and some man days (from the territory planning activity). This phase of the game is relatively calm.

Phase 2 also has four phases, each lasting 30 minutes. The planning continues with the demand-generation activities. However, instead of focusing on coaching the team through the territory plans and influence and discovery map, the activity centres on allocating the man days (awarded for the earlier activities) to pursue leads for generating opportunities and closing opportunities by answering questions. The questions test the team's knowledge of procedures, policies and how to deal with issues that their sales team might face. After each time period has expired, new demand-generation activities, leads and opportunities are released. This mirrors the changing landscape that the participants see in the real world but ensures their attention does not wander too far.

Score charts show what each team has in its pipeline and what revenue has been won; the charts are updated continually throughout phase 2. This creates a real buzz and sense of competition. The environment in this phase is more like their normal day-to-day environment. Since the game is built entirely around the audience's world, participants find it completely believable and they can easily relate to it.

Organizational game examples

The game was used in a two-day programme, allowing participants to experience some of the ideas offered in the more formal instructional sessions. The programme was run over 40 times, over a period of three years, across four continents – Europe, Africa, Asia and the United States – covering over 700 managers in the company. Over the lifetime of the programme, the business simulation was consistently rated as one of the best sessions, in terms of both content and relevance.

Although the game was originally designed for the sales management community, other business units wanted to attend as the programme spread; this was particularly true of areas that worked with the sales managers, so they could understand more about the sales managers' world. The game was therefore an excellent way to build understanding between functional areas, break down silos and create a common language within the organization.

The programme was also run in an abbreviated form for Oracle's Regional Management Team for EMEA. This not only showed real commitment from the top, but also meant the top team knew exactly what they were asking their staff to do. The core issues addressed in MySB apply to most sales teams and organizations. However, this product was really successful because it mirrored the real world of the client. The key areas and mechanism used in the game are transferable, but the factual content and figures need to be amended for each client. For example, this particular product incorporated methodologies that were relevant to the organization at a specific time period, such as categorization of customers as Invest, Milk or Hit. While this particular methodology might not be relevant to a different client, most sales organizations have a way of classifying their customers/prospects and a strategy for each. In contrast, the emphasis on balancing long- and short-term planning and the need for a sales manager to work through the team (coach) are issues immediately transferable to other sales environments.

Key gains that the game enables

Balance the long term and the short term

The sales environment can be very short term focused. However, successful sales managers must continually look ahead and invest in demand-generation and planning activities to produce the leads and opportunities that will bring them and their team success in the following quarter.

Develop sales management skills

Not all successful sales representatives make successful sales managers. This activity helps sales representatives to develop some of the skills they need to enhance their chances of being successful in a sales management role. These include:

- Recognizing the need to take a step back and focus their effort on coaching their team rather than trying to do all the work by themselves. This requires a different mindset and skills. Instead of knowing the details about every opportunity, they need to be able to identify the key areas where their input can make a difference.

- Focusing their efforts. There will never be sufficient resources or hours in the day to pursue every potential customer or sales lead. Successful managers use the tools available to them to assess the chance of success when pursuing potential customers and leads.

At Oracle, the programme and use of certain aspects within the game led to wide-scale adoption of particular tools and techniques throughout the region, along with a change in the language used for discussing sales activities.

Success factors

There are many factors that contributed to the success of the MySB programme at Oracle. These included:

- Support from senior levels in the organization – support from the top was evident from the beginning of the design process. Significant work was done, prior to beginning design work on the game, to assess the training need.

- Tightly focused material – in the early stages, the design team had numerous ideas about what should be included. When creating the game, the team continually questioned exactly what outcome they wanted and how success could be assessed. The result was a highly focused activity.

- Relevant to the real world – the material was entirely relevant to the real world of the participants. It was not an academic construct or something borrowed from another company or organization; it was totally real and believable for the participants.

- Profile of the programme within the company – it was made clear by the Executive VP for the region that attendance and participation in the programme was mandatory for all sales managers looking to advance within the company. It was also one of only a few programmes that was genuinely regional, so the opportunity for sharing across country borders was invaluable for the programme, the participants and the company.

About

Chris Elgood Associates Limited (Elgood Effective Learning) was created by Chris Elgood, MA, author of *The Handbook of Management Games and Simulations* (1976). The company's objective is to extend the use of games and simulations as an alternative to direct instruction. Christine Elgood, BA, MBA, took over in 1977 and has developed new material for the current environment and new methods that exploit up-to-date technology. The company's greatest strength remains treating each client as a special case.

References

Ansoff, I (1957) Strategies for diversification, *Harvard Business Review*, 35 (5) (Sep–Oct), pp 113–24

Henderson, B D ([1970] 1998) The product portfolio, *Perspectives on Strategy*, vol 35, Boston Consulting Group, Boston

21

Ocean of Culture

A dialogue tool for developing the organization's culture

LONE AAGAARD, Kommitment International ApS

#OrganizationalCulture #OrganizationalValues #OrganizationalStructures

Ocean of Culture unlocks sources of value within a company and identifies factors flowing from the company's culture that inhibit realizing that value. It is an experiential game that enables participants to encounter and confront both productive and unproductive aspects of their company culture, including both visible, deliberate aspects of the culture and those that may be more hidden and below the level of conscious choice and awareness. The goal of the game is to use the company's culture as a business driver through developing a shared understanding of, and commitment to, the alignment and coherence between market strategies and organizational structures and development (see Schein, 2010). As the name suggests, the basic metaphor throughout the game is that of an ocean. The metaphor operates at a number of levels, not least the image of an ocean being that which surrounds us and its very ubiquity being that which renders it difficult to see.

The game (Figure 21.1) can be facilitated by external consultants or in-house; in the latter case, Kommitment International can provide training. For such in-house training, Ocean of Culture provides a platform for human resources (HR) personnel and others concerned with organizational development to provide a clear, strategic underpinning and direction to their work.

Creating learning that results in change

The basic problem that Ocean of Culture seeks to address concerns how we design change processes so that the implementation, embedding and embodying of change actually happens. The game does so by reconfiguring

Figure 21.1   Ocean of Culture game board

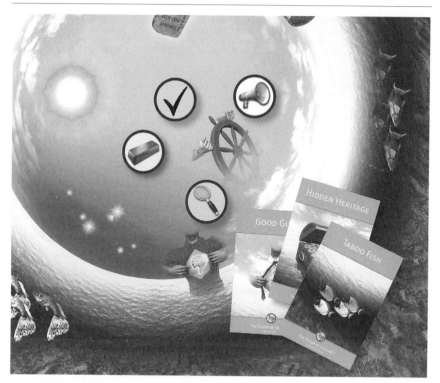

the dynamic of change, such that those organizational elements and features that are often seen as barriers to, and inhibitors of, change become the drivers and facilitators. The game process and structure are designed to promote individual and organizational learning through questions and material that challenge the participants' assumptions, while simultaneously generating understanding of the more fundamental patterns upon which these assumptions are grounded.

The gameplay encourages revealing and examining both explicit aspects of an organization's culture and those that are often more hidden. It can also throw into relief areas of discrepancy and contradiction, and points of dissonance between an organization's culture, its strategic aspirations and objectives, and its organizational structures and development processes.

The business development case

The Ocean of Culture game has been applied to situations in which a company appears to have reached some kind of limit to its development and needs a fresh framework for thinking about, understanding and acting strategically in relation to its business. Such was the case with a medium-sized manufacturing company that, while reasonably successful over the medium term, had seen profits reduced in recent years. This downturn had not responded to the haphazard strategic actions that had been determined by the joint chief executives/owners of the company, and the business was trapped in a cycle of cost-cutting – quality reduction – withdrawal from innovation that everyone involved could see would not end well; however, no one had the resources to stop the downward spiral.

As part of a broader process, Ocean of Culture was used by each of the functional teams, their managers and senior management. The ludic nature of Ocean of Culture and the specifics of the gameplay provided participants with both the space and the vocabulary to describe aspects of the organization's operations that contributed to its inability to reverse its falling profitability. A key element in this was the inability of strategic managers to stay in the strategic space to ensure the chosen strategy was implemented; there was an almost panic-driven return to operational detail as soon as tough strategic challenges emerged. As a direct consequence of the entire organization engaging with Ocean of Culture, the senior management roles were reorganized and redistributed to enable those with the capacity for driving strategy to do so without being constantly dragged back – as they saw it – by those whose concerns and knowledge lay in the details of operations.

The cross-function effectiveness case

The senior management of a large tertiary and vocational education provider had an objective that the institution's departments would improve interdepartmental cooperation to increase customer satisfaction. The Centre for Facility Services trains service assistants, property service technicians and security guards. The students' education is a combination of in-college study programmes and trainee periods in private and public companies. The educational institution therefore must address two specific customer groups: companies and students.

Ocean of Culture is, among other things, appropriate for creating correspondence and cohesion between different functions in an organization, providing the opportunity for employees to gain a greater mutual understanding of each other's functions, and developing a common language. It was therefore an obvious choice for this process.

It was clear that yet another 'top-down' initiative, designed to induce the various functions to 'play nicely', was not going to work in this situation. There was a fair degree of scepticism on the part of the staff, borne, not least, from an overexposure to initiative after initiative, which summarily failed to make the promised difference. It was clear that one of the major barriers to change was a lack of ownership of the process among those charged with implementing it. It is intrinsic to the nature of Ocean of Culture that those involved in implementing solutions are intimately involved in both defining the problems and designing the solutions. As the HR Manager of the institution said:

> After only a short time, everyone was involved in the process. You just cannot help getting stuck into it, as working with Ocean of Culture is so involving. Everyone must take part, and everyone must be heard, so you cannot avoid being a part of it. (personal communication)

Via the process, they identified several focal areas that could help strengthen collaboration, thereby improving long-term customer satisfaction. The manager of the centre for facility services expressed:

> We have already benefited a lot from it. People now have a greater understanding about why we each do as we do, and when something sometimes does go wrong, it is usually always about communication to some degree. One of the concrete initiatives is that we have decided to solve all the little issues that you always meet in day-to-day life. Every time we come across a challenge, we have to outline the procedures, so that everyone knows what to do and why. (personal communication)

The HR Manager also pointed out that employees' own sense of initiative is important in order to get as much involvement in the process as possible:

> It has inspired us and given us a taste for working intently on our collaboration and communication. People quickly saw the necessity of this, and everyone got stuck in because they think it's cool. We have ownership of the culture process, and we feel that it is our project. (personal communication)

Game purpose

Modern organizations face constant demands to develop, renew and push the envelope both externally, in relation to their customers and markets, and internally, with regard to their own organization and employees. Fierce competition on quality, efficiency and innovation demands that companies today focus on all links of the value chain, and that they continually work to raise the bar in all respects. Putting all the organization's efforts into the development of new technology, new products and marketing is no longer sufficient. The quality of the company's management and the skills, attitudes and behaviour of its employees, as well as its organizational structure and workflows, must all interact and develop in balance with its strategic decisions and business goals. An organization's culture has become a business driver.

Many executives, managers and HR departments are aware of this and invest large sums in preparing sets of corporate values and arranging management training courses, cultivating specific attitudes among the staff, skills development and organizational development processes, all intended to add impetus to the business strategy. Unfortunately, such efforts are all too often fragmented and short-sighted, and the focus shifts on the basis of personal preferences and skills, or according to the location of the latest 'brush fire'.

During one specific period, the organization may focus on internal service quality, staff satisfaction, competencies, optimization of business procedures, etc. During another, the emphasis may instead be on capturing market shares, sales promotions, branding and marketing efforts. The complexity can become overwhelming, and it may seem impossible to build up an overview and establish the required strategic balance between market, strategy, culture and leadership.

Ocean of Culture introduces an element of play into this complex situation. The simple acts of focusing attention on a brightly coloured game board, having counters to engage with kinesthetically, and using graphically attractive images and designs on the game board and cards encourage participants to bypass their often well-practised strategies for resisting or undermining change. The 'underwater' metaphor lends the game process an element of discovery and adventure. The sense of play means that it is OK to raise what might otherwise be points of dissonance within an organization and have them acknowledged, examined and responded to in an environment in which levels of engagement and commitment are raised by the very nature of the game.

Gameplay

Ocean of Culture unfolds as a voyage of discovery through the participants' own organization. It is designed to stimulate dialogue, reflection and action (Figure 21.2) with regard to both the constructive and the obstructive aspects of culture in relation to the growth and development of the organization. Play is focused on a game board in which 'the big picture' of the ocean contains 17 features or phenomena – aspects of organizational culture – that one might encounter, as shown in Table 21.1:

Table 21.1 The 17 features in the Ocean of Culture

The Ocean	The cultural identity of the organization
The Sun	The vision behind the organization
Hands on the Wheel	The management of the organization
Guiding Lights	The commercial objectives of the organization
Tablets of Stone	The set of values to which the organization subscribes
Good Guys	Who or what gets rewarded and accorded high status
Bad Guys	Who or what is accorded low status and how that is recognized
Habit Fish	Habits within the organization
Communication Fish	Language and communication within the organization
Hidden Heritage	History and experience within the organization
Hidden Skeletons	Unresolved conflicts within the organization
Taboo Fish	The taboos within the organization
Myth Fish	The myths within the organization
Ritual Fish	The rituals within the organization
Gathering Nets	The measurement and monitoring systems used
The Seabed	Basic assumptions and fundamental values
Team Fish	Working together within the organization

The game unfolds over four phases:

- exploration;
- prioritization;
- detailed consideration;
- decision plus a follow-up.

Figure 21.2 Discussion enabled by the play in Ocean of Culture

Phases one to four can take place as a full-day activity with a follow-up of at least a half-day within two weeks of the first part of the game. The game process is iterative and can become an embedded element of the organizational and human resource development cycle.

Key learning that the game enables

The game can be thought of as an iteration corresponding with a learning step. In the early stages of the game, activity is focused on creating a shared platform for exploring the organization's culture and becoming familiar with the 17 aspects of culture identified by the game. At this stage, participants begin to offer their initial observations.

As the game moves into the next stage, it is important that the facilitator supports the group to ensure their discussions about culture remain business-focused and to guide discussion towards the significance of the organization's culture for business growth and development. It is also important to establish a shared understanding that working with culture is a process, not an event; cultural change and transformation take time, energy and persistence.

Phase 3 focuses on achieving a deeper understanding of those aspects of culture that drive the organization, and coming to a common understanding of where they create opportunities for growth and where they function to inhibit growth. In the final phase, the group begins to lay the foundation for the decisions and subsequent steps they will take regarding the organization's culture, and create an action-oriented plan to promote the work of developing the organization's culture.

About

Kommitment International ApS is a consultancy firm that focuses on designing bespoke solutions for companies in the areas of strategy, implementation and culture. The core team comprises Lone Aagaard – the principal and owner of the company – a team of very experienced senior consultants, and a network of freelance and associate consultants abroad.

Reference

Schein, E H (2010) *Organizational Culture and Leadership*, vol 2, John Wiley & Sons, Chichester

22
Pitch Perfect
Reversing the sales process

ANN HANSEN, Concept and Competence
BO KRÜGER, Moving Mind

#TeamCo-creation #TeamOwnership #TeamCreativity

In the Pitch Perfect game, the participants do not listen to a pitch from a CEO or a salesperson trying to sell an idea or a product – they make the pitch themselves. The game is highly engaging and creative, and is designed to increase the participants' ownership of an idea, product or key message (Figure 22.1).

Figure 22.1   A group pitching

Case description

VisitDenmark and Wonderful Copenhagen hold several events every year, to which they invite international meeting planners and event organizers. In two days, they try to convince participants that they should use Copenhagen and Denmark as the next destination for their meetings, conferences and incentive trips. The events are called *famtrips*, as the aim is to familiarize potential clients with Copenhagen. During the trips, the participants usually eat Danish food, see tourist attractions, meet possible Danish partners (venues and suppliers), learn about the Danish meeting concept Meetovation, and visit numerous hotels and meeting venues.

The famtrips are of great importance for both Copenhagen and Denmark as they have the potential to attract millions of kroner from international business tourists. For example, Copenhagen hosted 20,500 delegates, who participated in a single business conference – the Wonderful Copenhagen (2016) oncology congress, in October 2016. For a week, the city was awash with conference attendees spending millions of kroner. The challenge of the famtrips is that all major meeting destinations around Europe and the world have similar promotional events. Meeting planners and event organizers are invited on amazing trips to cities and places like Barcelona, Vienna and Borneo, where they are plied with great food, cultural experiences and luxury hotels. Many of these destinations are cheaper, have more attractions and better weather. The competition is global and fierce.

In order to beat tapas, Sachertorte and orangutans, VisitDenmark and Wonderful Copenhagen decided that the Danish famtrips should stand out on creativity and a high level of participant engagement. Hence, they asked us to develop a gamification concept for the whole famtrip. We developed a storyline for the whole trip and a game for the final session, called the Pitch Perfect game.

The overall storyline

The basic idea of gamifying the whole famtrip is to reverse the sales process and let the participants pitch Copenhagen instead of having them listen to the usual sales loop from the Danish partners. To achieve this, we created a storyline that is introduced from the very beginning of the event. At the opening session, something unexpected happens. While the head of business events from VisitDenmark and the facilitator are introducing the programme, they are interrupted by some very important news. A video, with a (fake) message from the CEO of World Design, a furniture design company, is shown. The CEO explains it is not likely that World Design will organize their highly prestigious Innovation Conference in Copenhagen, as claimed earlier, because they have received other interesting offers. The Danes are shocked. The facilitator explains that it is of great importance for Denmark and Copenhagen to win this conference and that this can only be done with the help of the participants. The CEO of World Design will come to Copenhagen the next day, and their task is to pitch Copenhagen as the right place to have the Innovation Conference.

Participants are then divided into diverse teams, with a mix of nationalities and backgrounds, in order to enhance networking and creativity. They all receive a neckhanger, on which they can collect points during the two days of the game. The points can be won during different activities in the programme, many of them gamified. (I will not describe all these activities, as they are not important to the basic structure of the game and can easily be replaced with other activities.) The facilitator explains that the points can be used by the teams to 'buy' props that will be useful in the final pitch. The better the team performs, the more props they can buy.

Pitch Perfect game

The climax of the game was the Pitch Perfect game, in which the participants prepared and performed the final pitch. The game lasted about 1 hour 15 minutes. When they arrived at the final venue, owned by one of the partners, they were told that now was the time to win the Innovation Conference for Copenhagen. While shown around the venue, to see accommodations and meeting facilities, the groups collected cards with instructions that described how their pitch should be created and performed. The instructions actually functioned as obstructions that were designed to unleash the participants' creative talents and avoid traditional, boring sales pitches. The aim was to make the pitch fun, inspiring and sticky. There were four categories of obstructions:

The format of the pitch

This card described how the pitch should be delivered. Different formats were chosen to make the presentations diverse and entertaining:

- *Human slideshow* – one participant presented and the rest were frozen in different positions, like 3D slides.
- *Puppet show* – the presentation was done with hand puppets.
- *Poster* – a poster was created on a flip chart.
- *TV commercial* – presented as a two-minute TV ad, with the participants as actors.

Unique selling points (USPs)

These were USPs for Copenhagen and Denmark. The idea was to let participants take ownership and learn about the USPs of Denmark, such as *green and responsible* and *a top innovative country.*

Create a slogan

The idea was to invite the participants to create a compact, sticky tag line that could sell Copenhagen and Denmark.

A twist

This obstruction brings something surprising to the pitch, to break the habits of ordinary sales arguments. Twists were, for example, *a famous Dane*, *a mascot* and *use music*. After the tour of the venue, the points each team had earned were totalled. The teams used the points to buy props in special stores with items that fitted their presentation format (such as a toy store for the puppet show, a stationery store with pens for the poster, etc). After five minutes in the shops, the teams were given 15 minutes to prepare the pitch. The levels of enthusiasm and co-creation across nationalities at this stage were very high.

The Danish partners participated in the groups, which were supposed to help them build relations and create trust with the potential clients. When the teams finished preparing their pitches, the CEO of World Design (in reality, an employee at VisitDenmark) arrived with great fanfare. The groups then had three minutes to make their pitches. The room was boiling with excitement and energy. The participants laughed a lot and seemed to enjoy seeing each other presenting. Afterwards, each presentation received feedback from the CEO of World Design and the Head of Business Events at VisitDenmark. This was to enhance the learning and to make the participants feel their contribution was valuable.

The game finished with the final decision from the CEO of World Design, who, very surprisingly, decided that the Innovation Conference should be

Figure 22.2   Roll of group pitching

held in Copenhagen. Finally, everyone celebrated with confetti, loud music and champagne (Figure 22.2).

Effects of the game

The aim of the game was to:

- let the participants take ownership of the product (Copenhagen as their next meeting destination);
- learn about Denmark and Copenhagen;
- give the participants a fun, exciting and memorable experience;
- break the usual pattern of the sales pitch.

According to one evaluation (Enalyzer, 2016), the Pitch Perfect game succeeded in facilitating participants' ownership (other evaluations showed the same):

- 100 per cent found that the overall rating of the famtrip was *very good* (highest score).

- 87.5 per cent found it likely that they would use Copenhagen as a meeting and conference destination for their company/clients in the future.

- 66.7 per cent found the famtrip *very good* compared to other famtrips arranged by national tourist boards in which they had participated.

- 75 per cent found that the Pitch Perfect game session was rewarding to a *very high degree*, which was the highest score of all sessions. On the other hand, 25 per cent found it *neither nor* rewarding (which was the lowest score of all sessions).

The format really did seem to divide the participants. The high level of engagement and co-creation apparently seemed appealing to some and scary to others. We were aware that some participants would not like to present in front of the entire group, so we tried to create a structure in which not everyone had to perform. Somehow, almost everyone ended up performing anyway, which was a pleasant challenge for some and an unpleasant one for others.

One goal was for the participants to learn more about Denmark and Copenhagen, which they certainly did during the Famtrip. One participant wrote:

> Thank you so much for the invitation and opening my eyes to a destination that I wasn't well educated on. I do all of the sourcing for global meetings and assure you that Copenhagen will ALWAYS be at the top of my list when presenting to my clients! (Enalyzer, 2016).

However, it is impossible to say how much this was due to the game or to the famtrip as such. Apparently, some participants learnt other unintended things. One participant wrote:

> It was scary at times, but I came for business and personal reasons. I am taking away much more than just the destination. Rethinking how I approach the brief, thinking outside the box, asking better questions. (Enalyzer, 2016)

We wanted to give the participants a fun, exciting and memorable experience. Our observations on site were that the participants had a lot of fun and were highly engaged, some more than others. The many props and obstructions made a lot of the participants do funny things, like wearing wigs, funny glasses and silly hats – voluntarily. The general feedback in the evaluation (Enalyzer, 2016) was very positive and contained words like *fun* and *challenging*. One participant wrote:

> A wonderful concept, a great group of partners, a perfectly balanced itinerary and a valuable learning experience. Superb!

The evaluation also showed that the game was quite challenging for some participants. A smaller group of participants had difficulties with it. A participant commented:

> The pitch was a very good idea, but we should keep in mind that there are very shy people around... and I personally don't enjoy doing 'representations'... hence I got a laughing attack!

We wanted to break the usual pattern of the sales pitch. During a traditional famtrip, the participants hear numerous sales pitches. Many meeting planners and event organizers have reported they find the traditional sales pitch boring and monotonous, and they cannot separate one from another afterwards.

The different formats and twists definitely made the pitches very different from the normal destination pitch. The risk of a highly creative concept like the Pitch Perfect game is that the format shadows the content. This happened to some extent; sometimes the message was drowned in wigs and crazy body sculptures. On the other hand, the participants were engaged and focused most of the time, which is usually not the case when you are a passive listener to a sales presentation after two days of a tough programme.

Moreover, the same messages were repeated many times in many different ways, which enhanced key messages. For example, the message that Copenhagen and Denmark are innovative destinations clearly came across: 100 per cent thought to *a high* or a *very high degree* that the famtrip positioned Denmark as an innovative meeting and conference destination (Enalyzer, 2016).

Possible application areas

The overall storyline could easily be applied to many other areas in which clients or employees should take ownership of an idea, message or product. The storyline follows a very basic narrative structure. A 'hero' (the product owner) wants something (to sell the product) but an enemy (a competitor) or obstacle occurs, and the hero needs help. The clients become the helpers and help the hero overcome the obstacle by delivering the perfect pitch. The storyline could, for example, be used by a CEO who wants employees to take ownership of strategy development, or an HR manager who wants the employee to take ownership of the company's core values.

The Pitch Perfect game could be used to help clients, employees or students understand or take ownership of ideas, knowledge, concepts, messages and products. The game can, for example, be used in sales events, training and team-building days. We have used similar formats many times in many types of companies and organizations. In one example, a medium-sized company wanted the employees to engage in team building and discuss future opportunities for the company. The employees were split up into smaller groups and asked to prepare presentations with obstructions about various topics regarding the future of the company.

Motivational perspectives in the game

From a psychological, theoretical perspective, the idea of the game was to trigger intrinsic motivation. In the meeting industry, extrinsic motivation is very often used to attract the attention of potential clients. The industry is overflowing with goodie bags, gift cards, bonus systems, rewards and competitions. The result is that many meeting planners and event organizers are spoiled and very often expect to get something in return for participating in an activity. For example, the first question from several participants in the Pitch Perfect game was 'what can we win?' The problem of using gifts and rewards to motivate is that the motivation most likely disappears as soon as the reward is gone. Even worse, rewards often kill intrinsic motivation, meaning that people stop doing something they would usually do for free unless they receive something in return (Sheldon, 2012). Our aim was to create a game that was so interesting to play that participating would be rewarding in itself. We also hoped that the game could trigger an intrinsic desire to come back to Denmark and organize a meeting here. The theoretical framework for the Pitch Perfect game was the self-determination theory (SDT), a motivational theory created by Edward Deci and Richard Ryan of the University of Rochester. Deci and Ryan's massive research (Deci and Ryan, 2000) has shown that three basic human needs drive intrinsic motivation: competency, autonomy and relatedness.

Competency means that all humans seek to control the outcome and experience mastery with whatever they do. In the Pitch Perfect game, we teach the participants something that will help them do their jobs more effectively in the future.

Autonomy is the universal urge to be a causal agent in one's own life and act in harmony with one's integrated self; however, this does not mean being independent of others. In the game, we nurtured this need by giving a few obstructions and a lot of freedom to solve the task in whatever way the participants preferred.

Relatedness means that humans have a universal desire to interact, be connected to and experience caring for others. The games focus on team work and co-creation, providing plenty of opportunities for the participants to connect in constructive and meaningful ways.

We tried to keep both competition and rewards at a low level. On the one hand, we wanted to use the points as a feedback system; on the other, we did not want it to be a precise measure of winners and losers. We wanted the game to be fun for everyone all the way. We tried to avoid too much competition between the teams by introducing an outer enemy (another venue trying to win the Innovation Conference). We wanted the teams to fight on the same side and create a win/win situation. There was a small and harmless competition for achieving the most points. Eventually, it turned out that the game was so rewarding in which to participate that the participants chose to engage without being 'bribed' with lots of rewards.

Gameplay

The Pitch Perfect game is largely inspired by a game created by Del Close for improvisational theatre, called the Ad Game (Close, Halpern and Johnson, 1952). In five minutes, the actors should create an ad campaign for an ordinary product with an unusual quality, such as cornflakes playing music when you pour milk on them. The game focused on co-creation and cooperation. The game was non-competitive, as the goal for the team was to demonstrate outstanding creativity and to beat the clock rather than another team.

Goal

The goal of the Pitch Perfect game was not to beat the other teams, but to create a perfect pitch that could win the Innovation Conference for Denmark. It was also a subgoal for the teams to cooperate and co-create.

Game rules

The most important rule was that the pitch should integrate four different obstructions. This was to make the pitch challenging. It is not difficult for people in the meeting industry to make a pitch, but adding obstructions unleashes creativity and creative thinking. Game researcher Jane McGonigal (2011) writes:

> By removing or limiting the obvious ways of getting to the goal, the rules push players to explore previously uncharted possibility spaces. They unleash creativity and foster creative thinking.

Adding an obstruction is a technique that is widely known in the arts and is often used in improvisational theatre and movies. The use of the technique can be seen in the movie *The Five Obstructions*, by Danish director Lars von Trier (2003).

Procedures

Frequent time limits were used to eliminate critical thinking and analysis paralysis. Plenty of props were used to make the game playful and make the learning both tactile and kinesthetic.

Key gains that the game enables

Participants do not need rewards and hard competition to get engaged. It is a widespread myth that competition and rewards define a game. According to game designer and researcher Jane McGonigal, the four characteristics of a game are goals, rules, a feedback system and voluntary participation (McGonigal, 2011). Rewards and competition are not on the list. The best games are often those in which the activity is rewarding in itself. That is why the best games are not fun to win, because then the game is over.

In improvisational theatre, from where the Pitch Perfect game is inspired, most games are non-competitive and without rewards. According to creativity researcher Keith Sawyer (2007), most improvisational actors strive towards experiencing *group flow*, a mental state in which you are completely absorbed in the activity. A highly creative and engaging game format like this is very appealing to the majority of participants but can be a challenge to more introverted, shy types. The evaluation of the Pitch Perfect game showed that this was the case. However, if the alternative is to do traditional sales pitches, which do not really work anyway, it might be worth the risk. The participants accept that the sales process is reversed, even though it can feel like manipulation.

Our initial thought was that some participants would complain and feel forced into selling other people's products, but this never happened. One explanation for this could be that everyone had already voluntarily enrolled in a famtrip, which everyone knew was a sales concept. Hence, everyone went into the Pitch Perfect game with open eyes. If the game is used to induce the participants to take ownership of products or ideas that go against their own interest, it could become unethical. We therefore recommend that participation is always voluntary and that the aim of the game is transparent. Obstruction can simultaneously serve as a game rule and a creative technique. Game rules unleash creativity and creative thinking. This means that playing games and working with artistic processes are similar phenomena in many ways. This could lead to the provocative question: if a game means having goals, rules, a feedback system, and voluntary participation, is painting a picture, writing a novel, or directing a script then a game?

About

Moving Minds is a creative company with deep insight into what motivates managers and employees. They use this knowledge to create changes and learning that does not die in the boardroom but reaches every corner of the organization. Moving Minds specializes in designing and facilitating meetings, conferences and workshops. To that end, they design engaging games, both board and live games. The company has clients in more than 20 countries. The games it creates are based on the latest psychological research and thousands of hours of practical work.

References

Close, D, Halpern, C and Johnson, K (1952) *Truth in Comedy: The manual of improvisation*, Meriwether Publishing, Colorado Springs

Deci, E L and Ryan, R M (2000) Self-determination theory and the facilitation of intrinsic motivation, social development, and well-being, *American Psychologist*, 55 (1), pp 68–78

Enalyzer (2016) Famtrip Maj 2016, deltagerevaluering (participant evaluation), Visit Denmark 2016

McGonigal, J (2011) Reality is Broken, Penguin Group, New York

Sawyer, K (2007) *Group Genius: The creative power of collaboration*, Basic Books, New York

Sheldon, K (2012) *Motivation: Viden og værktøjer fra positiv psykologi* (Motivation: Knowledge and tools from positive psychology), Mindspace, Copenhagen

Von Trier, L (2003) *The Five Obstructions*, Zentropa, Denmark

Wonderful Copenhagen (2016) Copenhagen announcement autumn 2016, Newsletter

23

PublicProfessional

Know the effect of your communication

**LEIF SØRENSEN, CAMILLA BOYHUS MADSEN
AND MAJA SPANGSBERG KROGSTRUP,** Actee

#WorkplaceLearning #StakeholderCommunication #StakeholderAlignment

PublicProfessional is a conversation-focused, awareness-building concept for professionals who manage multiple stakeholders and must balance the interests of citizens, customers, politicians and regulations. This educational game teaches professionals about communication with the public and improves their analytical skills with regard to their own practice. The concept is centred around eight communication styles: problem solving, inspirational, developing, pace setting, advisory, affiliative, involving and framing. The game has been played more than 5,000 times in approximately 20 municipalities in Denmark. The game and concept are used as a framework to spark reflection and dialogue about how we as professionals address the person in front of us and what effect this approach has on the professional relationship.

Short description of case

One case used in the PublicProfessional concept is 'Sarah in the System'. The scene for the case is a residence called Klemmen, for young people with psychiatric diagnoses. It is located in an unspecified municipality of Denmark. In the case, you act as an employee at the residence and as a contact person for Sarah. She is one of the young residents, who are placed there voluntarily. It is your responsibility to make sure that Sarah's development plan is being followed.

Interesting moments in the case as part of the game

During the game, you face several challenges in which you need to communicate and work together with various authorities and professionals. At the beginning of the case, you find out that Sarah is harming herself. You feel it will be best to admit her to a hospital, but you know that the hospital might not agree with this. You are going to meet with the doctor and discuss the best solution for Sarah.

The next important situation is a team meeting, in which it becomes evident that your colleagues do not think you are setting strict enough boundaries for Sarah. The atmosphere in the meeting is tense, and you need to figure out the best way to communicate with your colleagues about this issue with Sarah. Sarah is in the 10th grade, and her teacher tells you she believes that Sarah, in spite of her problems, is able to take the exams. Sarah seems up for it. But you know the pressure might be too much for her to handle. How will you handle the dialogue with the teacher without Sarah feeling exposed?

Sarah and her mother have little contact. But the mother is suddenly accusing the Klemmen residence of preventing Sarah from spending time with her family. She has therefore complained to the municipality. How will you handle the dialogue with the mother from this point on?

The family has convinced Sarah's caseworker that it might be better for her to move to another residence. You believe this will create even more chaos in Sarah's life. How can you create a good dialogue with the caseworker about this? All these scenarios pose dilemmas that many employees working with a marginalized or vulnerable population can relate to. A job like this also affects you as a person. As part of the game, participants fill out this board to gain insight into their own reactions (Figure 23.1).

The game and concept have an impact on the player on two levels:

- On a personal level, the player tests several ways to solve specific dilemmas with no consequences for any real-life person. We can compare this to a flight simulation, in which the pilots can practise without worrying about crashing the plane. The professional working with vulnerable people is just as concerned with the quality of her work, since all actions related to her work will have a human impact. This is a barrier for innovating and trying new ways to improve the communication with the people she works with.

Figure 23.1   PublicProfessional game board

- On an organizational level, the game provides a common language and creates a shared frame of reference for actions involving a marginalized or vulnerable population. The professionals can use the style principles and the expected effect as a wall of qualification on their actions. This dialogue of communication styles and dilemmas unfolds in team conversations, in coaching dialogues and among colleagues in general.

In practice, the PublicProfessional game has been used in all sections of public administration and as a foundation for analysis to heighten social services.

Game purpose

Over the years we have observed the following participant gains:

- To give the organization's management insight into which communication styles the teams and employees use in their communication with the population with which they work – and which effects it creates.
- To give the management new tools to move the organization in the desired direction in relation to the communication.

- To give the management the opportunity to work on strengthening the correlation between the organization's goals and strategies, as well as the employees' professional repertoire and development.

- To give the organization a common professional language.

- To train employees and teams in analysing their communication and its effects.

- To give the employees the opportunity to look at their own repertoire and possibilities for development.

- To give the employees an opportunity to use the different styles of communication to achieve the sought-after effects in the work with the vulnerable population.

- To develop competencies for employees, teams and the organization.

Working with the various communication styles, the employees gain directly applicable tools to use in their daily communication with the population they work with and other stakeholders.

Challenges and conflicts in game topics

The main conflict in the game is to distinguish between the results the system wants you to create on the one hand, and to make choices that are in the best interest of the client you are trying to help on the other hand, which respect that person's needs and opinions. This dilemma plays out in the game when the player is faced with a specific situation, such as writing the first letter to call for a meeting with the client. Should the social worker emphasize the law and rules, or focus on the client's specific situation and consider his or her overall life situation? In some examples, the game requires focus on rules and laws, and in other examples the client's situation comes first.

Theoretical perspectives incorporated into the game

PublicProfessional is based on Daniel Goleman's (2006) theory about the correlations among leadership style, personal competencies of the leader, organizational results, employee welfare and service. With PublicProfessional, the participants learn more about their own competencies and what their strengths and weaknesses are.

Experience-based perspectives incorporated into the game

We worked with organizations in the senior citizens and work employment area. Based on the insights we gained, we developed and translated the theory into a concept about the communication and contact that social-work professionals have with clients. The level of engagement and transfer of the game's lessons is dependent on the design of the workshop process. The reflections of the committee build on participants' own real-life experiences, enhancing the opportunities to apply new knowledge in daily work routines.

Gameplay

One central aspect of the game is that instead of making one or two choices per round, the player has a limited amount of resources to use in each section. For example: 'You have 20 resources available and each choice uses 5, 10 or 20 resources. In the given example, how are you going to use your resources to solve the problem?'

Players must make one choice at a time, not all at once. But all of a player's choices affect the 'barometers' in the game; these barometers measure the extent to which the client's situation has improved. Making one choice at a time has the effect of creating a more focused and intense debate about how the player's style of communication, and thus the choices the player makes, affect the people the player is trying to help. When the player has used all his or her resources, they will see an option called 'cash in the effect'. This calculates whether the player's choices have had any effect on the barometers. The player receives points if he or she has managed to raise them. These eight barometers (Figure 23.2) are:

- Direction
- Responsibility
- Hope
- Openness
- Coping
- Resources
- Progress
- Overview

Figure 23.2 The eight barometers

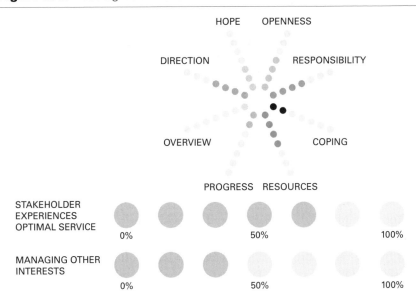

But the goal is not to raise all the barometers. It is more important to focus on which barometer the player wants to affect in the specific round/situation. This calls for strategic thinking and the need to prioritize, because it might not be possible to raise both the client's responsibility and his or her hopes at the same time. The eight barometers affect the two main goals for the client, which in the case of 'Sarah in the System' are 'Sarah's development' and 'Sarah's well-being'.

In each situation you, as the player, can click 'Thoughts' and gain insight into what your client is thinking at that point in the case. For example, in the first situation with 'Sarah in the System', you need to have a conversation with Sarah about how she is doing. By clicking 'Thoughts', you can see what Sarah is thinking at that moment: 'They don't care that my development has stopped and that I feel bad. How will they be able to help me?'

The four PublicProfessional cases available now target two different public areas. The case 'The Interests of the Main Street' and 'TurboTanken' take place in a municipality, where the employees want to improve communication with both citizens and local companies. The cases 'Sarah in the System' and 'Take Care of Sarah' are about Sarah as a vulnerable young woman in a residence. But we customize cases for all areas of the public sector. In each case, it is possible to track the sector's history and review the player's choices and the effects they have had. It is possible to access the simulator from all kinds of devices.

Key learning that the game enables

Understanding the effect of your communication

We all know that the way a person communicates affects how the message the person is trying to convey is received. But often our knowledge about the way we communicate and its effects are based on what can be termed 'tacit knowledge'. We are aware that we can use different ways to communicate to achieve different goals, but it is often knowledge that is difficult to articulate. It just lives inside us. In PublicProfessional, the link between the statements a person chooses and their effects on the game barometers make it clear how these things are connected.

For example, in the first conversation with Sarah, you can choose the statement 'I can help', which represents the problem-solving approach. If you choose this approach, it will have a positive effect on the Resources, Direction, Overview, and Progress barometers and a slightly positive effect on Hope, Openness and Coping; it will not have any effect on the Responsibility barometer. This emphasizes that if you as the professional help with practical arrangements, such as calling the dentist or filling out papers on behalf of your clients, then the clients do not have to take on the responsibility themselves. This might have consequences in the long run, where the clients might come to expect that you will solve more problems with a minimum of effort from them.

You cannot use all communication styles at once

The statement choices also show you that prioritizing is key when deciding how to communicate. You cannot communicate several messages in different ways. Or you might, but that could confuse the client more than help him or her. Thus, the game allows you to plan and prioritize the sequences of communication that you believe will have the greatest effect, in relation to your client's challenges and the situation at hand.

Communication style is not linked to personality

Many professionals in the public sector express that they feel most comfortable with certain ways of communication, on which they draw most of the time. For example, quite a few describe themselves as being first and foremost empathetic, where they tend to solve the problems for the client, and thus they spend much time listening and asking the client about his or her perspective. Of course, one's personality does play a role when it comes to communication style. But everyone can learn to use all the communication styles and work to apply the most suitable style to the situation in which it will bring the best results. It is just a matter of training and awareness about how to use the various styles and what characterizes them. PublicProfessional provides concrete tools for professionals to apply directly to their daily work. Therefore, the tool provides professionals with more opportunities to handle conversations with clients in the best possible way, adjusting the communication styles to the clients' needs and situation. In this way, it is a training tool for better communication, but is just as much about social intelligence.

About

Actee brings joy, excitement and curiosity to everyday learning. We advise, teach and coach organizations and companies on how to use games as a part of developing their workplace. We operate in the professional field of organizational development, change management and leadership development, where we have developed innovative educational game solutions for organizations, corporations and companies from around the world. We use games to give companies new knowledge about organizational development and change management. In both our board games and online games, players are presented with realistic dilemmas and challenges, and gain knowledge that can be applied directly to their daily work life.

Reference

Goleman, D (2006) *Emotional Intelligence*, Bantam, New York

24
Stakeholder Management
Moving people while building positive relationships

JAKE INLOVE AND SUNE GUDIKSEN, GameBridges

#StakeholderCommunication #StakeholderAlignment
#ConflictManagement

Stakeholder Management is a board game that helps project managers and team members find ways to deal with the stakeholder dilemmas they often face in their work. Stakeholder is here understood broadly as the people who affect our work – whether they are leaders, colleagues, partners or clients, etc. The game is developed as a hands-on, visual mapping tool to start a constructive conversation about the uncomfortable and complex dilemmas that we sometimes face with the stakeholders we are involved with. This can be dilemmas related to power relations and work-history conflicts, or simply dilemmas related to conflicting agendas, values or expectations. The purpose of the game is to give participants a variety of perspectives and strategies to deal with their stakeholders while reflecting on the most important gains and losses in the dilemma.

Why the game was made: we have all been there

Based on observation in organizations, most of us seem to have faced some kind of stakeholder dilemma at some point in our workplace experiences. Daily, most of us seek to move people to join our thinking, agendas or projects – we ask them to give us their stamp of approval, their energy or their resources. Daily, problems and conflicts occur at our workplaces – we seek to clean up the messes and make everyone cooperate again. These things do not happen without creating dilemmas occasionally. Dealing with stakeholders can be a complicated business. Achieving your objectives when there are potential conflicting agendas and goals, internal and personal conflicts, and scarce resources can be an overwhelming task. Yet, most of us 'have been there' in some fashion. Maybe you have faced the dilemma of being promoted to become your colleagues' new boss? Maybe you have faced the dilemma of co-workers violating safety regulations? Maybe you have been faced with the dilemma of negotiating a partnership agreement and contract?

No matter what kinds of dilemmas you have faced, you might have experienced how difficult it can be to have a constructive conversation about dealing with them. You might not be able to turn to your colleagues, if they are involved. Discretion issues might make it unreasonable to turn to your boss. Talking to our spouses usually lends us support and empathy but not always game plans for handling the dilemmas – spouses might understand the frustration but be unfamiliar with the details.

According to social psychologist Dacher Keltner: 'An individual's capacity for influence – power – is found in ordinary actions tailored to specific contexts that advance the group's interests' (Keltner, 2017). The problem is that since we are normally right in the middle of such dilemmas, it is rare to find a chance to discuss issues at the workplace or in the project team before taking actions. Here, Stakeholder Management offers a place outside the everyday work environment, where professionals from different departments and/or companies can discuss approach and strategies in discretion about these kinds of difficult issues.

Stakeholder Management aims at creating a safe space for professionals to have a constructive and qualified conversation about how a stakeholder dilemma can be handled. The reason Stakeholder Management can offer a constructive conversation is that the game helps participants to map stakeholders involved and evaluate possible strategies by the most important gains and losses at stake in the dilemma, so others can observe the dilemma as accurately as possible, which subsequently helps the rest of the participants to give constructive advice. The reason why Stakeholder Alignment can offer a qualified conversation is that the game offers a variety of stakeholder strategies – inspiration cards – to help participants reflect on possible approaches in action compared to what a participant seeks to gain and wants to avoid losing.

Gameplay

What is important to know when dealing with a dilemma?

A round in Stakeholder Management consists of five steps. Essentially, these steps are all about gleaning all the essential information when devising

Figure 24.1 Dilemmas, tactic pads, scoreboard, character cards

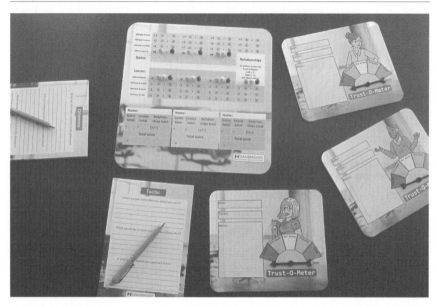

strategies to deal with stakeholder dilemmas. First, it is about figuring out who is involved and how good the relationship is to them. Therefore, the first thing the turn player does is map the dilemma by picking out character cards and writing essential notes about each stakeholder. Furthermore, on each character card, there is a 'Trust-O-Meter', which is a five-point scale to indicate the state of the relationship to this particular stakeholder. Here, other participants can get a quick overview of the people involved by literally having them mapped out in front of them with essential information (Figure 24.1).

Once everyone involved in the dilemma is mapped out, step two is about filling out the three most important things that could be gained and lost in the dilemma. Here, the turn player writes on the evaluation board the three gains and three losses that the dilemma is evaluated by – this is about figuring out the most important things that are at stake in the dilemma.

Then, in step three, all the other participants devise strategies to deal with the dilemma using their tactic pads. On the tactic pads, participants are encouraged to reflect on three things: 1) which people in the dilemma they would go to; 2) what they would say to them and how; and 3) in which sequence they would approach them. Here, the other players can draw inspiration cards to be inspired by some of the stakeholder strategies devised from stakeholder theories (Eskerod and Jepsen, 2013), influence theories (Cialdini, 2007; Yeung, 2011), and power theories (Keltner, 2017).

Tactic pads and inspiration cards help participants to see different stakeholder strategy options. This step is about getting the participants involved to reflect on what they could and would do in the dilemma and why.

When all the other participants have devised their stakeholder strategy, then, in step four, they share them one by one. Once a participant has shared his or her stakeholder strategy, the turn player evaluates the strategy and scores it according to the chosen gains and losses – is the strategy likely to gain a lot and lose a little, or lose a lot and only gain a little, or both? Furthermore, if the strategy affects the relationship one has with a given stakeholder positively or negatively, this is also taken into account in the evaluation. This step is about considering the consequences of specific approaches against certain gains and losses to investigate different stakeholder strategies' effectiveness in the dilemmas.

Finally, in step five, when all strategies have been evaluated and scored, the turn player writes down each player's total score and announces which strategy he or she finds most appropriate for the dilemma – which would be the highest scoring and sequentially the winner of the round (Figure 24.2).

Figure 24.2   A playing situation in Stakeholder Management

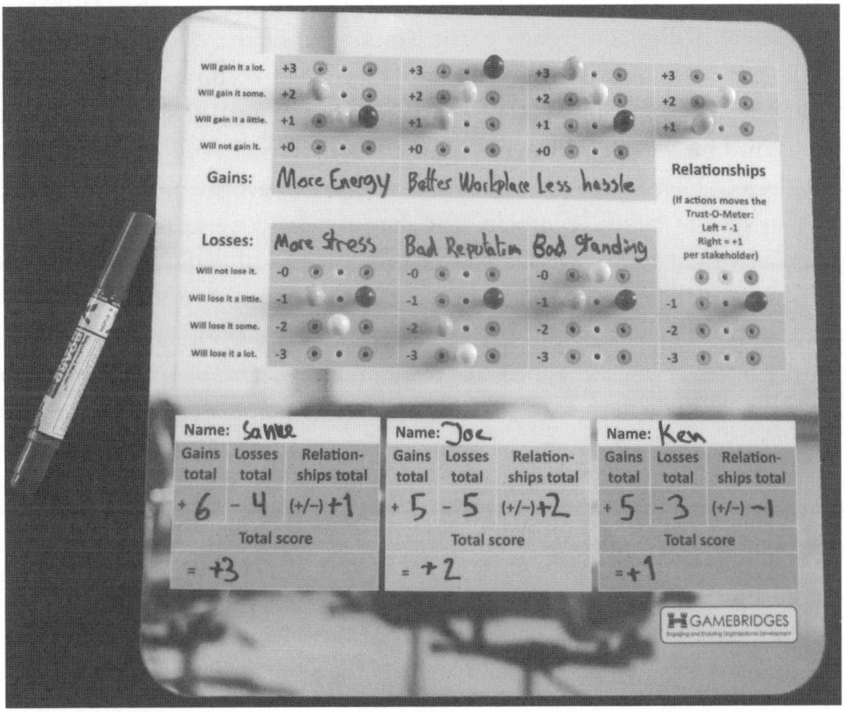

This step is about giving the turn player some perspectives and strategies to think about regarding the dilemma. This is a type of debriefing leading to a reflection that takes the best from each of the suggestions instead of necessarily choosing one specific approach. It also acknowledges that many approaches exist, and there is no single answer, but the game creates a needed space and opportunity to reflect on options identified and shared with participants outside the dilemma before taking action.

When the round is over, play proceeds by taking on the next player's dilemma. Once all four players' dilemmas have been played out, the game is finished – and participants can compare their stakeholder strategy scores across the three dilemmas they have participated in and see how well their strategies have been received. The final comparison can be a way to help participants reflect on their personal and habitual ways of devising stakeholder strategies and dealing with dilemmas in relation to a broader variety of possible beneficial approaches.

Case example: when being promoted is a dilemma

At an international play conference, Stakeholder Management was played with some of the conference participants. One of the dilemmas brought to the table was a Swiss woman who recently had been promoted to head of her department. This was, of course, a good thing. There was only one problem. One of her colleagues – anonymous in the case, of course, but here let's call her Sally – thought she was going to get the promotion. Sally was so sure of being promoted that she told everyone in the department that she would be. When she wasn't promoted, well, Sally wasn't happy. The Swiss woman being a new leader had enough to deal with, but Sally made it worse by obstructing her and creating a toxic working environment. As the Swiss woman mapped her dilemma, three groups of stakeholders emerged. First, there were her two superiors, a region manager and a region coordinator, both of whom she had a decent relationship with. Then there were the people in her department – her new employees – with whom she had a very good relationship. Finally, there was Sally, with whom she had a terrible relationship. These were all the people involved in and affected by the dilemma.

Once the Swiss woman had mapped out the dilemma, she revealed what she thought was at stake in the dilemma. The three most important things she could gain by dealing successfully with Sally's obstructive and toxic behaviour were: 1) more energy; 2) better workplace environment; and 3) less daily hassle. The three most important things she could lose by not handling Sally's obstructive and toxic behaviour were: 1) more stress and frustration; (2) gaining a bad reputation in the organization; and 3) getting in bad standing with colleagues.

As the other participants reflected on possible approaches, each participant came up with a different strategy for dealing with the dilemma. The first participant suggested that the Swiss woman consult her superiors and explain to them the situation. This might have relieved the Swiss woman of the pressure, but it could also make her look weak to her superiors. The second participant suggested that the Swiss woman confront Sally about her problematic behaviour, as she was now her new boss. This might make Sally act differently and could maybe improve their relationship, but it might also escalate the conflict, and Sally might use whatever she could against her to support her own cause. The third participant suggested that the Swiss woman should go to the colleagues in the department – her new employees. This could gain her the employees' support to help the Swiss woman make Sally behave differently, but it might also weaken her position as a leader for her employees.

After evaluating the strategies up against her most important gains and losses, the Swiss woman came to the conclusion that she would try to consult her superiors, as their relationship was good and they would probably empathize with her being new and help deal with the situation without escalating the drama. The Swiss woman was very grateful for the input she had got through the game and expressed that it had helped her to see possible options in her stressful situation – when she got back from the conference, she was determined to use the winning strategy.

Key gains from playing: experimenting with the difficult

One of the main benefits of playing Stakeholder Management is that the game helps people to distance themselves from their dilemmas, which enables them to experiment with their options and strategies for dealing with these difficult situations. The game is effective in creating an opportunity to discuss and subsequently act on an informed basis where at least three alternatives to one's own judgement can be weighted. As Keltner (2017) argues, there is power to be gained by asserting yourself:

People gain power as the result of small, everyday behaviours: by speaking up first, offering a possible answer to a problem, being first to assert an opinion, freeing up everyone's thinking by throwing out a wild suggestion, question or humorous observation that gets the creative juices flowing.

In many aspects of life, we are able to act rationally, think things through and experiment with strategies quite deliberately. Unfortunately, when it comes to uncomfortable people conflicts, we shy away and avoid it. This is, of course, the most comfortable thing to do, but not such a helpful thing to do. Without deliberation and experimentation, we will not improve our ability to handle stakeholder dilemmas, big or small. What Stakeholder Management can do is help participants take a playful approach to their dilemmas, which can open them up cognitively and help them to see other ways of doing things (Achor, 2013: 21–63). Seeing people be able to joke around and laugh about tough dilemmas in the game shows us that the game helps participants to create an emotional distance from the dilemmas – which is a healthy step in beginning to think rationally about how to act to best get through the situation. If people mentally stay in the mud, they will never fly up to get a bird's perspective with a clearer view of the situation – mapping the situation and having other people voice their perspectives on it all help to bring the dilemma into, well, perspective.

Furthermore, the game also empowers the participants to bring qualified third-party perspectives to the turn player's dilemmas, which help the turn player to see things from other people's perspectives. This can be a good foundation for learning experiences. Just as with the Swiss woman's case, Stakeholder Management can function both as a co-creation game, where participants co-create concrete outputs in the form of stakeholder strategies, but it can also function as a learning game, where people learn to see things from different perspectives and learn new approaches to handle tough stakeholder situations.

When to play: good times to experiment with the difficult

When should people sit down and play Stakeholder Management? We have found that the game works best in two situations. First, the game is highly relevant to people who are currently facing problematic stakeholder dilemmas. Here, the game's concrete output – generating possible stakeholder strategies – can be a tool to help people get through their dilemmas. What is important is not so much what they learn from the game but rather the input they get on how to handle their situation. In this situation, people are happy if they walk away from the experience better equipped to handle their current dilemmas.

The second relevant use for the game is in leadership or project management courses. Here, the game's structure helps participants systematically to reflect on different stakeholder strategies and how to evaluate approaches, which can create good learning experiences. Here, the focus is not so much on handling current dilemmas but rather on the reflective way of seeing a variety of options and evaluating them deliberately compared to the most important things at stake. As mentioned, a final step of comparing participants' scores across dilemmas can be a way to discuss preference strategies and how including a larger selection of perspectives and strategies can be a way to improve people's ability to deal with various stakeholder dilemmas.

A playful approach to dealing with stakeholder dilemmas, as exemplified in this chapter with Stakeholder Management, can be an engaging, creative and productive setting to learn about and generate new stakeholder strategies – and it is important to improve one's ability to handle stakeholders in the increasingly interconnected and complicated world of work in general, as well as in complex projects.

About

At GameBridges, we have an extensive overview of organizational tendencies, powerful theories and effective practices. We are future-focused in our approach, which enables us to identify upcoming millennial organizational challenges and we encourage our collaborators to think ahead. Our games blend concrete innovative actions with powerful learning perspectives.

References

Achor, S (2013) *Before Happiness: 5 actionable strategies to create a positive path to success*, Random House, New York

Cialdini, R (2007) *Influence: The psychology of persuasion*, rev edn, HarperBusiness, New York

Eskerod, P and Jepsen, A L (2013) *Project Stakeholder Management*, Gower Publishing, Farham

Keltner, D (2017) *The Power Paradox: How we gain and lose influence*, Penguin Books, London

Yeung, R (2011) *I is for Influence: The new science of persuasion*, Macmillan, Oxford

25

Strategic Derby

*Rapid strategic foresight with instant feedback
on potential competitor moves*

JAKE INLOVE AND SUNE GUDIKSEN, GameBridges

#StrategicForesight #CompetitiveAdvantage #StrategicThinking

Strategic Derby tackles the challenge of strategy development by visualizing the competitive advantages at stake and giving managers and business developers instant feedback on their strategic decisions. The purpose of the game is to give participants a sense of how future strategic scenarios could play out. It helps them to see that the results of their strategy are dependent on the quality of their own initiatives in correspondence with how significant competitors might act. In a concrete way, the game assists managers, HR managers and business developers in their efforts to come up with novel initiatives. It helps them to see these initiatives in light of competitors' potential moves, to reach an innovative direction that clearly demarcates from competitors. In other words, it helps in identifying a competitive advantage.

The challenge in strategic development

Strategic Derby offers companies a new way to tackle strategy development, rather than classic strategic planning programmes. Strategic planning programmes often consist of various analytical activities in which leaders and managers first analyse their industry (the market, trends, competitors, etc) and then their own organization and its capacities (finances, resources, values, culture, etc). The strengths, weaknesses, opportunities and threats (SWOT) analysis and Michael Porter's five competitive forces (Porter, 1985) are well-known examples of this approach. However, the ideation of new initiatives is difficult to spot with these approaches. In Strategic Derby, new initiatives are generated on the spot and evaluated against likely competitors' moves. The game is based on the idea that we need to do both to reach new initiatives with high innovation potential but with attention to rapid strategic foresight. The game relies on an understanding that strategy, in everyday conversations, can mean many things, but at a minimum can be described by Mintzberg's five P's (Mintzberg, Ahlstrand and Lampel, 1998):

- Strategy as a plan.
- Strategy as a position.
- Strategy as a pattern.
- Strategy as a perspective.
- Strategy as a ploy.

These five insights all illuminate different aspects of strategy and are important to consider when a company is developing its strategy – whether it is the company's plan of action, position in the market, perspective on the world, ploys to gain advantage, or decision patterns. These five insights are all present in Strategic Derby and the participants move between them as they progress through the game.

Gameplay – customer value propositions

Strategic Derby is a board game with the appearance of a horse race. Participants can write directly on the board with proposed initiatives and supporting arguments. This board gathers information about what moves players made, when they made them and by how much. It also records the gains earned in each turn, as well as the ideas accompanying each move. The board is divided into three columns. Each column represents a set of potential customer value competitive advantages. The three main customer value categories on the board are:

- Lowest total cost.
- Product leadership.
- Customer solutions.

These three categories are based on David Kaplan and Robert Norton's (2004) categorization of customer value propositions. The first category has the competitive advantage of being the cheapest, the second of offering the best product, and the third of being most relevant to the customer. On the Strategic Derby game board, three ways to establish and substantiate these value propositions are listed below them (as seen in Table 25.1).

Table 25.1   Customer value propositions and subcategories

Lowest Total Cost			Product Leadership			Customer Solutions		
Lowest sales cost	Lowest production cost	Lowest supplier cost	Best quality	Best functionality	First on the market	Best service	Best customer relationship	Best customization

These nine categories are the outset for play in Strategic Derby. However, in a different version, nine business-model components can also be used as categories to work with both internal and external value. Participants or groups can choose the categories on which to move forward. Participants are rewarded points relative to their competitors based on their position on the game board. How many first, second, third places, etc, a participant or group has on the nine competitive parameters determines how many points the player earns.

Because of this game reward system and instant feedback on participants and competitors' action, players are pushed to think about what competitive parameters they can beat their competitors on and how they can implement them. This makes them think in terms of their own capacities (already established positions and earned points) as well as in terms of their competitors' capacities and their possible ploys. In this way, Strategic Derby simulates market mechanisms and gives players instant feedback on chosen competitive parameters.

Participants also disconnect from their daily practices while playing and tap into a more future-oriented way of thinking. This happens because Strategic Derby has a different time perspective. A turn in the game can represent six months, a year, or even a decade in real time. This feature can help players to think further into the future, envision various scenarios and come up with big ideas that could take a good deal of time to realize. This means a different kind of perspective is added – a time perspective. When time is introduced to the game, it can help players to articulate their estimations of the future and what kinds of actions should be performed there. Suddenly, changing technology and environment are discussed, along with ideas on how to use them as a competitive advantage.

Telecom case

Two versions were applied in a large telecommunications (telecom) business case. In the first version, participants played in four pairs. One pair was the telecom company, while the other three pairs were competitors with a

Figure 25.1 Telecom setting

significant difference in foundation. In the second version, participants also played in four pairs. Each pair had an internal perspective on the telecom company (Figure 25.1). In the competitor version, the participants gained awareness of how their competitors might steal customers by launching various initiatives, products and services that the telecom company would not be capable of launching itself. Furthermore, they articulated the fears they had for the future of the telecom company, facing such harsh competition.

As they played, they grew creative and came up with many initiatives that could enhance competitive advantages and help the company be able to compete in the future. One of these was an idea to negotiate a partnership with fitness businesses and, through this partnership, offer new customer telecom packages. Afterwards, these ideas were further developed in other settings and brought along in the follow-up strategic road-map work for the company.

In the other version, in which Strategic Derby was played with four internal perspectives on the telecom company, the participants avoided moving on the cost competitive parameters; they avoided this even when clear opportunities occurred in the game. This elicited discussion about how the company had turned a blind eye towards the fact that the company's costs were becoming too high and it was harming their ability to compete in the market. As the game progressed, participants became better and better at coming up with initiatives to improve the cost parameters. For a company that had been the market leader, but was now pressured harshly by competitors, this turned out to be a serious shift in mindset for them. While many participants were already aware of this, the shared communication through the game raised awareness of the importance of focusing more on lowering costs; thus, a common ground was established. Both game versions produced valuable insights for the telecom company. The initiatives that emerged during play were captured; they laid the groundwork for the company's further strategic development on that specific day and over the long haul. A department manager at the telecom company expressed that:

> Everyone was very excited and we got a lot of insights to our Roadmap 2017 with new product directions and strategic positioning, and what needs to be done in order to change it. (personal communication)

Game versions and layers

Strategic Derby can be played in two versions: a light version that can be played quickly, and a more thorough version that takes a little more time. In the light version, participants only have to argue why they moved as they did. This means they explain why they believe it is important to invest in the competitive advantages they chose on the board. This version can help participants to reflect on their estimations of future scenarios and their beliefs about the importance of certain types of competitive advantages.

In the more thorough version, participants have to come up with concrete initiatives that enhance a competitive advantage. This means if they want to move on 'best service' they have to have an idea that can improve their service. This might be a new newsletter, customer awareness training for the sales personnel, etc. In addition, the competitive parameters in the game can be changed in order to keep up with current market trends and conditions. We have created versions in which business-model issues – backstage and frontstage – were the central concern. Customer value parameters can also be replaced beforehand with more tailor-made categories in a specific market.

In one case, Strategic Derby was played with an education institution and tailor-made categories were created to accommodate their specific quasi-market situation. Here, the price categories were replaced with capacity parameters, where participants could reflect on how they were using their institution's resources to offer value to the organizations that needed their training.

Key gains that the game enables

Via Strategic Derby, managers and business developers have a so-called safe place to test various scenarios before deciding on the best ones. Participants can instantly see which moves paid out and which did not. As Mintzberg, Ahlstrand and Lampel (1998) pointed out, when strategies are analysed they appear to be patterns of decisions and actions. Ordinarily, these patterns can only be analysed from the past; in Strategic Derby, however, they can be analysed from the future scenarios that were played. Participants typically question whether their moves in the industry were beneficial. Did they bet all their resources on the same competitive advantages as their competitors? Or did they position themselves differently from their competitors and earn more points (in the game) and profit (in real life)?

The game mechanics of Strategic Derby mean players readily go into 'game mode' and seek to earn more points than their competitors do; however, the game reward system is only the means by which to advance their idea generation. It works in the sense that they need to generate ideas for each move as well as argue for their idea's potential. Participants quickly begin trying to impress their competitors with increasingly brilliant and innovative ideas. Sometimes, players are persuaded by their competitors' ideas and follow along by using the same idea or an adjusted version of it to move ahead. Agreement arises. Participants compliment each other for their good ideas or creative interpretations. Often, participants will begin to talk about their game company's image, brand values and strategy, creating an imaginative narrative of what their company would be like and in which direction it could go.

This competitive nature of the game elicits a playful attitude from participants, high engagement and, often, laughter. Most importantly, they develop new strategic initiatives and elaborate high-quality ideas. They see their ideas in connection with competitors' suspected moves. The competitive parameters are open for interpretation. For example, the parameter 'Best customer relationship' is vague, which means that players have to be creative in trying to interpret and substantiate it. Remember Mintzberg's P's for strategy? One of them was *perspective*. This is when strategy is discussed in terms of how players' perspectives through game action lead to convincing competitor advantages. The game moves beyond the ploys participants make to win points and conquer certain positions on the board.

As one can imagine, this is a very different kind of setting for talking about strategy than a traditional meeting based on charts and mappings. Because of the game format, players can bring up strategic issues in a low-risk manner. Power relations in the group can be somewhat levelled in play, so all participants have a say and can promote potential innovative inputs. The game board creates a visual overview of proposed ideas and scenarios. This allows groups and facilitators to discuss and qualify the strategic thinking that each player demonstrated during the game. It allows facilitators to trace patterns in action (possibly subconscious patterns) that might surprise participants.

The ability to continually experiment with strategies is highly important in a world in which competitive advantages, as influential business thinker Rita McGrath (2010) argues, are no longer sustainable, but rather temporary. The game approach is one way to begin implementing Henry Chesbrough's (2010) notion of an adaptive platform, in which strategy and business experimentation takes place on a regular basis. Game rules and procedures provide constraints that can engage a cross-disciplinary circle of stakeholders, challenge business assumptions, elicit surprises and elevate new scenarios for serious consideration. A playful approach to strategy, as exemplified in this section with Strategic Derby, can create a more engaging, imaginative and concrete productive setting for developing strategy.

About

At GameBridges, we have an extensive overview of organizational tendencies, powerful theories and effective practices. We are future-focused in our approach, which enables us to identify upcoming millennial organizational challenges and we encourage our collaborators to think ahead. Our games blend concrete innovative actions with powerful learning perspectives.

References

Chesbrough, H (2010) Business Model Innovation: Opportunities and Barriers, *Long Range Planning*, **43** (2), pp 354–63

Kaplan, R and Norton, D (2004) *Strategy Maps: Converting intangible assets into tangible outcomes*, Harvard Business School Press, Boston

McGrath, R G (2010) Business models: a discovery driven approach, *Long Range Planning*, **43** (2–3), pp 247–61

Mintzberg, H, Ahlstrand, B and Lampel, J (1998) *Strategy Safari*, The Free Press, New York

Porter, M E (1985) *Competitive Advantage: Creating and sustaining superior performance*, The Free Press, New York

26

Tango

A pivotal element in change to develop leadership culture

WOLFGANG KARRLEIN AND LARS KRONE, Canmas GmbH

#LeadershipAttitude #LeadershipStyles #LeadershipCulture

The goal of this game is to develop leaders and put them in charge of leading people. This highlights the role of Celemi Tango™ in a change project to strengthen leadership and HR development processes, and align them with the business strategy. Participants are in the driver's seat as executives to experience causes and effects of their business and HR decisions in a fierce, competitive environment.

The case: a leadership change process

The starting point

The company is an international leader in its industry (components and engineering) with 3,000 employees and some €300 million turnover. It has production sites in Europe, Latin America and Asia. Its products find a ready market in various industries, ranging from automotive and IT to wholesalers. It is a leading international player in its market segments. New developments in technology (eg internet of things and IT), business models (eg service models) or demographics (eg striving for new talents) will have an effect on how they sustain their business success. Hence, they realized it is key to position now for the changes these developments may bring. The focus is on the people. The board members are thoroughly convinced that motivated employees will have a significant effect on how the company will identify, develop and benefit from future technological developments, trends and new business models. Leadership, competence management and employee development are key areas for the change process. Examples of the goals in these fields are:

- Strengthen the attractiveness of the company for new talent (employer branding).

- Provide stringent and transparent personnel development, comprising a systematic identification of competencies and career goals, and matching these with the company's strategic goals.

- Develop a strong, convincing leadership culture by expanding the current strong managerial and technological know-how of the managers into a future-oriented understanding of leadership.

- Aligning the technological and business strategy with HR and competence management to enable acting in a proactive, agile manner for future developments and challenges.

The change process – overview

The change (like all change endeavours) was partly a project as well as an ongoing process. In the first phase, the focus was on activating a group of 20+ key players comprising first-line executives to high-potential middle managers. They prepared themselves to act as change agents and role models, through the activities of intensive leadership interval trainings in several groups. One goal (among others) was to establish a common understanding for their role in the forthcoming process and create an open atmosphere and culture of discussion. In hindsight, this turned out to be crucial for all successive phases.

The second phase was considered to be an incubator in developing the conditions for change. It started with understanding the big picture of what was going on and eventually evolved to preparing for concrete actions and taking the initiative to prepare the entire organization. The third phase concentrated on rolling out the change to the entire organization, involving an increasing number of people to actually live the change.

Pivotal role of Celemi Tango in the change process

Celemi Tango was a pivotal and significant element for the activities described below. This board-based business simulation served several purposes with both its content and its method.

The 20+ leaders were grouped into teams of four, acting as top executives of their company in the simulation (Figure 26.1). They were the ultimate decision makers, managing and controlling the financial and operating policies of the company. They were the ones being held accountable for the results in the simulation, revealing their business and customer strategy, financial management and market position. They decided and acted accordingly because they were the ones in the driver's seat. All participants found themselves and their companies in strong competition for customers and talents. These included strategy, managing the projects with customers, strengthening their people's know-how and leveraging project successes to increase the company's image; in short, the market valuation was the winning formula.

One crucial aspect in Celemi Tango that made it the perfect tool for this endeavour was that managing the economic side was only one side of the game (the tangible aspects). However, with this simulation, the culture, people, competence and intangible side likewise played major roles in striving for success. A second aspect was that it required and promoted intense discussion and decision making within the teams. The subjects to be discussed, pondered, decided upon and implemented were similar to the discussions all

Figure 26.1   Running the game simulation

employees experience on a daily basis in their actual role in real life. So this simulation not only provided a reasonable replica of everyday challenges, but it also impelled the participants to action, to strengthen their ability and competence in making decisions. While this happened first in the simulation, this 'blue print behaviour' was transferred into their real role in the subsequent change process. The large work-mat board shows several dimensions and items, which the participants discussed during Celemi Tango. Now they had to discuss their assessment of the status in their own organization at the time of the workshop versus their common vision of a target status (Figure 26.2).

Last but not least, given the transparent yet complex events during the simulation, it became possible to receive immediate feedback on the outcomes of considerations, discussions and decisions. So the simulation also led the participants to a more agile way of managing and leading. The beneficial features of Celemi Tango can be used repeatedly with the same group; since the dynamics differ with each game, it produces new situations each time it is played. This provides the opportunity to highlight different topics and introduce various additional features that a company encounters in the real world. For example, automation (representing the internet

Figure 26.2 Transfer from simulation into reality: current versus target

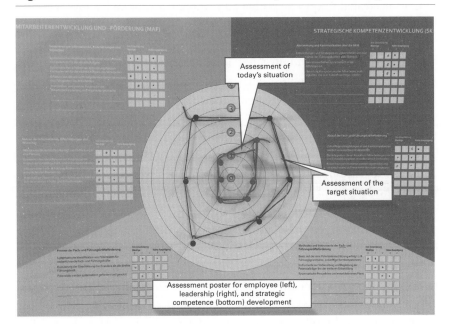

of things) and new business processes (eg digitization of processes) can be introduced and the search for talent (eg headhunting) can be enhanced. This made Celemi Tango an even more important asset in this change process as it provided the flexibility to increase the challenge as the company proceeded with its change.

'Leading others' as a special part in the change process

The leadership training mentioned above as the kickoff of the change process focused intensively on the perspective of 'leading the self'. Based on this, 'leading others' was a specific topic, which we integrated as a tailored enhancement in Celemi Tango. To better illustrate this enhancement, we first briefly describe Celemi Tango in its usual version. Then we turn to the specific enhancements and cover 'leading others' in this context. Some additional background models are captured below.

Celemi Tango in action

Power of learning – basic principles of Celemi simulations

The core belief on which Klas Mellander (1993), the mastermind and co-founder of Celemi, created the product some 30 years ago, is captured in one line:

> You cannot absorb other people's knowledge – you must create your own.

Back when he was a schoolteacher, Klas observed that what one learns is much less important than how one learns. This has been established through neuroscience many times ever since; the conditions for learning are much more important than the content. Today, it is widely known and accepted that the human brain processes information in a highly flexible way to be able to learn and adapt, even through old age. Our brain is always curious and eager to learn by nature. This can be combined with another very strong impulse: to be part of a (social) group, to belong somewhere. Both conceptual ideas are integrated in Celemi's philosophy and business simulations. It is not about spoon-fed information, but about discovering, discussing and experiencing with peers. Celemi's simulations are characterized by being practical, mobilizing participants to explore, discover and build their own mental model of the content. It uses highly visualized material and transparent mechanics (no black boxes in the simulations) to support participants in grasping content (literally, ie, to touch; and figuratively, ie, to understand).

It starts with the belief that people have the desire to learn. If they have the desire, they will eventually succeed. The art lies in creating the right environment to stir motivation. The second step is to provide content information. Here, the trick lies in the way this is presented. Presenting every bit of information at once is a recipe for confusion and demotivation. People need time to swallow and digest, ie process information, put new information into a mental framework or correlate it with existing frameworks. Supportive activities during this process are discussions, dialogue, play and reflections. Only then is the chance to create an 'Aha!' effect high. It is a metaphor of the feeling that someone truly has created understanding and new insights. Only then can you expect common understanding and purposeful, target-oriented, aligned actions. This is what leadership is about: aligning people to act in coordination with one another.

Celemi Tango – it takes two to tango

Like almost all simulations from Celemi, Celemi Tango also falls into the category of being a board-based, highly interactive business simulation. The subtitle reads: success through people. It is about managing both tangible assets (eg finance, profitability) and intangible ones (eg knowledge, IP, competence); a company's sustainable success depends on both sides of the coin. It takes two to tango. The effectiveness of Celemi Tango with regard to increasing awareness, especially of the intangible aspects, has been documented and proven (Bontis and Girardi, 2000). Let us now focus on the key elements and mechanics of Celemi Tango. In the usual settings, six teams (with four people each) form six knowledge-based companies competing in the same market. It is about balancing, attracting, building and retaining the suitable employees and customers while increasing profitability and market value.

Challenge 1

Attract and retain key employees. This is tied into concepts of talent management, competence and leadership development, and builds a corporate culture that is highly influenced by the people. People are characterized by three traits:

1 Career expectation and orientation: for example, a high flyer is highly focused on developing his or her competencies, learning, and making a difference. Being a low flyer does not imply low quality of work; it merely indicates a lower focus on professional development. As in real life, there are people who want to do a good job, but are less oriented towards seeking promotion at all costs.

2 Decision preference: if people are attracted by a company, it is always for a combination of reasons and gut feelings. In this simulation, there is a ranking of decision criteria by which people differ. Given a choice (and concrete offers), one is more attracted by the know-how focus and culture of a company. Know-how focus may be represented by investing in research and development (R&D). Or the person may be more interested due to the company's image. For example, BMW and Google are companies that are attractive (not only but to a high degree) because of their image. A third criterion in the decision may be a greater focus on monetary incentives.

3 Chemistry: the third characteristic, chemistry, refers to personal (psychological) traits. In Celemi Tango, this serves two purposes: first, to highlight that a company's culture is formed largely (but not only) by the kind of people it employs. So to join (or leave) a company, it is often that the chemistry between people is hampered. The saying 'People join organizations – but leave because of people' reflects the importance of this. The second function targets team dynamics and customer fit. The better the chemistry among project team members, the stronger the performance. The better the fit between a customer's people and culture in a project, the easier it will be when the project road becomes bumpy. We are accustomed to trusting people who are more predictable.

Challenge 2

Win the right customers. The customers and the deliverable they want to buy are characterized by three aspects:

1 Required competencies of the people delivering the value (for key customers there are always two people with different levels of competence required). To provide the appropriate project teams, management must ensure that they have two employees who at least match this minimum competence requirements – otherwise they would not be able to run the project and would lose the customer with negative effects, eg on financial figures as well as in image in the market.

2 The decision criteria with which company they will sign the contract. This can be price, know-how or image. But it can also be 'chemistry', ie a cultural fit between both companies.

3 The 'chemistry' of customers is likewise indicated as geometrical symbols. To determine the fit with a potential supplier, the culture is determined by the highest number of its employees with the same chemistry. Example:

a customer has a 'circle-culture' and can choose between two suppliers. One has three 'circle' employees and the other has only one. The better fit then would be with the supplier with three 'circle' employees.

Given these first two challenges, each team must develop and try to implement a market as well as a people strategy. But that is not the end of the story.

Challenge 3

Invest in tools and processes. For example, by investing in R&D, a team can increase the know-how level of its company. But investing in R&D would mean that some employees are not able to serve customers while being connected to such a project. Of course, investing in R&D leads to the question: will this team be able to generate sufficient money to cover the outlays, and to what extent, without running out of cash?

Challenge 4

Create sustainable profitability. It is a business, and business is also about cash flow, cost structures, profits, etc. So the teams must balance everything (strategy, employees, investments, etc) while ensuring that they can afford it (Table 26.1).

Table 26.1 Summarizing the challenges

Challenge #1: Attract and retain key employees	Challenge #2: Win the right customers
Ensure competence and expertise Create the right mix of people Train and develop your people Build corporate image and know-how *Example of a decision:* *Would you hire only one highly competent employee or two less experienced at half the cost?*	Build the right competence Match with employees' chemistry Have the right image and know-how *Example of a decision:* *Do you see challenging customers as a risk – or an opportunity?*
Challenge #3: Invest in tools and processes	**Challenge #4: Create sustainable profitability**
Allocate resources to R&D projects to: Build internal processes Create operational efficiency *Example of a decision:* *Should you wait with the investment until you have the money?* *Or invest first, so you can make money later?*	Cash flow and profit Improve business decision making Pricing, cost structures, capacity utilization *Example of a decision:* *What is the bottom-line effect of a 5% discount?*

While each team starts from scratch on an equal footing, it will not be long before they will differentiate, experiencing independent development. It is not unusual for a team to hit bankruptcy, possibly because they were too aggressive in the short term, or possibly too overoptimistic in pursuing a strategy that was almost a self-fulfilling prophecy. Celemi Tango is highly flexible and similar to real-life experience, so that in handling such a dismal situation, everyone might learn something from the setback. This snapshot lays the foundation for the add-on and extension we developed for the above-mentioned change process. The extension drills down into what chemistry is and how one can handle it in real life.

Developing interpersonal competencies for leaders in change

For both the customer and the change process described at the beginning of this chapter, a key issue was to create and increase the managers' awareness of people in order to improve their ability to lead others. This was especially important since change has a significant emotional side, which requires more than just tools – even field-tested managerial tools. The concept of chemistry in Celemi Tango that was described in the last section provided the basis to elaborate and integrate an add-on, closer to the way leaders treat real people. Abilities such as perception, awareness and effective communication are emphasized.

The idea was to combine a scientific, psychological motivation model with the individual chemistry symbol (such as circles, squares and triangles) assigned to the employees in Celemi Tango. To account for the degree of matching between people and the customers' corporate culture, we use an organizational culture model that aligns well, heuristically, with the motivation model.

PSI model to account for people's chemistry

Personality-system-interaction (PSI) model was mainly developed by Kuhl and colleagues (2001). It focuses on motives as the main internal driver and psychological energy of people to act. The practical advantage of this model is its integration of different cognitive, motivational and volitional models, such as the 3K-model by Kehr (2005), and others mentioned below. PSI uses four motivational types defined by two dimensions – how people perceive versus how they decide:

- One dimension is the 'perception filter'. In short, it highlights where people put their main perception focus: it can be either on specific tasks, which provides the motivation, or on the context, ie the overall big picture in which specific tasks are embedded.

- The second dimension is called decision filter, which highlights whether the motivation is extrinsic (is triggered from outside) or intrinsic (is triggered by one's own internal causes).

Both dimensions span a two-by-two matrix resulting in four basic motivation types:

- Task filter and extrinsic motivation results in being motivated by results (which is related to Vroom's expectation theory).

- Task filter and intrinsic motivation results in being motivated by learning and gaining new insights or experiences (which is related to Herzberg's job design).

- Context focus and extrinsic motivation results in being motivated by the effects that one's activities inspire (which is related to the goal-setting theory by Locke and Latham (1994).

- Context focus and intrinsic motivation – an integrative kind of motivational energy (that is related to the equity theory by Adams and Freedman, 1976).

Based on these four motivational types we assigned the three symbols in Celemi Tango to three of the motivation types (see Table 26.2).

Table 26.2 Celemi Tango symbols corresponding with PSI motivation types

Motivation type	Corporate culture	Symbol
Result-oriented	Market, Hierarchy	●
Effect-oriented	Adhocracy	■
Learning-oriented	Clan	▼

CVF to account for corporate chemistry

The competing value framework (CVF) developed by Cameron (1988) and Quinn (1988), provides us with a suitable model for company cultures.

The model is characterized by four culture types which results from two dimensions (see Table 26.3). For more information and in-depth description of these four culture types, see Cameron (1988) and Quinn (1988).

Table 26.3 Different culture types in the Competing Value Framework

	Dimension 1	**Dimension 2**
Culture type	Flexibility, freedom of decision, dynamics *versus* Stability, order and rules, controls This dimension ranges from flexibility and malleability to stability and reliability	Internal focus, integration, unity *versus* external focus, differentiation, competitiveness This dimension ranges from organizational glue, consonance to organizational differences, independency
Clan	Flexibility, freedom of decision, dynamics	Internal focus, integration, unity
Hierarchy	Stability, order and rules, controls	Internal focus, integration, unity
Adhocracy	Flexibility, freedom of decision, dynamics	External focus, differentiation, competitiveness
Market	Stability, order and rules, controls	External focus, differentiation, competitiveness

Integrating the models in Celemi Tango

Using these two models, we heuristically defined the suitable matches (see Table 26.2). For example, the so-called result-oriented motivation type, who is prone to a Management-by-Objective approach, fits well with a Market corporate culture, which is (among others) characterized by a strong, result-driven attitude and leadership style.

Having established this background and matching model, we then created question-and-answer statements. The people in Celemi Tango gave the answers in interviews before the teams decided whom they deemed suitable for their HR strategy and their customers. The chemistry and other characteristics, such as competence level and so on, were disclosed only after a job was offered (as per the usual rules).

With the simulation, we did not introduce the underlying models, but provided information to the participants about manners and patterns of behaviour; such information included, for example, how a 'circle' person might typically speak, behave or act. Next, they received a record of important questions and answers from the people whom they could hire as new employees. Based on this, the teams were encouraged to discuss whom they wanted to hire because of his or her fit to the strategy, HR road map, culture and customers. Only after a job was offered was the 'truth' revealed to the teams.

Key gains for the leadership change process

As mentioned, we used Celemi Tango as a pivotal element in a comprehensive leadership development and competence management change process. After the managers underwent a leadership interval training session, it became clear that the key purpose was to experience how leading people is essential to any change in and of itself as well as specifically crucial for the corporate goals at hand. The simulation in its regular form provides elements such as emphasizing the role of people and aligning business strategy and customer segments with personnel development. In the simulation, paying less attention to talent and know-how management might trigger strategic disadvantages, leading to fewer growth options, reduced competitiveness, and being stuck in the middle of a crisis with effects on financial performance as well.

To emphasize even more important leadership attitudes, such as perception and awareness of people, as well as abilities like listening and asking about competence and communication skills, we expanded the simulation based on two models: motivation types and corporate cultures. The learning effect for the participants was increased, as they experienced the ambiguity inherent in speaking and dealing with people. This was especially true since we provided people's answers to specific questions, as well as discussions of who may fit the strategy, HR road map and culture in the company and at the customer; decisions of whom to offer a job could only be based on what people said.

It happened that some teams hired people who turned out to be a less-than-perfect fit to what the team had envisioned. The team then had to live and cope with this situation, just as in real life. Two examples may illustrate this:

Example 1

The team hired a person they thought to be a high flyer concerning his competence level. Because of that, the team planned to assign this person to a challenging project right away. Now, however, after hiring, it turned out that the person was less competent. In this case, an assignment would not be accepted by the customer. The new employee would have to be sent to training that would help him achieve the expected level. In consequence, this meant reassigning other employees to serve the customer, thereby rescheduling other projects. Given all this reshuffling, it could mean not being able to serve a customer at all. In any case, paying less attention led to higher costs, more stress for the employees and, potentially, to image damage if a customer could not be served.

As a key lesson, the group of leaders mentioned that it would be okay to hire a less competent person if there was a strict plan in place for how to develop the person while balancing revenue and costs and leveraging the personal development to improve the company's know-how.

Example 2

One team paid too little attention to the chemistry (ie motivational type) of the person to be hired. As it turned out, this new employee was of a different type. This caused trouble during a challenging project, as the cultural and personal fit was disadvantageous when the project came to a rough patch. In effect, this led to higher stress for the team and a prolonged project time span, causing higher costs and loss in image. In the following business years, it was tricky to find appropriate assignments, especially for challenging customers for whom chemistry would play a vital role. As for the key learning point, the leaders experienced the value of creating a substantiated assessment about a person, and the importance of involving additional colleagues for a broader perception when doing so. A second learning point was to pay close attention to the other person, listening with an open mind and without assumptions. As one participant put it, with a smile: 'I always thought that engineers and physicists think alike. But – well – it seems that even those people are human' (personal communication).

About

Canmas – Business Learning and Consulting Ltd is a change facilitation company that provides proven customer-tailored methods to mobilize leaders, change agents and employees in business organizations. Our clients are mid-sized and large corporations who have the challenge to change and transform their business. We provide support to activate people for the change as facilitators, act as pilots for substantiating change initiatives and programmes, and as a partner when it comes to mobilizing the organization as a whole. Our facilitators have gained their experience over more than 20 years in various leadership roles in international companies. Celemi is a strategic partner to us whose business simulations have been globally successful for more than 30 years in making corporate learning more effective. We share the same understanding concerning the key success factors for effective change.

References

Adams, J S and Freedman, S (1976) Equity theory revisited: comments and annotated bibliography, in *Advances in Experimental Social Psychology*, vol 9, pp 43–90, ed L Berkowitz and L Walster, Academic Press, New York

Bontis, N and Girardi, J (2000) Teaching knowledge management and intellectual capital lessons: an empirical examination of the Tango simulation, *Int J Technology Management*, 20 (5/6/7/8), p 545

Cameron, K S and Ettington, D R (1988) The conceptual foundations of organizational culture, in Smart, J S (ed) *Higher Education: Handbook of Theory and Research*, Volume 4, Kluwer, Norwell, MA

Kehr, H M (2005) Das kompensationsmodell von motivation und volition als basis für die führung von mitarbeitern, in *Motivationspsychologie und ihre Anwendung (The Compensation Model of Motivation and Volition as a Basis for Managing Employees)*, ed R Vollmeyer and J Brunstein, pp 131–50, Kohlhammer, Stuttgart

Kuhl, J (2001) *Motivation und Persönlichkeit: Interaktion psychischer Systeme (Motivation and Personality: Motivation and personality: interaction of psychic systems)* Hogrefe Verlag, Göttingen

Locke, E and Latham, G (1994) Goal-setting theory, *Organizational Behavior 1: Essential theories of motivation and leadership*, pp 159-83

Mellander, K (1993) *The Power of Learning*, McGraw-Hill Inc, New York

Quinn, R E (1988) *Beyond Rational Management: Mastering the paradoxes and competing demands of high performance*, Jossey-Bass, San Francisco, CA

27

The Meeting Design Game

A dialogue tool to improve the process of planning and designing meetings and conferences

ANN HANSEN, Concept and Competence
BO KRÜGER, Moving Minds

#TeamDialogue #TeamPrioritizing #TeamAgreement

The Meeting Design Game is a card game (Figure 27.1). The game comprises more than 100 different meeting design elements, divided into 12 main categories (Table 27.1).

Each category has approximately eight to ten subcards. 'Meeting design' is a fairly new term and a topic garnering a lot of attention among people working professionally in meeting and event planning. It is a complex term comprising many components and topics from various fields of psychology research, learning studies and social science; hence, it can be complicated to explain what it is. On various occasions, we have been tasked with explaining what meeting design is, with very little time available. This challenge made us experiment with many different ways to communicate the messages most effectively. The aim was always to avoid one-way communication and traditional PowerPoint presentations and focus on involvement and

Figure 27.1 The Meeting Design Game: card deck and box

Table 27.1   The 12 categories in the Meeting
Design Game

1	Objectives
2	Content
3	Meeting flow
4	Evaluation
5	Social activities
6	Participant involvement
7	Physical set-up
8	Venue
9	Sustainability
10	Technical solutions
11	Food and beverage
12	Local inspiration

engagement instead. The creation of the Meeting Design Game is the result of an alternative format used during a meeting design training session.

The case

The training comprised 12 multicultural meeting professionals, all with different job descriptions, levels of experience and roles. After introducing the participants and the training programme, the game was played. We wanted to see whether the game itself was able to clarify the complex question: what is meeting design?

The participants were placed in groups of three, given a full set of cards and informed of the simple game rules. Then they were asked to select a current meeting or conference on which a group member was currently working. Afterwards, the group was asked to prioritize how important the 12 main cards were to making their meeting successful. The cards were prioritized from most important to least important.

Game effects

The immediate responses from the participants were positive. They intuitively knew what to do. The elements on the cards fitted directly into their reality and were experienced as relevant, challenging and inspirational.

Figure 27.2   The Meeting Design Game in action

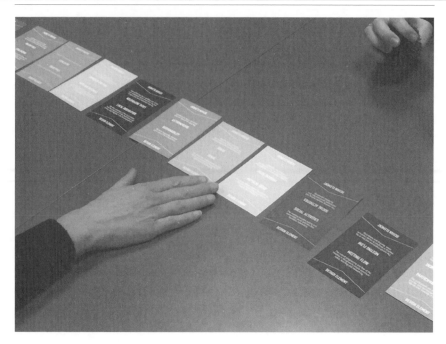

The direct effects of the game were:

- discussions about the perception of the design elements, which led to clarification and common understanding of different elements and terms;
- clearer priorities and identification of the most important elements in the planning and design process;
- a structured dialogue about relevant content;
- agreement on which elements to investigate further or not;
- distribution of tasks and responsibility.

Several 'Aha' moments from the participants were observed, and we became almost indispensable as meeting experts and facilitators. The level of engagement and focus on the task was overwhelming. When the time allocated for the exercise was up, participants insisted on more time to delve deeper into the design process. There were several other exercises and formats throughout the training, all with a high level of interaction and engagement. At the end of the training, there was an evaluation of the working methods that had been most valuable for the participants and most likely to be applied afterwards. The feedback was clear – out of approximately 15 different working methods, the Meeting Design Game received the highest score. After the initial use of the game in the training, we conducted several tests of the game with groups comprising a broad selection of nationalities, industries and job functions. We asked them how the game could be useful to them. The following feedback was received:

- help clarify objectives;
- start the planning of the meeting/event;
- repeat during the planning process and afterwards to review and evaluate;
- with attendees to design next event;
- for students, as an educational tool;
- with clients and stakeholders, to gain common understanding with the client;
- for lack of clarity/confusion in the team;
- for further inspiration and generation of ideas;
- to help codify or challenge normal processes;
- team building;
- introduction of new employees;
- as a checklist and to delegate tasks.

Possible application areas

The format of the game is very simple and could easily be applied to many other areas where the objectives are to create, for instance, common understanding and clarification, discussion about perception of issues and terms, priorities and identification of key issues, distribution of task and responsibility, among others. The format could be used with a variety of content and adapted to theoretical models, preferably in areas in which the complexity is high. Examples could be processes relating to recruitment, strategy development, company values, communication planning, among others.

Game purpose

The purpose of the game was to create a tool that, in simple terms, consolidated and captured all of our complex knowledge and experience about meeting design. There is a striking contrast between the simple structure of the game and the large amount of knowledge encapsulated in the cards.

This makes it easy to start the game with very little instructional assistance. The aim of the game is to create flow triggers, thereby creating a flow experience for the players. Flow is a mental state characterized by complete absorption in what one does. Findings in the 'flow in work' research by Wheal and Kotler (2016) show that flow leads to:

- heightened creativity;
- increased performance;
- accelerated problem solving;
- cutting the path to mastery in half and accelerating performance up to 500 per cent.

Observing and interviewing the people playing the game showed that the game was able to create a state of flow. The game accommodates the logic of the players. All the expert knowledge on the cards is selected and prioritized by the player; this creates a logic connected to the reality of the player and not to any theory of design thinking or fixed linear process. A high level of co-creation, creativity and autonomy is an important element in the format.

Challenges and conflicts in game topics

The game has no defined end. It is up to the players to decide when the game should end. This enables flexible autonomy, but also risks leaving the players with a feeling of not having completed the task. The idea of returning to the game when you are ready or need it again could complicate the sense of achievement. Some players might lack cards with different content; hence, blank cards are a part of the game, for the players to make their own content. The game has proven to be less valuable if there is no concrete case involved.

Gameplay

The format of the game (Table 27.2) is somewhat inspired by a game from Workz, another contributor in this book. But an important development in the structure is the ability to return to the game when your design and planning process has moved on. In that respect, it serves as an ongoing tool.

The gameplay is flexible as it can be played alone or in a group of up to six people, once or multiple times and for one hour or longer, depending on your needs.

Table 27.2   The steps in the game

Step 1	• Take the 12 main cards, named *Design Elements*, from the box.
	• Spread the cards out on the table.
	• Ask yourself: which *Design Elements* are the most important in order to make your meeting successful?
	• Prioritize the *Design Elements* in a row, with the most important to the left and least important to the right.
Step 2	• Now ask yourself: do you know what to do with this *Design Element* in your meeting?
	• If yes, move the card towards you; if no, move the card away.
	• Do this with all the *Design Elements* cards.
	• To capture for future reference, take a photo.
Step 3	• Choose a *Design Elements* card that you moved up and wish to explore further.
	• Take the corresponding *Sub Element* cards from the box, in the same colour.
	• Repeat Steps 1 and 2 with the *Sub Elements*.
	• Finish Step 3 by deciding which actions you will take from here.
	• If desired, put together **an action plan** and delegate tasks.
Step 4	• If needed, repeat Step 3 with other *Design Elements* that you do not know what to do with.

First, the participants think of an event or meeting they are currently working on; alternatively, they make one up.

Key gains that the game enables

Dialogue across cultures, experience and industries

Having facilitated the game in multicultural and diverse groups, we have discovered that the game creates a common language and a dialogue that overcomes the potential cultural differences. The cards make it easy for a group that has not previously worked together to start a dialogue. The content of the cards opens the dialogue and helps to focus on all aspects of a meeting. It invites everyone to share experiences and opinions.

'Free consultants'

The participants who do not have a case themselves serve as consultants and offer great value to the case holder. They challenge old habits, ask the important 'why', and share their experiences and knowledge about the case in play. The result of the role of the consultant has left them with a sense of self-efficacy and they leave the game situation with a sense of accomplishment and confidence. The activity in itself is engaging, even though there are no competitive elements and no winners.

Tactility/design of the game

The tactility in the game, the cards, and the box with the dividers creates curiosity and motivation to see what is in the box and on the cards. For instance, a participant remarked: 'It is hard to keep your hands from it' (personal communication).

The design of the cards also triggers an urge to pick a card that is important to a player and can emphasize the value of the card, just by holding on to it.

About

Bo Krüger and Ann Hansen – two of the world's leading meeting designers – have joined forces, creating the Meeting Design Game. Ann and Bo have trained people all around the world in Meeting Design for years. They have continually worked on methods to make it as easy as possible for meeting and event planners to apply Meeting Design principles and create great events. After years of testing, they have found that the Meeting Design Game is by far the most effective method.

Reference

Wheal, J and Kotler, S (2016) [accessed 9 March 2017] European Flow Research Network – The Flow Genome Project [Online] https://blog.bulletproof.com/jamie-wheal-steven-kotler-high-consequences-hacking-flow-state-216

28

The Way Forward

Develop and communicate a coherent strategy

CHRISTOPHER ELGOOD AND CHRISTINE ELGOOD,
Elgood Effective Learning

#BusinessDevelopment #ManagingGrowth #StrategicThinking

The Way Forward was commissioned by the MBA Alumni Association of Bradford Management Centre for a national competition. The simulation was designed to provide MBA students with the experience of running a business at a strategic level. It involved moving away from individual functional disciplines to a more holistic view of a business and the role of senior leaders in developing and implementing a strategy.

The design was based on long experience of modelling business situations for educational purposes, especially in regard to balancing realism and credibility against playability. The game rejected the prevailing view of the time that a model should accurately reflect a specific real industry. Instead it encouraged participants to use core economic theory, such as the laws of diminishing marginal utility and of supply and demand, and game results as data rather than importing specific industry knowledge (see Locke, 1989). The Way Forward is now widely used to increase business acumen and sensitivity in a fast-changing, global world.

Gameplay

Participants are divided into teams of four to six players, with up to six teams competing against each other. The participants receive a written brief about a fictitious company that trades a product of varying quality in different markets. The teams take over existing companies, all of whom are in the same situation. The teams are encouraged to create a strategy for their business based on the information provided in the player brief and the decisions they can make. There is then a series of up to five rounds, each representing a half-year of real time, during which the teams make decisions of both a quantitative and multiple-choice style and receive the results from their decisions.

The decision variables include company image, degree of central control versus delegation, and degree of effort to be devoted to each of 45 markets, defined by region and product type. The economic model reflects the belief that in today's world, there is no great difference between large, reputable companies in terms of what they offer, but that customers tend to buy from the supplier with whom they feel most comfortable. This means more importance is attached to the overall image presented and to consistent behaviour by a company. This then needs to be backed up by a consistent approach throughout the company, so that all staff understand the company's strategy and the activity in which they need to engage to make it successful. This is modelled through the use of management priorities. The game also includes an agenda item feature, which presents three problems that might arise at a board meeting. These are not based on an economic model but are external matters that might affect any company. They require a choice from among several given options (usually three). Each choice has a consequence, which is expressed through a financial impact on cost, revenue or competitiveness, so that it can be integrated with the outcome. The results of the agenda item decisions are made known to the playing teams. The consequences of agenda item decisions can be delayed for one or more periods, or have secondary effects.

The agenda items can be changed and new ones created to reflect the specific concerns of a customer or industry. An up-to-date example of an agenda item might be doubts about the ethical status of a supplier or the use of fleet cars with a poor record of exhaust pollution. The agenda item feature has a major impact on acceptance and enjoyment of the game because it invites value-based decisions that can be linked with discussions about the image the company seeks to project.

The international environment portrayed by the game increases student awareness of commercial and cultural differences and of the issues surrounding globalization. It is permissible, for instance, to operate only in foreign countries and ignore the home market, if it is thought profitable to do so.

Once each team has made its decisions (Figure 28.1), they are evaluated by the computer model. The model includes an interactive element, so the team's decisions are assessed on a team-by-team basis. All the strategies are then compared, so that a team with better decisions in one area will perform better than a competitor. This mirrors competition between competing companies in the real world. The team's results are returned in the form of a profit/loss account, balance sheet, cost information and market statistics.

Figure 28.1 Player decision sheet completed each period

DECISION SHEET

HALF-YEAR:	COMPANY NAME:

DECISION 1 - CONTROL CODE. Circle one of the numbers.

1   2   3

DECISION 2 - GEOGRAPHIC AREA DECISIONS

- MARKET IMAGE. Circle one of the codes in each geographical market.
- SEGMENT/SECTOR STRATEGY. Enter 0 to 5 in each position.
- PRICE STRATEGY. Enter P or M or R in the space provided

UK

Market Image:	CL	CO	DI	EL	EX	FA	GL	GR	OP	PO	RE	RO
Strategies	Popular				Standard				Executive			
Government												
Big Firms												
Retail												
Direct												
Price Strategy P/M/R												

Western Europe

Market Image:	CL	CO	DI	EL	EX	FA	GL	GR	OP	PO	RE	RO
Strategies	Popular				Standard				Executive			
Government												
Big Firms												
Retail												
Direct												
Price Strategy P/M/R												

Eastern Europe

Market Image:	CL	CO	DI	EL	EX	FA	GL	GR	OP	PO	RE	RO
Strategies	Popular				Standard				Executive			
Government												
Big Firms												
Retail												
Direct												
Price Strategy P/M/R												

DECISION 3 - MANAGEMENT PRIORITIES

	Priority Number	Priority Number	Priority Number	Priority Number
UK				
Western Europe				
Eastern Europe				

DECISION 4 - AGENDA ITEM CHOICES. Enter numbers for the items and options relevant to your team for this Half-Year.

AGENDA ITEM NO.   OPTION NO.

....

....

....

DECISION 5 - DIVIDEND

Enter your Dividend in Pence per Share for the half year just completed: ....p

DECISION 6 - SHARE CAPITAL SOUGHT FROM NEW SHARE ISSUE

Enter the number of new shares you wish to issue: ....

Between decision periods, there may be an input session focusing on a particular area of the simulation, to help the players develop their understanding. For example:

- The difference between a volume or margin strategy – how to determine whether the decisions the team has made are producing the expected results.

- Marketing strategy – the 4 Ps – product, price, promotion and place (see Perreault and McCarthy, 1996).

- The importance of staff motivation and how the actions of senior management impact it.

- The role of senior managers in setting the strategy and of middle managers in implementing it.

- The information about their own company – the data provided in each half-year contains information about the competitor's position in each market and the sale prices being won. In addition to this, some limited data about the competitor's financial performance can be shared. The share price for each team is provided in each period; this is the winning criterion (Figure 28.2).

How and where it is used

The original business game was part of a national competition run by the MBA Alumni Association at Bradford Management Centre. It took place at the end of the MBA course, when students had returned to their place of work. There was a schedule for decision making and processing spread over an eight-week period. The competition was sponsored by Barclays and Royal Mail. The Way Forward is embedded in the qualification programme of The Institute and Faculty of Actuaries (UK), where it is used in a face-to-face training environment. It is also part of the qualification programme for The Institute of Actuaries (India); here, it is run virtually, with the participants based in India and the processing and facilitation provided using a cloud application. It has also formed an integral part of a commercial awareness programme for CPA Global, with events held in North America, India and Australia. In each instance, the core economic principles and structure of the game remain the same, but the board papers and associated consequences are adjusted to reflect topical management dilemmas relevant to the organization and country.

Figure 28.2 Share price information and competitor information displayed

THE WAY FORWARD

TEAM NAME	NOW	HALF YEAR 1	HALF YEAR 2	HALF YEAR 3	HALF YEAR 4
	£2.50				
	£2.50				
	£2.50				
	£2.50				
	£2.50				
	£2.50				

THE WAY FORWARD

TEAM NAME	SALES (REVENUE)	SALES (UNITS)	PROFIT AFTER TAX	DIVIDEND (PENCE PER SHARE)

Key gains that the game enables

Creating and communicating a strategy

Many organizations fail not because they do not have a strategy, but because that strategy is not clearly communicated to everyone within the organization. With The Way Forward, participants are encouraged to develop a strategy for their business and to consider how they would communicate the essential elements of it to their team. Participants invariably realize that: 1) it is more difficult to create a winning strategy than they first imagined; 2) a strategy in itself is not sufficient; it must be communicated and implemented by individuals within the business.

This experience is essential for middle managers, who often do not understand their own company strategy or how their actions connect with it. It is also important for those stepping up to a senior role, who need to let go of the tactical decisions and develop a more holistic approach.

Analysis of company and market information

In some situations, participation in The Way Forward provides participants with a basic understanding and ability to use the data a company has available to it to help with decision making. For participants who are already familiar with the type of data available, it is about focusing on the right data elements. The amount of data provided and the time available for decision making means it is impossible to analyse everything; participants need to make a judgement call. Instead, they must focus on what is really important and useful; otherwise, they risk analysis paralysis. It also introduces participants to the idea they will never have all the information they want to make a decision. As senior managers, they need to become comfortable using their judgement.

Trade-offs – cause and effect

Through the cycle of decision making and results, participants are encouraged to think through the decisions they make and the consequences of those decisions. They are then encouraged to really examine their results. Have the decisions they made had the expected impact? If they increased their sales in one area, did they have to divert resources from another area to achieve it? Was it worth it? There is also the element of competition. Have a team's results been affected by the decisions of a competitor? Such questions demand a debriefing and thorough reflection on the decisions.

About

Chris Elgood Associates Limited (Elgood Effective Learning) was created by Chris Elgood, MA, author of *The Handbook of Management Games and Simulations* (Elgood 1997). The company's objective is to extend the use of games and simulations as an alternative to direct instruction. Christine Elgood, BA, MBA, took over in 1977 and has developed new material for the current environment and new methods that exploit up-to-date technology. The company's greatest strength remains treating each client as a special case.

References

Locke, J (1989) Some considerations of the consequences of the lowering of interest and the raising the value of money, *The Two Narratives of Political Economy*, pp 47–55, London

Perreault Jr, W D and McCarthy, E J (1996) *Basic Marketing: A global-managerial approach*, Irwin, Illinois

29
Quick games
Power-up group dynamics

BO KRÜGER, Moving Minds

#TeamCo-creation #TeamEnergy #TeamCommunication

Quick games are short games that last from two to thirty minutes. They are usually aimed at creating learning readiness and positive, constructive group dynamics (Figure 29.1). Sometimes a number of quick games can be applied one after the other to create a stronger effect.

Applied situations

I have used quick games at numerous sessions and events, such as innovation workshops, management seminars, off-site company days, training

Figure 29.1   A typical situation from a quick game

programmes, scientific conferences, etc. I have used the games with all types of target groups, from CEOs, bankers, politicians and researchers to teachers and students. I have used the games with Europeans, Americans, Asians and multicultural groups. My general experience is that if the game is experienced as meaningful by the participants, fits the target group, and is well facilitated, there are very few limits to where the games can be applied. It is often claimed that games should only be used if they connect directly to the content of the meeting, event or training session. I often hear condescending comments about quick games, like they are 'childish' or 'meaningless'. In my opinion, there are two reasons for such criticism.

The first reason is that many people, unfortunately, have experienced bad games that were badly facilitated. I have, like too many people, participated in games that I experienced as forced, too difficult, out of my comfort zone, or just plain stupid. However, this does not prove that quick games should not be used; it just shows how difficult it can be to design, facilitate and choose the right games, so they will have the desired impact and be experienced as meaningful.

The second reason is that the critics apparently do not understand the deeper effects of games. As I will explain more thoroughly later, play is one of the easiest ways to raise the number of positive emotions in a group. Barbara L Fredrickson is one of the world's leading experts on positive emotions. Her research (2009) has shown that a high positivity ratio has numerous positive effects such as increased learning, creativity and performance. Moreover, I assume that many of the critics of quick games take no issue with accepting that performance is increased by warming up prior to a sports match, or taking breaks during a hard workday, activities that are not connected directly to the content of what they are doing. In my experience, quick games have similar and even stronger effects on an event as warming up or taking a coffee break.

Lack of words can lead to resistance

Often the language used to describe quick games is very imprecise. They are often referred to as icebreakers or team-building activities. The term 'icebreaker', for instance, is often used to describe all kinds of games and playful activities, without distinguishing between different game dynamics or objectives. This generalization can often lead to resistance from both participants and facilitators to the use of quick games, as one previous bad experience with an icebreaker can result in the notion that all other icebreakers are the same. This reasoning would be equivalent to claiming that if you had one bad meal, then all other meals are probably bad, too. We know logic like that does not hold true, as we all have very differentiated language to describe and classify food. Our advanced food vocabulary gives us a clear understanding that meals can be extremely different, and just because a person does not like raw sushi does not mean that the person does not like tapas.

Moreover, the word 'icebreaker' carries the underlying assumption that there is ice or resistance in the room, which is not necessarily the case. I believe that a more precise and differentiated vocabulary to describe quick games could prevent a lot of resistance and many misconceptions. Hence, I will try to develop a taxonomy or classification that can help us distinguish between different types of quick games.

Quick game taxonomy

The classification in my quick game taxonomy is based on what the main objectives and expected outcome of the games are (Table 29.1). This is helpful because the expected effects of the game, in most cases, are the most relevant criteria for deciding which kind of game to use. Hence, other relevant classification criteria, such as game mechanics or props used, are not helpful. Most games have many different effects, such as creating learning readiness and a good mood in the group. In the taxonomy, the games are classified according to the main objective of the activity. A side-effect of Co-creation Games, for example, is increased networking and team spirit; in actuality, the main aim of the games in this group is to create new content together.

Below, I will review each group of games and give an example of a game that suits the category.

Jolt

A jolt is an activity that is designed to shock someone in order to change his/her behaviour or way of thinking. Jolts are often used to make participants understand, remember and reflect on an important learning point or message. An example of a game that can be used as a jolt is the Tap Game.

The Tap Game

I used the Tap Game in a workshop at the International Congress and Convention Associations (ICCA) World Congress 2016 in Kuching, Malaysia.

Table 29.1 Quick game taxonomy table

Type	Main objectives	Game example
Jolt	Understand, remember and reflect on an important learning point or message.	The Tap Game
Brainbreak	Sharpen the brain to create learning readiness.	Switch Fingers
Networking game	Increase networking. Build high-quality Connections.	Namefeud
Co-creation game	Create new content together.	One Word at a Time
Energizer	Have fun, increase positive emotions, create learning readiness.	Grab It
Team-building game	Increase team spirit, communcation and cooperation.	Sudden survey

Participants included 100 congress organizers, venues and suppliers from all over the world, mainly Asia. The objective of the game was to enable the participants to experience how difficult it is for others to understand what they try to communicate. This is a useful lesson when, for example, a person organizes scientific congresses, which are aimed at communicating complex content among peers. The game was played as described below:

- Participants were asked to work in pairs.

- They were then asked to think of a melody that they were very sure their partner knew (for example, 'Happy Birthday').

- They were asked to tap the melody with a pen on the table. The partner's task was to guess which melody was being played.

- After the game, they were asked how many managed to guess the melody (less than one in four).

- I told them a similar game has been created as a part of a scientific research project (Heath and Heath, 2007), which showed that most people thought there would be a 50 per cent chance that the other person would guess the melody. In reality, only 2.5 per cent guessed the song (3 out of 120).

- I asked the participants why there is such a big difference between what we believe the other person will guess and what they actually do.

- A likely explanation is a bias called 'the curse of knowledge' (see Heath and Heath, 2007), which means we assume that other people have the same knowledge as ourselves. When we tap the melody, we can hear all the instruments and the complete song in our heads, whereas the other person only hears a monotonic tapping sound.

The effects of the game were very positive. There was a lot of interaction and laughing. Shortly afterwards, I received an e-mail from one of the ICCA organizers, with the evaluations. She wrote: 'Your presence definitely made a lasting impact on our (hard to please) delegates!'

The overall evaluation of the 90-minute workshop was very positive (ICCA, 2016): 19 out of 26 respondents found the content of the session *excellent* and 7 found it *good*; 25 respondents found they had gained new ideas or skills from the session. One participant wrote:

> Via the use of creative games and devices (backed up by facts) I feel capable now to handle a large group of people – so they can learn more effectively and with meaning. (personal communication)

Brainbreak

Brainbreaks are short, two- to five-minute activities or games that are aimed at sharpening the brain to create learning readiness. Brainbreaks often do not have a direct link to the content of the event. Brainbreaks can be compared to warming-up activities before a football match. Many brainbreaks include auto-motoric skills and are often used to break up a long, tiresome session. An example is the Switch Fingers game.

Switch Fingers

Switch Fingers is a game that can be done while sitting, in just a few minutes. The objective is to create learning readiness and capture the participants' attention, as the game forces them to put away their devices or other distracting things. The game goes as described below:

- The participants are asked to put the thumb up on the right hand and the little finger up on the left hand.
- They are then asked to shift quickly, so they put the thumb and the little finger up on the opposite hand.
- The game is about shifting as many times as possible, as fast as possible, without messing it up.

The game is very easy to use, and I have played it at numerous sessions. On one occasion, I used it at a conference I was facilitating at the Danish Technical University (DTU). The participants were about 80 researchers and professors from DTU, along with researchers and senior managers from Siemens. The aim of the conference was to find opportunities for cooperation between the two organizations. At the conference, there were tandem speakers. First, there was a speaker from Siemens and then a speaker from DTU. After several lectures, the audience began to grow tired. I decided to play the Switch Fingers game, as I thought it would fit the target group and the situation.

The game worked well. Almost everyone participated and seemed refreshed. Afterwards, one of the professors from DTU came to me and said he liked the game, and would use it in his teaching in the future.

Networking games

These games are aimed at helping the participants network and create high-quality connections with other participants. One of the main reasons why people attend meetings and conferences is to network with other participants (American Express, 2016). Research has shown that most people do not excel at networking unless it is facilitated (Ingram and Morris, 2007).

Namefeud

This networking game is inspired by the popular games Scrabble and Wordfeud. The aim of the game is to learn the names of other participants in a fun way. The game is often used as an opener with new groups that do not know each other, but can also be used as a fun game with people who already know each other. The participants are asked to write the first letter of their name on a piece of paper. In the lower corner, they write the number of letters in their name (in my case it would be two, for Bo). The number represents the points they can achieve from using the letter.

Then the participants are asked to get together with four people they do not know. Each group is given five vowels (for some reason most names start with consonants). They now have five minutes to create a word landscape (as in Scrabble), using the letters they have in their group. The winning team is the group that scores the most points (following the same rules as in Scrabble). I have used Namefeud, for example, with high-school teachers, in a training course on innovative teaching methodologies. The aim was to let them network quickly. Moreover, the main message of the training was 'innovation is not a spectator sport', meaning that you cannot become innovative if you only talk about it, you have to do it. The co-creating nature of Namefeud was a great way to get that message across from the beginning of the training. The intriguing letter game worked well with teachers. I have also played the game successfully with other groups of people. The pace and the energy of the game is calm compared to many other network games, such as Network Bingo (a game in which participants are asked to fill out a bingo card, with interesting facts about the other participants, as quickly as possible).

Co-creation games

These games are aimed at having the participants create new, original material together. The games are typically used in innovation workshops or in seminars where the group is looking for common ground.

'One Word at a Time' game

This game is inspired by improvisational (improv) theatre, where it is used to train the 'yes and' principle. This is a creative that forces players to accept other players' ideas ('yes') and add their own ideas ('and'):

- Participants work in pairs.
- They are asked to tell a story, one word at a time.
- The aim of the game is to build meaningful stories together.
- The stories can be fictional, but they can also be linked to a relevant topic, for example 'how should we cooperate in the organization?'
- The 'yes and' principle can also be used for brainstorming, where participants are required to build on each other's ideas.

I used this game during a seminar with 120 health-care professionals from a Danish municipality, including doctors, nurses and physical therapists. One of the aims of the seminar was to increase cooperation between different units. I used the game to show the participants how they can easily cooperate and co-create, if they are open to one another's ideas. I also asked them to tell stories one word at a time, about how they would like to cooperate in the future.

The game created a lot of energy and laughter in the room. I asked the participants to pair up with people they did not know, which also helped them to build stronger relations; this could make it easier to cooperate after the seminar. The feedback was very positive, and many said it was the best theme day they had ever had.

Energizers

Energizers are games or activities that aim to energize the participants. Energizers are often fun and usually include some physical activity. In many ways, they are similar to brainbreaks but usually last longer. Energizers increase positive emotions, raise the energy level of the group and create learning readiness. They do not usually have a direct connection to the content of the event. Energizers are often used to kickstart activities and to raise the energy level during or after a long, tiresome session. If well chosen, energizers can have an amazing positive impact on the group dynamics. On the other hand, a badly chosen and facilitated energizer can easily be experienced as stupid or silly and lead to resistance.

Grab It game

The Grab It game is an easy game that works with most groups:

- Participants get together in pairs.
- Participant A holds his/her hand flat in the air. Participant B points his/her index finger towards A's palm.
- B's task is to touch A's palm five times without getting caught.
- When done, they shift.
- In the final round, they try to catch and touch at the same time, using both hands.

I used the game during the 5th European Conference on Positive Psychology in Copenhagen (2010). This was a scientific conference with approximately 400 psychologists and researchers from Europe and the United States. The participants included some major names in psychology, such as Mihaly Csikszentmihalyi and Howard Gardner. I was asked by the congress organizers to facilitate small brainbreaks and energizers between speakers in plenary sessions. There was no formal evaluation of the games and activities, but the reception was very positive. One of the keynote speakers, Professor Barbara L Fredrickson, specifically asked me to facilitate one of my games before her keynote address. When I asked her afterwards why she wanted to give some of her precious speaking time to me and my games, she said, 'I talk about how positive psychology works, but what you do shows it' (personal communication).

Team-building games

The aim of these games is to increase team spirit, communication and cooperation. They are often used on company days or as part of a training programme. There are many team-building games in use all over the world. Some games are disconnected from the content of the event; few are directly connected to the content.

Sudden Survey

Sudden Survey is a game created by the Indian learning expert Thiagi. The aim of the game is to explore a topic quickly in a group. The game has a clear team-building effect, but at the same time is closely connected to the content of the event:

- Participants work in groups of three to five people.
- They are given four minutes to create a strategy for how to collect data from the other participants, about the topic at hand (eg gamification or company values).
- They then spend five minutes collecting data.
- They are given five minutes to analyse the data and write the three most important findings on a poster.
- The facilitator reviews the findings with the groups.

The game can be used anytime during a session to explore a given topic. It is also very suitable at the beginning of a programme, to replace the tiresome 'Nameround'. Sudden Survey is a very effective way to kickstart group dynamics and let people interact with each other. I used the game as an opening activity in facilitation training courses with journalists and communication consultants from various organizations. There were usually 15–20 participants. The training course was only one day, so it was important for me to get the group on their feet right from the start. The game proved successful every time. In a very short time, we managed to generate a lot of energy, do some networking, and gather knowledge about the group and team spirit.

The feedback was extremely positive. The training course got the highest possible ratings from all participants several times in a row. According to K-Forum, a professional training provider, it was the first time ever that this happened in any of their training courses.

Key gains that the game enables

Quick games can be very effective tools to enhance learning and nurture positive group dynamics, if used the right way. The points below further argue for the beneficial use of these:

- A more precise language to distinguish between different kinds of quick games can reduce resistance and increase the chances of success.
- There are good games and bad games, and just because a person experienced one bad game does not mean that all games are bad.
- Good facilitation of a quick game is just as important as the game itself.
- In order for a quick game to be successful, it usually has to be challenging to play. If it is too easy, it is boring and might seem childish; if it is too difficult, it can generate fear and take participants too far out of their comfort zone.

Theory behind

Many different theories can be used to explain the effects of quick games. Below are some examples.

Positivity ratio

Barbara L Fredrickson's (2009) research has shown that if people and groups experience a high ratio of positive emotions compared to negative ones, they flourish and become a better version of themselves. The optimal positivity ratio is most likely 3:1 or higher. This means that, to flourish, we should experience at least three positive emotions for each negative one.

When we flourish, a number of positive things happen to the group dynamics. For example, we become more creative, open to other people, perform better, learn more and become more action-oriented. Hence, a high-positivity ratio is desirable for most kinds of group activity. According to Fredrickson (2009), most groups and people have a positivity ratio of around 2:1, well under the 3:1 tipping point. In an interview I did with her, she said that play was the easiest way to increase the amount of positive emotion (Krüger, 2011).

Movement increases learning

There is much research to support the idea that movement increases learning and creativity (Ratey, 2008). For example, a study from Stanford showed that walking and talking can increase creativity by up to 60 per cent (Oppezzo and Schwartz, 2014). Since many of the quick games involve movement, it is most likely that such games will have an overall positive impact on the event in which they are applied.

About

Moving Minds is a creative company with deep insight into what motivates managers and employees. They use this knowledge to create changes and learning that do not die in the boardroom but reach every corner of the organization. Moving Minds specializes in designing and facilitating meetings, conferences and workshops. To that end, they design engaging games, both board and live games. The company has clients in more than 20 countries. The games it creates are based on the latest psychological research and thousands of hours of practical work.

References

American Express (2016) [accessed 9 March 2018] Doctor's Orders: The Physician's Perspective On Meetings and Events [Online] https://www. amexglobalbusinesstravel.com/content/uploads/2017/12/Pharmaceutical-Conference-Planning-The-Physicians-Perspective-On-Meetings-And-Events.pdf

Fredrickson, B L (2009) *Positivity*, Crown Publishers, New York

Heath, C and Heath, D (2007) *Made to Stick: Why some ideas take hold and others come unstuck*, Random House Books, London

ICCA (International Congress and Convention Association) (2016) Evaluation of World Congress 2016, Kuching, Borneo, internal document

Ingram, P and Morris, M (2007) *Do People Mix at Mixers? Structure, homophily, and the 'life of the party'*, Columbia University, New York

Krüger, B (2011) *Kontorets Indiana Jones: Loer at improviser på arbejdet (The Indiana Jones in the Office: Learn to improvise at work)*, Gyldendal Business, Copenhagen

Oppezzo, M and Schwartz, D L (2014) Give your ideas some legs: the positive effect of walking on creative thinking, *Journal of Experimental Psychology: Learning, memory, and cognition*, American Psychological Association, 40 (4), pp 1142–52

Ratey, J (2008) *Spark – The Revolutionary New Science of Exercise and The Brain*, Little Brown, New York

PART THREE
A Core Understanding of Business Games

30
Structure in business games
Five cores

All the games in the book are built around game structures consisting of five cores: 1) framing metaphors; 2) rules; 3) materials; 4) challenges; and 5) participation. These structures govern how the games unfold and what players can do in the games, all of which affect the outcomes the games can produce. Before elaborating on the cores, we first briefly investigate the relationship between structure and outcome.

A game researcher named Jesper Juul (2011) has made a thorough analysis of what structures games are built around. Although the analysis is mostly related to games in the entertainment industry, we can still use it for starters. Juul found that there are two archetypes of game structures, namely a progression structure and an emergence structure.

The progression structure is based on sessions where the player must perform a predefined sequence of events—this is evident when there are steps (e.g., 1, 2, 3) or levels (e.g., 1, 2, 3). Games built around a progression structure are usually fairly predictable because players always go through the same sequences in the same order. The progression structure yields a great deal of control to the business game designer and facilitator as he or she controls the sequences of the events. This type of game often has a strong pre-made storytelling ambition.

The emergence structure is based on a few initial structures that, combined, generate many possible situations in the game. Games built around an emergence structure are usually unpredictable because patterns and possible directions combine and interact in ways that no one can foresee. Where progression games can be illustrated as a straightforward staircase, emergence games can be viewed as a huge grid with many intersections – as you can see in Figure 30.1, the players navigate these two game structures very differently.

In all the games in this book, the game flow advances in steps; however, there is variation in how fixed these are and in the way a particular ludic space is constrained (towards progression) or deconstrained (towards

Figure 30.1   Progression versus emergence game structures

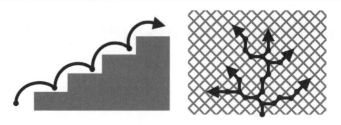

emergence) from the start and along the way. The two game structures presented above are extremes. Many games have elements of both progression and emergence, where sequences of events are predetermined while, at the same time, there is room enough at each step to enable multiple scenarios. What is interesting about how these game structures relate to the games in this book is that the choice of game structure has a close connection to the outcomes each game seeks to produce. If the purpose is competence development, the game structure usually leans towards progression structures. These games are also based on pre-made content based on theory or observations experienced over time. If the purpose is primarily organizational development, the game structure usually leans towards emergence structures, wherein some content is created beforehand, but most of it is created through gameplay. Some games can be used for both competence development and organizational development, but even in this case, one purpose is still prioritized higher than the other. To summarize these connections, see Table 30.1.

After analysing the games in this book, we found that the training games were connected to methodological considerations about creating personal experience formation for the participants through practice and repetition in games. These games were based on progression structures, which function as training exercises. The training games in this book are often based on representative fictional cases, which are used as the basis for a transfer of learning. Moreover, we found that the co-creation games in the book are connected to methodological considerations about creating innovative ideas through games based on emergence structures; these function as ideation exercises and co-creation activities. Both types of purposes aim to support learning, but they do so in different ways. They seek to create an informal atmosphere wherein participants can co-create, and organizational members can engage in dialogue with each other across departments, teams

Table 30.1 Training games and co-creation games

Game Type	Training Games	Co-Creation Games
Game Purpose	Competence development.	Organizational development.
Organizational Problem	Incompetent or dysfunctional behaviour from organizational members.	Integration and risk management in a massive economical pressure.
Game Function	Clarification of responsibility placement and exercise of correct behaviour.	Internalization of organizational agendas and creation of opportunities.
Game knowledge	Derived from theory or experience and incorporated into the game beforehand as fictional content, but often as realistically as possible.	Invites local, situated knowledge unfolded through gameplay. None or little content, rather the game creates a frame for discussion.
Game Structure	Progression structure based on fixed sequence of events that the player must go through via predetermined actions.	Emergence structure based on few rules that allow several different situations and player actions to occur.

and professions through common metaphors and language created from visual elements and tactile materials.

As mentioned earlier, five core elements in the games can be identified (Table 30.2), and these are used by all applicators and facilitators. These cores also determine whether a given part of the game seeks to advance through progression or open up for emerging themes:

- framing metaphors (initial framing);
- rules (what participants are allowed to do or not do);
- materials (functions and aesthetics);
- challenges (challenges given during gameplay);
- participation (arrangement of the people involved).

Table 30.2 List with all five cores and all games

	Framing Metaphors (initial framing)	Rules (what one can do or not do)	Materials (how the game is built)	Challenges (in-game struggles)	Participation (the arrangement)
08: The Acid Test	Based on the analogy of excavation when one stratum gives way to another.	Remove the fewest counters to uncover the 12 red counters to win the game.	Counters in three different colours placed in 23 plastic siloes.	Puzzle challenge – uncover the 12 red counters in fewer moves than competitors.	Divided into teams and competition based.
09: Add Value	A train track that symbolizes the customer journey.	Go through the four steps: 1) Personas; 2) The User Tour; 3) Prioritizations; and 4) The Star Round.	Board with writable pieces, cards and personal cards.	Mapping and answer challenge – fill out and answer questions about customer.	All working together, inviting multiple stakeholders and co-creation based.
10: Align	The name of the game indicates the purpose with the game.	Multiple-choice based with ranking algorithms.	Digitalized board game played on tablet that records choices.	Decision challenge – based on dilemma cards, challenge cards, chance cards and event cards.	Both individual competition and working together and sharing results.
11: Bizzbuilder	The game itself works as a metaphor for synergy and long-term and short-term thinking.	Multiple-choice based with score algorithms.	A digital tablet game with challenge algorithms and a fixed number of choices.	Decision challenge – based on scenarios and consequences of previous decisions.	Both individual competition between pairs and working together across pairs and sharing results.

12: Business Branching	Representing a company as a tree trunk with branches representing business areas.	Mapping out the company and going through a series of tasks per round.	Writable board with pieces and challenge cards.	Mapping and decision challenge – map out company and decide resource allocation.	All working together, inviting multiple stakeholders and co-creation based by playing against the game.
13: Changesetter	Representing change management as a question of getting everyone on board the boat.	Multiple-choice based with a score algorithm that moves the boat and the people.	A digital board game with a circular board, boats and people.	Decision challenge – based on game scenarios and consequences of previous decisions.	Teams working together competing against other teams.
14: Changeskills	Using questions to explore ways to implement policies.	Try to interpret a question the same way as the other groups.	Board, three different types of question cards, and a jury.	Answer challenge – answer questions in the same way as the majority.	Competition between teams who are scored by a jury.
15: Exploring Change	Travelling metaphor with a navigator, west, east, north and south.	Based on a series of steps where participants sort out cards with statements.	Cards with statements, mats and posters.	Mapping and organizing challenge – organize and map cards on mats.	All working together.
16: Innovate or Dinosaur	The metaphor of either innovating or becoming extinct.	Write out a problem and use inspiration cards to make solutions.	Inspiration cards, two boards and dinosaur tokens.	Answer challenge – problems to solve using creative techniques.	Working together in teams, but there can be competition between tables.

(continued)

Table 30.2 (Continued)

	Framing Metaphors (initial framing)	Rules (what one can do or not do)	Materials (how the game is built)	Challenges (in-game struggles)	Participation (the arrangement)
17: Innovation Learning Diamond Game	A diamond to represent four archetypical innovation roles of a jester, detective, gardener and conceptualizer.	Choose a challenge and four task cards, then lay them out and solve them one by one.	Task cards, a centrepiece, drawing materials, clay, picture cards and writing pads.	Task challenge – solve a task and reflect on the associated reflection questions.	All working together.
18: Leadership development simulations	Build around name metaphors, such as Wallbreakers and Bridgebuilders.	Multiple-choice based.	Boards, booklets, pieces and computer programs.	Decision challenge – based on game scenarios and consequences of previous decisions.	Working together in teams, but competition between teams.
19: Linkxs	Name metaphor related to creating links in the puzzle and in the team.	Put the puzzle pieces correctly together in the group.	Cardboard-based puzzle pieces.	Puzzle challenge – figure out how the pieces fit together with an instruction.	Working together in teams, but competition between teams. Observers see how it all plays out.
20: Managing Your Sales Teams	The game works as a metaphor for managing sales teams over longer periods of time.	Multiple-choice based.	Booklet with information, a playing mat, counters and computer calculation program.	Decision challenge – to optimize scores across different variables.	Working together in teams, but competition between teams.

21: Ocean of Culture	Using an ocean metaphor to represent an organization's culture.	Go through tasks and answer questions.	Board, question cards, counters, a task booklet, a text booklet, a process booklet and notepads.	Mapping and answer challenge – fill out and answer questions about customer.	All working together.
22: Pitch Perfect	A metaphor of reversing the sales process and a metaphor of buying assets.	Collect cards indicating how to perform pitch and perform pitch with certain constraints.	Necklaces, cards and props, like wigs and masks etc.	Answer challenge – create a pitch while being obstructed by constraints.	Working together in teams, with illusory competition between teams.
23: PublicPro-fessional	Scenarios representing real-world cases and challenges.	Multiple-choice based, where scores are calculated on many parameters.	A digital game with multiple graphics.	Decision challenge – choose which communication styles to use with stakeholders.	Individual players play against the game.
24: Stakeholder Management	A metaphor for level of trust called a 'Trust-O-Meter' and bar-chart style scores to show gains and losses.	Map out a stakeholder dilemma, come up with strategies, and evaluate strategies with scores.	A score board, character cards, inspiration cards, a 'Trust-O-Meter' arrow, and dilemma and tactic pads.	Mapping and answer challenge – map out dilemmas and make strategies to handle them.	Individual players play against each other. Important that people are from different organizations.

(continued)

Table 30.2 *(Continued)*

	Framing Metaphors (initial framing)	Rules (what one can do or not do)	Materials (how the game is built)	Challenges (in-game struggles)	Participation (the arrangement)
25: Strategic Derby	Uses the derby metaphor of horse racing to indicate strategic advantages.	Decide parameters to invest in and come up with ideas, get score based on market situation.	Writable board, investment cards and whiteboard markers.	Decision and answer challenge – choose parameters and come up to ideas of how.	Working together in pairs, but competition between pairs.
26: Tango	Uses a tango dance metaphor to represent change management.	Multiple-choice based, where scores are calculated on different parameters.	Board, cards, coins, coin holders, tokens, writing pads and pens.	Decision challenges – to optimize scores across different variables.	Working together in teams, but competition between teams.
27: The Meeting Design Game	Use meeting design terms to clarify the games subject.	Take 12 cards and sort them according to priority.	Different types of cards.	Organizing challenge – sort out cards according to priority.	All working together. Can be played alone or in groups.
28: The Way Forward	Market mechanism theories used to represent markets.	Multiple-choice based, where scores are calculated on different parameters.	Booklet and programme to calculate scores.	Decision challenges – to optimize scores across different variables.	Working together in teams, but competition between teams.
29: Quick games	Usually strong metaphors to quickly let people know the character of the activities.	Different depending on game, but usually simple.	Usually simple materials such as pen and paper or no materials at all.	All kinds of challenges.	Can be both working together and competition.

Framing metaphors

In all of the games, players explore the meaning of the game in light of the supported materials. Sitting around a table in a workshop situation with various people whom one has not met before can create nervousness, which prevents participants from airing their ideas. Warm-up sessions might do the trick, but a game metaphor can establish an initial informal atmosphere and mutual understanding – a place to start from. Linguistics professors George Lakoff and Mark Johnson (2008) state that a metaphor is: 'A way of conceiving of one thing in terms of another, and its primary function is understanding.'

By using the metaphor 'Innovate or dinosaur' (C16), for instance, players instinctively grasp the meaning of the game. In other types of games, especially video games, there is a story, which is a main part of the game. However, in business games, the story can be more like a metaphor or an analogy providing an initial understanding, or it can be a fully fictional story, developed with characters and so forth. Several of the games rely on pre-made scenarios with included dilemmas. Some already, through the name of the game – for instance, Ocean of Culture (C21), or Linkxs (C19), where puzzles are to be linked and teams are to be linked – establish a guiding analogy. Others have in-game core metaphors like Changesetter (C13), with a boat where people can either be on-board or off-board. Game boards are used to manifest the metaphor through visual means such as Business Branching (C12) that builds on a centreboard (tree trunk) and eight branches. Because participants are also developing the story in the process, the story can also be provided through templates that are partly filled out, but not completed.

Familiar analogies or metaphors create initial understanding. Conversely, using an unfamiliar metaphor from a field far removed from the normal company setting creates wonderment and attention towards understanding what might be behind this term: what does it mean? How can we understand this? The idea of basing the Acid Test (C08) on excavation is the core element that holds the game together. Due to the use of an unfamiliar metaphor, participants are more likely to question its use to begin with, and this initiates participants' own understanding of it. Therefore, depending on the metaphor and how participants understand it, it can start with familiarity and work towards unfamiliarity or vice versa; but in general, metaphors can provide a strong initial framing.

Game rules

The rules are the actions that players can or cannot take. The procedures outline how to proceed with the game. This includes the starting action – for instance, who begins or what to begin with. This is followed by the ongoing procedures, the progression of action and, finally, how to bring a game towards closure, which could be called resolving actions (Fullerton, Swain and Hoffman, 2004). The rules and procedures determine how the gameplay will unfold; in a sense, they are the glue that ties the gameplay together.

Many of the games guide participants through a series of steps – for instance, Add Value (C09), in which the teams are to follow the customer's footsteps through four parts, or the Innovation Learning Diamond game (C17), in which four tasks are to be completed in a specific order. These types of sequences – which can be more or less fixed – are found in all of the games. Another main component of many of the games is the use of a multiple-choice system – a limited number of options to choose from, with some answers being better than others based on the game algorithm (C6, C14, C18). But then we have specific rules providing further game structure. PublicProfessional (C23) has a twist in which participants are given a total number of resources, meaning that more can be used for a specific round if the participants choose this. Strategic Derby (C25) has a gameplay without turn-taking – participants work in pairs and must reveal their movements on the board at the same time, each thereby avoiding disadvantages in being the first to reveal his or her strategic moves. Gamechangers, in the Workz Leadership development chapter (C18), does not reveal all content information from the beginning; instead, the participants are to explore how most of the fictional organizational actors in the game feel. Pitch Perfect (C22) revolves around collecting cards with specific rules for a final pitch the participants have to perform – here, everyone has a chance to win right to the end.

As described above, rules lead to a specific form of gameplay and thereby have a major influence on the outcomes. A careful design and selection for each situation is therefore needed. Certain types of rules are more appropriate for certain types of outcomes and certain types of content.

Materials

From a designing point of view, the selection of materials to use in a given situation plays a major role and should align with the game rules. Materials such as foam, cardboard, fabric, felt and glass each have different advantages and disadvantages or constraints. In the words of Gibson and Walker (1984), they have different affordances. The tangible elements in the game can be open for an exploration of specific meanings beyond those that the participants have already within their minds.

In digital games, on the one hand, one loses the tangibility of physical materials and the learning quality of thinking with one's hands and body, but on the other hand, one can gain graphical and informational feedback; it is also easier to retrieve and save information before, during and after gameplay – and on a large scale. Unfortunately, today, looking at screens is a common part of work as well as a distraction – social media, news and entertainment games all steal employees' energy away from their work. Here, physical games can offer an effective dear revisit to the real world in a working life that is becoming more virtual than physical already.

In the games, materials come in the form of familiar objects such as boards, cards and other resources – but also a number of other materials tied to a purpose within the specific game. Examples include a specific number of counters in the Acid Test (C08) and a variety of forming materials in the Innovation Learning game (C17). As the participants move through the steps in the games, they earn more resources and moves – or such is the case in many of the games wherein each round has an algorithm indicating what can be gained.

Challenges

In all games, there are challenges to overcome. However, the types of challenges to overcome can vary greatly from game to game. In the business games in this book, six types of in-game basic challenges are used (Table 30.3).

Table 30.3 Six types of in-game challenges

Decision challenges	Deciding between two or more predefined options.
Answering challenges	Coming up with answers to questions.
Mapping challenges	Mapping out how something looks.
Puzzle challenges	Figuring out how something should be.
Organizing challenges	Sorting and categorizing things.
Task challenges	Doing some predefined task.

These types of challenges manifest differently in the various games in the book, but there are some clear patterns in how they function. Decision challenges are the most common type of challenge across the games, but it works differently in the games. For example, decision challenges with multiple-choice systems are implemented in several games (C10, C11, C13, C18, C20, C23, C26, and C21) with a variety of options, scores and consequences – but even these multifaceted multiple-choice decision challenges are quite different from those in Business Branching (C12) and Strategic Derby (C25), wherein decisions need to be made, but there are no pre-made options, so the players need to create the options themselves. Usually, decision challenges are connected to ambitions to improve players' ability to fulfil their designated organizational positions.

Answering challenges are also quite common in the business games in this book; C09, C14, C16, C22, C24 and C25 have answer challenges. Here, players need to come up with answers and solutions themselves; they cannot decide on a pre-made option or move a token and see what happens – they have to be creative and use their knowledge. Often, answering challenges are used to elicit co-creation and creativity by summoning players' perspectives and ideas.

Mapping challenges are used by some of the business games in this book. Here, players need to map out an organizational process together to get a broader, more actionable overview of it. Commonly, mapping challenges are used to bring siloes together and get enough perspective to work with complex challenges, such as service design (C09), temporary business advantages (C12), change processes (C15), culture (C21) or stakeholder management (C25).

Puzzle challenges are less common in this book, but they are used to help players reflect on their approaches to solving problems (C08, C19). Organizing challenges are also quite rare in this book (C15, C27), but they are used to help players categorize organizational phenomena and help them approach the challenges in question methodically.

Finally, two examples of task challenges can be found in this book (C12, C17). Here, the game challenges the players to do specific predefined tasks and then reflect on them. These tasks are metaphors for processes and help players to learn specific things.

As outlined above, different kinds of challenges are often used with different ambitions, which in turn affect which kinds of rules and materials are appropriate.

Participation

The last core is related to the people at the tables, their competencies and the existing power relations between them (as was also described in Challenge 6, Part One). This also relates back to the importance of a boundaryless internal–external organization (see description of Challenge 1 in Part One); however, here it is discussed from a concrete participation perspective. To level power relations within a company, outsider participants are important. These external actors tend to take the customer's perspective or a thought-provoking partner perspective, which enables company insiders to discover and bring about different viewpoints internally. Arranging the initial participation can be difficult; often, all the relevant actors cannot be present – and it is not always best to include all. Careful reflection on participation set-up can lead to a highly successful session.

The games also explore this participation and closely tie it to the rules. Align (03) creates a flow where individual achievements are to be balanced with shared organizational results. The Changeskills game (C14) includes a jury. Bizzbuilder (C11), in later parts of the game, challenges pairs – who had otherwise worked on their own agendas – to collaborate. In Linkxs (C19), some participants are selected to be observers in a given round. Also in Linkxs, participants who work together in real life and therefore know each other well are needed to form the groups. Conversely, in Stakeholder Management (C24), participants must come from different organizations to enable a freer sharing space.

Coherence between cores

The cores mentioned here have to play together. Specific rules can lead to a specific set-up with the participants – for example a division of a group in pairs or role play, which is a specific kind of turn taking with two-and-two playing together. Resources need to match the rules and so on. This is where the game concept needs to be iteratively developed and tested to find working generic forms.

In the framework (Figure 30.2), we can see how the five cores are the glue in the games. All of the games balance the knowledge incorporated by the game designer and facilitator with the local, situated knowledge coming from the ones who chose the game and the participants, but the control of the elements in the game determines whether a game situation moves towards progression or emergence in a given moment in the gameplay.

Figure 30.2 Structures and five cores

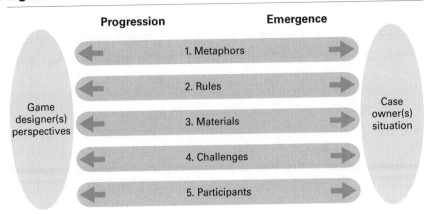

References

Fullerton, T, Swain, C and Hoffman, S (2004) *Game Design Workshop: Designing, prototyping and playtesting games*, CRC Press, Florida

Gibson, E J and Walker, A S (1984) Development of knowledge of visual-tactual affordances of substance, *Child Development*, 55 (2), pp 453–60

Juul, J (2011) *Half-Real: Video games between real rules and fictional worlds*, MIT Press, Cambridge, MA

Lakoff, G and Johnson, M (2008) *Metaphors We Live By*, University of Chicago Press, Chicago

31
Facilitation in business games
A flow between progression and emergence

So far, Part Three has mostly described how the cores are used in the making of the games and how we can think of progression and emergence, but what can be done during play? As game researcher Marc LeBlanc (2006) argues, there are two separate factors that provide the dramatic tension of a game. The first one is uncertainty, 'the sense that the outcome of the contest is still unknown' (LeBlanc, 2006: 445). The second factor is inevitability, 'the sense that the contest is moving toward resolution' (LeBlanc, 2006: 445). In games generally, inevitability emanates from the game mechanic of a ticking clock, but it does not have to be a clock as such – it can also be, in the words of LeBlanc, 'non-renewable' resources. A way to reach closure is also to provide limited game-piece materials, for instance, a maximum of five resources for each potential participant or group. The facilitator sometimes elicits feedback, either by reinforcing uncertainty through new objectives, rules, and so on, or by deciding on how long a game should proceed. We view the facilitator as the prolonged arm of the game. In fact, the major difference between computer games and business games is that, in a computer game, the feedback is provided by computation (Juul, 2011), whereas in a business board game, the facilitator is part of the feedback – a co-enabler of the feedback.

Business game tuning instrument

The presence of a facilitator who, together with the participants, can determine what is needed in specific situations does normally lead to the best outcome, even though some games are virtually self-explanatory. Whether a facilitator chooses to assist in providing direct content or not is up to the facilitator's personal style and opinion – one must determine in each situation if the knowledge the facilitator possesses on a given subject matter will help or not.

We suggest extending the aforementioned framework also to be used as an instrument that can be tuned during play. If you listen carefully, you can hear when specific instruments are out of tune, and the same goes for game situations – one can focus on the atmosphere and the interaction to observe whether tuning is necessary. After all, none of these games are 100 per cent fixed if the situation calls for a change.

In general, to accomplish a strong outcome it is the act of constraining (progression) or deconstraining (emergence) the business game during play; a business game facilitator with a trained eye can help the game produce the optimal outcome (Figure 31.1). What can be changed during gameplay to tune towards a specific outcome is directly linked to the five core elements.

Core 1: metaphor – deliberate or emerging

Corresponding with Kensing and Madsen's (1992) metaphorical interventions, metaphors can, on the one hand, be applied during play to further advance perspectives. On the other hand, metaphors can also arise because of incidents during play. For instance, participants can provide new metaphors during play, which happened during a session with Strategic Derby (G18) where participants uttered that 'the reason their company's strategy lost was because they tried to capture the whole board'. A variety of resources or materials as a kind of selection pole usually advances such potential in-game emerge metaphors, which can become strong points in follow-up activities.

Core 2: rules – exogenous or endogenous

During play, the facilitator might observe that a specific rule or procedure is not beneficial or fruitful for a certain case. In these cases, he or she can make the choice, together with the participants, to omit this procedure from the game. We call this endogenous because these are rules and procedures that the case owners feel comfortable with and that facilitate quality dialogues. This will usually lead to a more emergent structure. On the other hand, it might also happen that the participants have too many options; therefore, adding a rule or a procedure – that is, one more constraint – makes sense in such a case. We refer to this as exogenous, meaning that the facilitator provides an extra external factor (ie adds a rule).

Core 3: materials – fixed or flexible

Adding or removing materials during play is another way to either constrain or deconstrain a business game session. For instance, participants can be

Figure 31.1   Facilitator tuning instrument

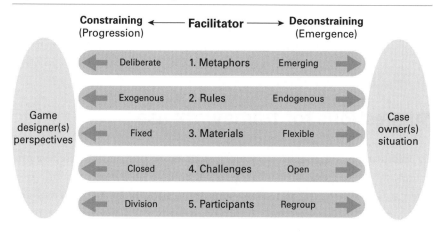

allowed to use whatever resources are within range, or the facilitator can restrict material choices to only one type of resource, or a limited number if the dialogue tends to go in circles. Cards can be added, or metaphor-inspired materials as surprise elements.

Core 4: challenges – closed or open

It is good to have in the backhand ways to reduce cognitive load if challenges are too hard for participants and frustration takes over. In *Linkxs* (G12) the authors argue that a reasonable level of conflict is Ok, but it can also become non-productive. As facilitator, it is possible to direct such heated conflicts to a state where it becomes a winning activity through running attention and reflection. It counts the other way as well; challenges can be on a level where they do not provide the struggle that a game needs for it to last. Every participant goes to a challenge in a unique way and it can be hard to tell beforehand what they are capable of and the level of difficulty one can insert.

Core 5: participation – division or regrouping (not done)

One never really knows how participants function together when put into new groups. During gameplay there are reasons for a *division* of the participants. In a situation where the authors worked with a Danish company having a Czech department, they worked together closely at the workshop for the first time. They started in two groups with participants from each department in both groups. However, as the workshop progressed it became clear that the CEO had to leave for a while to avoid beginning to dominate (he indicated this himself). At the same time we also had to switch participants around – aka *regrouping* – in the next activity in order to achieve better group dynamics. This can be difficult without evoking strong feelings, but can turn out to be better than continuing with a non-working situation.

Suggestions for framework use

In presenting a component framework such as the one set out here, we find it important to suggest how it can be used. First of all, it illustrates the cores one can work with in the making and application of business games and how a decision on one of these components leads to specific effects in terms of both progression and emergence. Therefore, the component framework can be used to determine which kinds of effects business game facilitators could pursue in a specific situation.

Intended uses for the framework are as follows: 1) to provide an understanding of which components to consider when making and applying a business game; and 2) to use the components as instruments to tune during gameplay, eliciting specific effects and a positive change in direction. It can work as inspiration for those lacking ideas on which elements to include in a game and how to run these, even though it should not be viewed as a step-by-step process model. Thus, it serves as a guideline for the cores to include, as well as provide the knowledge of what one can expect to achieve from doing so. During play, it can work as an instrument for the facilitator in terms of guiding participants' dialogue towards a specific effect.

References

Juul, J (2011) *Half-Real: Video games between real rules and fictional worlds*, MIT Press, Cambridge, MA

Kensing, F and Madsen, K H (1992) *Generating Visions: Future workshops and metaphorical design*, L Erlbaum Associates Inc, Hillsdale, pp 155–68

LeBlanc, M (2006) Tools for creating dramatic game dynamics, in *The Game Design Reader: A rules of play anthology*, pp 438–59, ed K Salen and E Zimmerman, MIT Press, Cambridge, MA

32

The history and future of business games from a Dutch perspective

Understanding and influencing complex systems

THOMAS BENEDICT, InContext Consultancy BV

The Dutch market has seen strong development in organizational gaming, beginning in the 1960s. This chapter provides some historical perspective on how this industry evolved.

Monodisciplinary to multidisciplinary

Business gaming outside the military began with the adoption of the Beer game by different multinational companies. This game was created by a group of professors at MIT Sloan School of Management (Sterman, 1989) and is focused on understanding the supply chain as a complex system. In the sense that the Beer game focuses on just one organizational function, this game is monodisciplinary. The first multidisciplinary management game in which coordinated decisions needed to be made in all functional areas was the Philips Electromotorenspel. Developed in the 1970s, it was used for decades in Philips management and leadership development. Many more versions of multidisciplinary decision-based management games followed and were adopted by many companies and universities.

From generic to company-specific

The original management games were built as extensive computer programs. This meant that, except for predefined parameters, they were not adaptable to company-specific circumstances or requirements. Professor Léon de Caluwé from the Twijnstra Gudde consultancy firm (Caluwé, Geurts, Buys and Stoppelenburg, 1996) began building extensive simulations based on company-specific issues. His approach relied on dividing players into groups that reflected the organizational structure and processes. By a careful analysis of the organizational issues, reality could be simplified into a playable but relevant model, often without any computerized support. This type of game became very popular in the 1990s, despite the high development cost.

Behaviour in gaming

Until the mid-1990s, most management games were decision-based and therefore focused on cognitive development. The behavioural element was missing, so that facilitators and observers provided feedback to the playing teams. This solution was merely a quick fix and a strong demand developed for games with behavioural elements built in to the game design itself. In the mid-1990s, various management games were developed to focus on organizational learning, conflict management, quality improvement, cross-functional collaboration and handling ambiguity. Early examples of these games were Metamorphose, commissioned by Philips Electron Optics and Linkxs (see C19), which was originally built for the Dutch Post Office. Piet Vergunst, a philosopher and consultant at InContext Consultancy Group, infused business games with a radically different approach. These games were less focused on cognitive content and more on presenting behavioural, ethical and philosophical challenges. The game design became less numbers-focused and more creative, often using puzzles to simulate complexity and challenge problem-solving skills. Even so, these management games are still perceived as highly relevant, as they reflect recognizable organizational systems. In addition, training actors were used during games so that skill areas such as management and sales could be added to the learning experience.

Systems thinking

Peter Senge (1990), in his highly influential book *The Fifth Discipline*, applied systems thinking to the business world. In the Netherlands, systems thinking for organizations had already been introduced by Professor A C J de Leeuw (1986; 1994). Beginning in the mid-1990s, games were used to experience tough but highly applicable concepts such as systems archetypes and learning disabilities. Conversely, organizational systems thinking was used to build and enrich new management games and simulations, deepening the learning experience and increasing the take-home value for participants. By the start of the 21st century, computer systems were becoming more flexible so that various developments fuelled a boom in the gaming industry. Many different tailor-made games were developed to reflect a multitude of organizational challenges, not only from a content perspective, but also focusing on interaction, system dynamics, organizational learning and behaviour. This type of game is currently used in almost every industry in the Netherlands.

Serious games

The (entertainment) gaming industry has been earmarked by the Dutch government as a growth area and has received much attention and support, especially towards developing serious games. This has led to a multitude of successful game development companies in the country. Some of these have moved into the realm of organizational gaming. An early example of a fully digital serious game, called The Game, was developed by game development company Ranj for leading law firm Houthoff Buruma (Ranj, 2010). However, this type of game has not had a major impact on business as of yet. This may be due to high development costs, lack of customization, and the unfamiliarity of game designers with the complexity of business issues.

Future orientation

Individual online games

Business games have proven their value in the market. Clients have a strong desire to reduce learning costs by developing fully online solutions that can be played by individual learners. So far, no individual online games have been successful. Development is currently focused around intelligent story-based simulations that allow players a great degree of freedom and integrate content and behaviour (the latter via video role-playing). It remains to be seen whether this type of game will become a serious alternative for the live gaming experience.

Mass customization

A growing trend in the business games industry is mass customization. This means that games are developed in such a way that customer-specific content can be loaded into an existing game platform or engine. This allows for cheap, rapid development, combined with a high level of customized content. Align (see Chapter 10) is an example of such a game. This approach is currently working and growing.

Phygital games

Business games still benefit from the physical proximity of players. While digital elements enhance gameplay, we do not want players staring at a screen and not interacting with each other. The most recent games and simulations are built using a digital system. This system interacts with each player individually, giving specific information, allowing individual input and enabling players to interact with virtual counterparts. Each player can also physically interact with other players, effectively playing in a combined digital–physical environment. This development is new and therefore comes at a high cost. Where these games have been implemented, extreme learning returns and high customer satisfaction are achieved. Economically viable 'phygital' gaming environments are becoming possible due to the developments in mass customization technology. The Netherlands boasts a thriving and creative organizational gaming industry that has been in development since the 1960s. Many Dutch design games are successfully applicable around the world.

References

Caluwé, L, Geurts, J, Buys, D and Stoppelenburg, A (1996) *Gaming: Organisatieverandering met spelsimulaties* (*Gaming: Organisational change by using a simulation*), Delwel, The Hague

De Leeuw, A (1986) *Organisaties: Management, analyze, ontwerp en verandering*, Van Gorcum, Assen, pp 60–203

De Leeuw, A (1994) *Besturen van veranderingsprocessen*, Van Gorcum, Assen, pp 56–69

Ranj (2010) [accessed 10 March 2018] Houthoff – The Game – Walkthrough, *YouTube* [Online] https://www.youtube.com/watch?v=AhNW4uV-hro

Senge, P (1990) *The Fifth Discipline: The art and practice of the learning organization*, Currency Doubleday, New York

Sterman, J (1989) Modeling managerial behavior: misperceptions of feedback in a dynamic decision making experiment, *Management Science*, 35 (3), 321–39

33

The history and future of business games from a UK perspective

Encourage novel, imaginative and subversive thinking

CHRISTOPHER ELGOOD, Elgood Effective Learning

Games are studied here as a means of preparing for a future situation by increasing knowledge or skill. The situation being considered is one that is dangerous, expensive or impossible to create in reality. A game gets closer to reality than instruction or demonstration: it 'shows' rather than 'tells'. It allows players to practise and explore in safety. Game playing has been around for so long that it is close to being instinctive human behaviour.

Games are developed in response to a perceived need and generally represent reality through a medium. At the most basic level, hide-and-seek can be seen as preparation for encountering a strange tribe. No artificial representation is needed because the existing physical environment serves. At a more complex level, chess can be seen as practice in deploying mixed military resources. The representing medium is a playing board with movable tokens. Even more complex are the flight simulators used for training airline pilots. The medium employed is virtual reality.

Games, as used for learning, respond to the needs of the time, the currently suitable media of representation and the intended learners. What is it that presently needs to be learnt? Who needs to learn? How can the situation be represented in a way that is recognizable and playable? All have changed over the years. In the Middle Ages, knights armed with lances rode at each other with intent to kill. They practised on a quintain, an upright post with a horizontal beam pivoted in the middle on top. From one end of the beam hung a target and from the other end hung a sandbag or a bucket of water. The knight who failed to strike firmly and accurately got sandbagged or drenched.

Early games were played by people who could not read or write and had limited resources. In remote parts of Africa, games are still played by scooping small pits in the sand and moving stones from one pit to another. Noughts and crosses (tic tac toe) can be played the same way, without even needing stones. The next development in gaming was the use of a range of different tokens that represented real people or objects. Sometimes the tokens were recognizable models of the real thing. Board and token games have been dated to the period 2050–1800 BCE (the Middle Kingdom in Egypt). Simple board games (such as draughts, or checkers) do not need writing. The same is true of the simpler four-suit card games that originated in China prior to 1000 CE. Pictures are quite adequate.

Board games became much more sophisticated when literacy became common and print, paper and pencil became readily available media. Events could be scheduled by instructions on a playing board or by small cards. Development had reached the stage in which games like Monopoly were possible. Board games have a lasting appeal because of their convenience and flexibility; the tokens, locations and event cards can represent any chosen reality. Every Christmas sees new board games in the shops.

The fact that games are developed as a result of need shows why games about business and commerce were preceded by war games. War was seen as requiring study and analysis at a time when business learning came into being through trial and error. This is dramatically illustrated by the fact that the Prussian Military College was founded in 1810, Harvard Business School in 1908, and The London Business School only in 1964. War games, or *kriegsspiel*, were divided into 'rigid' and 'free' types, depending on whether the rules were predetermined or subjective.

Learning about work situations was, for many centuries, a matter of separating out distinct tasks and teaching/learning a single task only. Awareness of how that task related to other tasks was not a priority. In the era after the Second World War, governments decided that it would be advantageous if people knew why they were doing something, why it was important and how it fitted into the larger picture. The age of industrial training had begun. There was a need for wider understanding.

In the 1960s, a small firm in England called Management Games Ltd published a range of business games concerned with fundamental business concepts. These games described an imaginary situation and called for decisions, in numbers, about what should be done in certain areas. They were largely paper-based. Only a few used display boards. The outcome for the decisions (such as 'items produced' and 'cost') was worked out by a set of mathematical rules, called a 'model', usually with the assistance of hand calculators.

The scope of many such games was restricted to a single business function, such as production or purchasing. A notable exception was the Small Business Management game by Clive Loveluck. It placed a heavy emphasis on marketing at a time when the UK was not greatly aware of the need for it. For many years after the Second World War, there was a huge emphasis on exporting goods; the domestic purchaser was lucky to buy anything that was vaguely suitable. As the situation improved, finding a customer gradually became a problem. The game addressed that issue.

There were also games that featured physical activities, such as the manufacture of paper pamphlets of a certain number of pages, cut to a prescribed size, stapled together and hole-punched to fit into a cover. These were elaborate and time-consuming, but offered dramatic learning experiences, such as discovering that a minor error at one work station made the work of a later station impossible. In 1976, Gower Press published *The Handbook of Management Games* (Elgood, 1976), which collected descriptions of available games and listed creators and suppliers. The games listed were mainly of the type described above.

Technology then took over. The advent of the computer made it possible to administer game rules of great complexity and to suggest that playing the game was seriously akin to managing a real business. Many games of high economic reality were developed (mainly in the United States, which was far ahead in that field). The physical activity of participants centred upon preparing data for a computer, or actually entering it. The down side was that no game was deemed credible unless it used this technology.

A different development was also under way during those years. In 1947, Kurt Lewin founded the National Training Laboratories (NTL) in the United States. This was not connected with war games or management games, but was very much concerned with human behaviour and effective cooperation. NTL significantly influenced ideas about learning; in 1969, William Pfeiffer published his first collection of structured experiences for human relations training (Pfeiffer and Jones, 1969). These were non-numerate, easy to operate, and offered self-knowledge to participants. The playing mechanisms were tangible materials or role play. The concept was developed further by David Kolb in *Experiential Learning* (1984). Such devices are well within the popular definition of 'games' and belong to the pragmatic learning tradition.

So in the later years of the 20th century, there was one group of people building complex numbers-based simulations and another group (from a different discipline) building 'experiences' (and other instruments, such as psychological questionnaires) that focused on human behaviour. It has since been widely recognized that the most sophisticated business plan is likely to fail unless the people involved understand what it means and cooperate to make it work. This need has caused two traditions to draw together.

In this century, the Digital Revolution has caused massive changes. In some respects, it has favoured complex computer-controlled games.

They can be played internationally in real time and, for instance, in-game financial transactions can use up-to-the-minute exchange rates. In another respect, such games have suffered, because workers, in their normal work life, are frequently screen-bound – to a PC, a laptop or a tablet. They are devoid of human contact for long periods. They welcome the social experience that goes with standing together around a board display and moving objects upon it. The cycle has come around through physical equipment, board display, simple sums and electronic computation, and come back to representation by tokens.

Historically, the benefits that games brought to organizations largely accrued when game players gained seniority and opportunity. For what was to be taught (and was therefore the subject matter of a game) was defined by authority and did not include novel, imaginative and, perhaps, subversive thinking. Yet the game environment encourages such an attitude and this is one of its great benefits. Participants come out of it with concepts new to those who sent them for training. When promoted, they have a wider vision than their predecessors. That is a risk with 'top-down' education. Most people only learn what they are taught. The difficulty of novel thinking can be illustrated by the well-known Nine Dots puzzle (Figure 33.1), currently discussed online at www.Brainstorming.co.uk.

The task is to join all nine dots with only four straight lines without taking the pen off the paper. The middle diagram shows the best that can be done with five lines and the right-hand diagram uses just four. The constraints of conventional thought impose an assumption that the nine dots indicate the boundaries of the task and make it unlikely that one will consider extending the lines outside it.

The situation has changed with increasing use of games and with participation by high-level decision makers. Creative thinking is highly valued, because organizations face challenges greater in number, variety and complexity than ever before. It all happens in a rapidly changing world.

Figure 33.1 Nine Dots puzzle

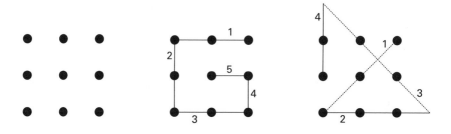

It becomes essential to use a pragmatic approach and study the world as it now exists and not rely too much on past trends. Gerald Gutek (2014) has commented, 'Pragmatism focuses on a changing universe rather than an unchanging one.'

Before a strategy can be devised to meet a need, that challenge must be recognized. Today, it is as likely to be recognized by forces outside an organization as by executives within it. These forces may be governments, the media, commissions of enquiry or 'think tanks'. However a challenge is recognized, games are a valuable way to examine it because they extend the boundaries of permissible thought.

Examples of problems for which a strategy is needed include globalization, change, ethics, compliance, cyber warfare, productivity and leadership. An example from the UK is the national publicity given to productivity per worker compared with that of Germany. The fashionable method of representation in the future will be virtual reality and social media. Board games and tokens will still have a role, perhaps in combination with technology. It is already possible to have an onscreen board display that shows the immediate 'now' to all users, wherever they are, but updates as each player in turn makes a move.

Novelty is also influential. Globalization means increasing contact between people of different languages and cultures. Signs, icons and pictures, being more international, are sometimes preferred to words. Social media already use images like 'smilies' to show personal emotions. There are several online dictionaries of them. Games might well use them. One party might make suggestions to another. The second party could demonstrate an emotional response by showing a 'smiley face' or a 'frowny face'. Such games would be responding to a learning need, and also to a fashionable way to communicate. Game designers are imaginative folk, and we are now in an age where it is dangerous to label anything as impossible. Novelty plays a part in encouraging participation and game designers need to be aware of it.

References

Elgood, C, ed (1976) *Handbook of Management Games and Simulations*, Gower Publishing Company, London

Gutek, G (2014) *Philosophical, Ideological and Theoretical Perspectives on Education*, Pearson, New York

Kolb, D (1984) *Experiential Learning*, Prentice Hall, Englewood Cliffs

Pfeiffer, J W and Jones, J E (1969) *A Handbook of Structured Experiences for Human Relations Training*, volume I, University Associates Press, California

34

The history and future of business games from a Nordic perspective

Towards New Nordic management

In the Nordic countries, the use of games in organizations has grown steadily throughout the 1990s and in the 21st century, but it has exploded in broader innovation and change application in recent years. To take a quick tour back in time, two main purposes have driven forward the use of games in organizations in the last 30 years. These two directions – namely, 1) inclusion and later co-creation, and 2) change behaviour and training – correspond fairly well with the discussion on emergence and progression that we took up in the first part of Part Three.

Inclusion and co-creation (leaning towards emergence)

The field of participatory design emerged during the 1980s and took off during the 1990s as a counterposition to traditional system development at that time. Proponents criticized traditional development for not involving the workers who were going to use the system in their everyday work lives. Early arguments in this research were related to 'users having a say', operating with more democratic development set-ups, and creating ownership for those who were going to incorporate the system into their daily work lives (Ehn, 1993; Bødker et al, 2000). One of the inclusion approaches was dubbed 'participatory design games'. These were used to invite user practices and perspectives, to encourage collaboration on directions and solutions, and to create means for ownership, thereby subsequently building motivation and follow-up actions afterwards. Ehn was inspired by Wittgenstein's notion of *language games*, which the philosopher conceived as the way we learn to participate in human activities, following the model of a mock-up or prototype. An important part of the organizational kit game was, therefore, to provide simple materials for mock-ups, but which still resembled the language games of workers' everyday practice. One challenge Ehn and Kyng (1991) sought to explore was how to 'create a design language game that makes sense to all participants'. Brandt and colleagues used the term 'exploratory' and suggested that design games can be both a way to reach mutual understanding and a means for future scenario exploration (Brandt, 2006; Brandt and Messeter, 2004).

As the development problems and challenges increased in complexity, and participatory design received attention outside of system development circles, the names of these approaches were slightly altered – for instance, to participatory *innovation* instead of design (see Buur and Matthews, 2008), because the subject matter was broader, involved more professional disciplines, and in general was characterized by the presence of a circle of diverse stakeholders. With this movement into broader innovation agendas, the games likewise acquired new names, such as game tools, innovation games and business games. In addition, the games had a different look and were adapted to fit situations with broad stakeholder negotiation and new subject matter, such as service, business model and strategy development (Gudiksen, 2015; Inlove and Gudiksen, 2017). However, the game design was still in a manner that complemented the strong qualities that the designers already were equipped with (for instance, visualization and tactility competencies, as well as working in situations with uncertainty and ambiguity). Although games are used regularly in the private sector, the purpose of *inclusion* and the act of co-creation through games have received increased attention in the public sector in recent years. Public organizations – municipalities, regions and agencies – are trying hard to find ways to become boundaryless organizations (see Challenge 1 in Part One).

Behaviour change and training (leaning towards progression)

Historically (see Andersen, 2009), training and behaviour-changing games grew out of management studies in the 1950s, when the number of management games and business games boomed. Here, they were present at many conferences and the topic of many articles. Since then, they have evolved with the capacity of the computer, which is the reason that many of the games that come from this tradition are digital today and benefit in their game mechanics from everything today's technology can offer – quick process-ing, complex algorithms, generating player statistics, and more attractive graphic design.

Around the beginning of the 21st century, a series of change-related games surfaced in the industry in Sweden and Denmark, most of them with a focus on larger organizations and work practices found here. For instance, company contributor Workz in this book grew out of the film company Zentropa as a specific unit with a focus on innovation and co-creation. Eventually, this unit separated from Zentropa and moved towards a focus on more change- and training-related games. Likewise, in Sweden, a company called Celemi (contrib-utor Canmas's consultant partner) was started based on Klas Mellander's (see Celemi, 2018) proposition for a different learning approach with a focus on *thinking*, *exploring* and *discovering* rather than simply receiving information. Since the millennium more companies have emerged, creating and apply-ing games that train participants in a specific topic that is often related in some way to change processes in organizations. These companies build on a number of learning models from various influential scholars and sources from early war games, and they do tend to overlap in game format.

In comparison, the two directions – inclusion and co-creation, and behav-iour change and training – have some of the same goals: both seek to involve participants, drive engagement, build up human relations, and bring forth new learning, which could result in practice change. However, the *inclusion and co-creation* direction does lean more towards a bottom-up approach (more options, content and design are in the hands of the participants), whereas the *behaviour change and training* direction tends to start with a top-down agenda (fewer options, content and design are in the hands of the game applicators). However, in both directions, one can observe that the applicators learn from each other and begin to coalesce in a type of yin–yang relationship.

Aligning with 21st-century skills

Much talk surrounds what skills are needed in the future, but a common recognition in the discussion is that 21st-century skills differ from traditional academic skills in that they are not primarily content knowledge-based. These skills do not necessarily replace the old ones but rather complement them.

In 2015, the World Economic Forum published a report titled 'New vision for education: unlocking the potential of technology' (World Economic Forum, 2015). The extensive research in the report finds that most educational technologies are focused on developing foundational literacies, missing out on four competencies that are central leading to 21st-century skills: 1) critical thinking/problem solving; 2) creativity; 3) communication; 4) collaboration. Games, especially business games, can play a central part in building these four competencies. First, as many games in the book have demonstrated, business games can help develop critical thinking and problem-solving skills by acting as reflective frameworks and methodical systems for dealing with issues. Second, games can foster creativity and collaboration by acting as co-creation forums that gather people and help them enter a ludic learning space, where they are no longer bound by the typical barriers to creativity. Third, games help people to develop communication competencies by giving them visual and metaphorical aids and showing them the strengths in using more than just a verbal medium for communication. Fourth, games help people collaborate by being a third space with shared interest for participation.

Resurrection of a board game movement

In the Nordic countries, board games are more popular than ever, and a retro movement can be observed. Board game cafés, festivals and all types of events are held every year. Why is this? There seem to be at least two reasons we can identify here.

The first reason relates to media and technology constantly either taking our attention or interrupting our focus. In opposition, board games and associated acts such as role-playing remain a way to find space for social interaction and immersion in an interesting topic. Another reason is that materials are easier to get; guidance on game design can be found quickly, and games tap directly into maker movements – that is, an interest in creating enjoyable experiences through craft.

Even though these board games do not address organizational challenges, and classic entertainment game designers cannot easily move into a field like business games without years of practice and understanding of how organizations work, the movement towards, and increased interest in, board games is helpful in finding a format that many are familiar with. Games continue to be a common denominator that works well in organizational challenges.

As business games become more popular, an increase in the number of internal organizational process facilitators and external consultants who create their own games for use in organizations can be seen. For instance, daily news feeds that the authors receive contain new, tailor-made games created for an organizational challenge at hand. Therefore, we look to the future and welcome a greater variety of games – and a new age for the use of games in organizations.

Future organizational challenges

As we have illustrated, games have proven to be a useful and effective vehicle to connect silos and create communicative space for mutual learning and shared communication. Games are also useful for reflecting on past operations, getting an overview of the present, and enabling future-scenario exploration. What can be observed from the business environment from the early 1990s onwards is an increasing interest in how to tackle innovation and change challenges that arise because of the introduction of new technologies and rapid market changes, more global/glocal-oriented companies, and a multitude of cultural aspects present in business organizations. Examples of innovation and change challenges are included in Table 34.1, but they are not limited to these.

Table 34.1 Potential upcoming organizational challenges

Complex matrix structures	Cultural differences because of global orientation and an increase in complex structures.
Conditions for innovative environments	Companies will continue to promote their workspaces and design them to facilitate interpersonal relationships between employees.
Stakeholder or crowd-based management	With the increase of stakeholders involved in projects and initiatives stakeholder relation management is more important than ever.
Building up and manage relations	Since networking and collaboration are central in the future world of work, workers' ability to connect with others becomes their main asset.
Self-directed learning	Curiosity-based exploration, gathering and combining knowledge are precursors for innovation; hence self-directed learning becomes essential for creative workers.
Artificial intelligence in the workplace	Working together with learning algorithms and intelligent machines will soon be normal in the workplace, which will lead to new management challenges.

As we focus more on 21st-century skills and new organizational challenges, it becomes clear that games and playful activities are here to stay as a key component in New Nordic management approaches in the years to come.

References

Andersen, N A (2009) *Power at Play: The relationships between play, work and governance*, Palgrave MacMillan, Houndmills

Bødker, S, Ehn, P, Sjögren, D and Sundblad, Y (2000) Co-operative design – perspectives on 20 years with 'the Scandinavian IT design model', in *Proceedings of NordiCHI, 2000*, pp 22–24

Brandt, E (2006) *Designing Exploratory Design Games: A framework for participation in Participatory Design?* Proceedings from the ninth conference on participatory design: expanding boundaries in design, volume 1, ACM

Brandt, E and Messeter, J (2004) *Facilitating Collaboration Through Design Games*, proceedings of the eighth conference on participatory design: artful integration: interweaving media, materials and practices, volume 1, ACM

Buur, J and Matthews, B (2008) Participatory innovation, *International Journal of Innovation Management*, **12** (03), 255–73

Celemi (2018) [accessed 9 March 2018] Our Mission and History [Online] https://celemi.com/our-mission-history/

Ehn, P (1993) Scandinavian design: on participation and skill, *Participatory Design: Principles and practices*, **41**, p 77

Ehn, P and Kyng, M (1991) Cardboard computers: mocking-it-up or hands-on the future, in *Design at Work, Cooperative design of computer systems*, ed J Greenbaum and M Kyng, pp 169–95, Lawrence Erlbaum, New Jersey

Gudiksen, S (2015) Business model design games: rules and procedures to challenge assumptions and elicit surprises, *Creativity and Innovation Management*, **24** (2), pp 307–22

Inlove, J and Gudiksen, S K (2017) *Strategic Derby: A game tool approach to support strategic foresight*, proceedings of ISPIM Conferences, 2017, Vienna, pp 1–14

World Economic Forum (2015) [accessed 9 March 2018] New Vision For Education: Unlocking the Potential of Technology [Online] http://www3.weforum.org/docs/WEFUSA_NewVisionforEducation_Report2015.pdf

INDEX

Note: page numbers in italic indicate figures or tables.